Property in the Body: Feminist Perspectives

New developments in biotechnology radically alter our relationship with our bodies. Body tissues can now be used for commercial purposes, while external objects, such as pacemakers, can become part of the body. *Property in the Body: Feminist Perspectives* transcends the everyday responses to such developments, suggesting that what we most fear is the feminisation of the body. We fear our bodies are becoming objects of property, turning us into things rather than persons. This book evaluates how well-grounded this fear is, and suggests innovative models of regulating what has been called 'the new Gold Rush' in human tissue. This is an up-to-date and wide-ranging synthesis of market developments in body tissue, bringing together bioethics, feminist theory and lessons from countries that have resisted commercialisation of the body, in a theoretically sophisticated and practically significant approach.

DONNA DICKENSON is Emeritus Professor of Medical Ethics and Law at the University of London. She received the 2006 international Spinoza Lens Award for contribution to public debate on ethics, becoming the first woman to receive the award.

Cambridge Law, Medicine and Ethics

This series of books was founded by Cambridge University Press with Alexander McCall Smith as its first editor in 2003. It focuses on the law's complex and troubled relationship with medicine across both the developed and the developing worlds. In the past twenty years, we have seen in many countries increasing resort to the courts by dissatisfied patients and a growing use of the courts to attempt to resolve intractable ethical dilemmas. At the same time, legislatures across the world have struggled to address the questions posed by both the successes and the failures of modern medicine, while international organisations such as the WHO and UNESCO now regularly address issues of medical law.

It follows that we would expect ethical and policy questions to be integral to the analysis of the legal issues discussed in this series. The series responds to the high profile of medical law in universities, in legal and medical practice, as well as in public and political affairs. We seek to reflect the evidence that many major health-related policy debates in the UK, Europe and the international community over the past two decades have involved a strong medical law dimension. Organ retention, embryonic stem cell research, physician-assisted suicide and the allocation of resources to fund health care are but a few examples among many. The emphasis of this series is thus on matters of public concern and/or practical significance. We look for books that could make a difference to the development of medical law and enhance the role of medico-legal debate in policy circles. That is not to say that we lack interest in the important theoretical dimensions of the subject, but we aim to ensure that theoretical debate is grounded in the realities of how the law does and should interact with medicine and health care.

General Editors
Professor Margaret Brazier, *University of Manchester*
Graeme Laurie, *University of Edinburgh*

Editorial Advisory Board
Professor Richard Ashcroft, *Queen Mary, University of London*
Professor Martin Bobrow, *University of Cambridge*
Dr Alexander Morgan Capron, *Director, Ethics and Health, World Health Organization, Geneva*
Professor Jim Childress, *University of Virginia*
Professor Ruth Chadwick, *Cardiff Law School*
Dame Ruth Deech, *University of Oxford*
Professor John Keown, *Georgetown University, Washington, D.C.*
Dr. Kathy Liddell, *University of Cambridge*
Professor Alexander McCall Smith, *University of Edinburgh*
Professor Dr. Mónica Navarro-Michel, *University of Barcelona*

Property in the Body: Feminist Perspectives

Donna Dickenson

CAMBRIDGE UNIVERSITY PRESS
Cambridge, New York, Melbourne, Madrid, Cape Town, Singapore, São Paulo

Cambridge University Press
The Edinburgh Building, Cambridge CB2 8RU, UK

Published in the United States of America by Cambridge University Press, New York

www.cambridge.org
Information on this title: www.cambridge.org/9780521687324

First published 2007

Printed in the United Kingdom at the University Press, Cambridge

A catalogue record for this publication is available from the British Library

Library of Congress Cataloguing-in-Publication data
Dickenson, Donna.
Property in the body : feminist perspectives / Donna L. Dickenson.
   p. cm. – (Cambridge law, medicine, and ethics)
Includes bibliographical references and index.
ISBN-13: 978-0-521-86792-4 (hardback)
ISBN-10: 0-521-86792-4 (hardback)
ISBN-13: 978-0-521-68732-4 (pbk.)
ISBN-10: 0-521-68732-2 (pbk.)
1. Biotechnology – Moral and ethical aspects.   2. Body, Human.   3. Feminist theory.
I. Title.   II. Series.
TP248.23.D53   2007
174'.957 – dc22
2006035152

ISBN 978-0-521-86792-4 hardback
ISBN 978-0-521-68732-4 paperback

Contents

Acknowledgements

Grateful acknowledgement is made to the *Journal of Bioethical Inquiry* for permission to reprint sections of my article 'The lady vanishes: what's missing in the stem cell debate' in chapter 3, and to *Medical Law International* for permission to reprint sections of an article which appeared in (2005) 7(1), as part of chapter 7. Shorter sections of chapter 8 also appeared in (2005) 1(1) *Genomics, Society and Policy*. Parts of chapter 2 appear in several chapters of my earlier *Property, Women and Politics* (Cambridge, Polity Press, 1997), but without the links to modern-day biotechnology.

Preface

In the two years since I started writing this book, property in the body has become the most topical of topics. Two recent scandals, in particular, have elevated it to a dubious pre-eminence: the theft of the late broadcaster Alistair Cooke's bones by a criminal ring which sold them for US$7,000 to a dental implants company, and the revelation that the supposed stem cell breakthroughs by Prof. Hwang Woo Suk used 2,200 ova in the course of research that turned out to be entirely fraudulent. From its earlier low obscurity, property in the body has risen to such heights of interest that the reader could be excused for asking, 'What more could I possibly want to know about this topic?'

Luckily, or unluckily, there is still a great deal to bring to light, and a particular kind of illumination required. The rise of private umbilical cord blood banking, for example, has not yet made the media headlines. What coverage it has received in the popular and scholarly literature has been based on false assumptions, including what I present in chapter 4 as the mistaken presumption that the cord blood is the baby's and not the mother's, even though she puts effort into its extraction. Why that assumption has taken root has to do, along with other large misconceptions and abuses such as those perpetrated by Hwang, with particular blind spots: gendered ways of thinking about property in the body. As I argued in my earlier *Property, Women and Politics,* the common law, liberal and Marxist political theory, and even many second-wave feminists have presented women as having no relation to property except as its objects. Here, in this new book, I build on that insight, and on the counter-attempt I made in *Property, Women and Politics* to lay the foundations for a theory of property that would count women in. Property in the body was not my sole concern there; here it is, but the practical questions about ethics, law and politics of human tissue raised in this book are analysed using the philosophical and jurisprudential model I developed earlier.

But my theoretical thinking did not come to a premature halt ten years ago. This book takes both the theory and the practice further, with the applied questions compelling further refinement and rethinking of the model towards which I was groping then. That sort of symbiosis between theoretical and applied ethics is what I always aim to do: call it phenomenology, narrative ethics, feminist ethics, casuistry, Aristotelian *phronesis*, or what you will. I have never accepted that theory can flourish apart from practice, or the reverse.

The theoretical foundations which I laid almost ten years ago are now urgently required to deal with the welter of practical issues that have arisen in recent biotechnology. With its novel and solid feminist theoretical position, I hope that this book will transcend two dominant but ill-thought-out responses to the private enclosure of the genetic commons and tissue in the body. These are, first, the cynical shrug: 'we live in a capitalist society, so what do you expect?'; secondly, its neo-liberal counterpart: 'we live in a capitalist society, which will bring us great medical and scientific progress if we just leave well enough alone'. Both responses are far too simple and in fact pernicious. The rest of this book will show why.

I have benefited throughout the writing of this book from the generosity of many colleagues, who have manifested the altruistic qualities of a genuine 'gift relationship' in making their expertise, advice and kindness freely available to me. During my stay in 2004 at the Columbia University Institute for Scholars at Reid Hall, Paris, where this book was begun, I was given a great deal of support by Danielle Haase-Dubosc and Mihaela Bacou. Former and current members of the French CCNE (Comité Consultatif National d'Ethique) were equally generous with their time: among them, Nicole Questiaux, Simone Bateman and Anne Fagot-Largeault, to whom I am also grateful for her invitation to present a seminar on my work in progress at the Collège de France. Jean-Paul Amann, her deputy, was enormously helpful in setting up and chairing the session. At the CCNE library near the Invalides, I was warmly welcomed by staff and benefited from their excellent collection of bioethics literature, as well as from the specialised search facilities which they graciously make available to foreign scholars. Jennifer Merchant, professor at the Université de Paris II Panthéon-Assas, gave me a very great number of valuable 'leads' into the French bioethics and biolaw literature, which is still too little known outside France.

Chapter 8 could never have been written without the remarkable opportunity graciously afforded me by Nga Pae o te Maramatanga, the New Zealand National Institute for Research Excellence in Maori Development and Advancement. Their conference on 'Research ethics, tikanga Maori/indigenous and protocols for working with communities', held in Wellington in June 2004, was not just a scholarly gathering, but rather a collaborative venture with Maori communities all over Aotearoa/New Zealand. Invited speakers were sent into local groups to work together in identifying the most pressing research ethics questions, then brought back to the plenary conference together with their hosts for an open discussion. I have never before given a conference paper which was followed not by the attack-and-defence style of questioning all too common among philosophers, but rather by a song from my hosts on the platform. It was one of the most moving experiences of my academic life, because it was much more than just academic. My deepest thanks to my hosts at the Bluff *marae*, Te Runanga o Awarua, particularly Sumaria Beaton, and to Mera Penehira, Sharon Hawke and Paul Reynolds of Nga Pae o te Maramatanga for their good company and excellent organisational skills. My deepest thanks also to Lopeti Senituli for presenting me with a copy of his paper on Tonga at this conference and for his helpful answers to my questions. I am grateful as well to John Pennington, Executive Officer of Toi Te Taiao/the Bioethics Council, who was hospitable and helpful in providing me with materials and explanations concerning the human gene transplantation consultation exercise. Most of all, I am very deeply honoured to have been ritually welcomed into the Bastion Point and Bluff *marae* by my hosts, the *tangata whenua: karanga mai, mihi mai.*

Rightly or wrongly, I like to think that my slant on bioethics issues is unusually global, but I could never have transcended the narrow bounds of liberal Anglo-Saxon thought without help from many friends abroad. Besides my Maori and French colleagues, I would particularly like to thank the organisers of several European Commission projects in which I have been involved, particularly Heather Widdows, Caroline Mullen, Helen Harris, Itziar Alkorta Idiakez, Aitziber Emaldi Cirion, Urban Wiesing, Christian Byk and Ruth Chadwick. It was thanks to my dear friend Ron Berghmans of the University of Maastricht that I first made these Europe-wide acquaintances. Other Dutch and Belgian colleagues also deserve a mention, particularly Ruud ter Meulen, Geertrui van Overwalle and Guy Widdershoven, all of whom have been, as the saying goes, a great pleasure to work with. I would also like to express my deepest thanks to the jury and organisers of the international Spinoza Lens award, particularly Marli Huijer and Rene Foqué, for the way in which they have helped me to see continuities in my work, of which I myself had been unaware, and to venture further into the Forbidden Forest of phenomenology.

I owe a very great deal to Dr Susan Bewley, chair of the Royal College of Obstetricians and Gynaecologists Ethics Committee, without whose assistance I would never have had access to the clinical evidence base about cord blood, used in chapter 4. I respect a great many clinicians for their commitment to serious ethical debate, but perhaps Susan most of all. My thanks should also go to the librarians at the Royal College, to my colleagues on the Ethics Committee, and to my former student Saskia Tromp for first alerting me to the issue of cord blood during our supervisions.

I am also very grateful to Onesimus Kipchuma, associate editor of the *University of Nairobi Law Journal*, for providing me with a copy of the journal containing an article on 'The tragic African commons' by Prof. H. W. O. Okoth-Ogendo, which I found invaluable in writing chapter 8. Among many other colleagues whose comments have helped me to refine my ideas, I would particularly like to thank Catherine Waldby, Lori Andrews, Susan Dodds, Francoise Baylis, Carolyn McLeod, Catriona MacKenzie, Jane Kaye, Mary Mahowald, Carole Pateman, Alan Ryan, Jennifer Hornsby, Diana Coole, Susan James, Ingrid Schneider and Sarah Sexton. Thanks should also go to anonymous referees at Cambridge University Press, as well as to Margaret Brazier, Finola O'Sullivan and Brenda Burke.

And finally, once more with feeling, *con brio, affetuosamente:* to Chris, Anders and Pip.

DONNA DICKENSON
Beckley, Oxford
June 2006

1   Do We All Have 'Feminised' Bodies Now?

It is widely feared that we no longer possess a property in our own bodies. Instead, it has been argued, 'what we are witnessing is nothing less than a new gold rush, and the territory is the human body'.[1] Tangible rights in human tissue and intangible rights in the human genome have been said to be the subject of a new enclosure movement by researchers, biotechnology corporations and governments.[2] Commodification of the body, broadly construed to include private property rights by third parties in tissue, DNA samples, umbilical cord blood and other substances derived from individuals' bodies, has caused great, if sometimes belated, outrage among patients' rights organisations, academic commentators, journalists and the general public, in both the developing and the developed worlds.[3]

---

[1] Suzanne Holland, 'Contested commodities at both ends of life: buying and selling embryos, gametes and body tissues' (2001) 11 *Kennedy Institute of Ethics Journal* 283–4.

[2] James Boyle, 'The second enclosure movement and the construction of the public domain' (2003) 66 *Law and Contemporary Problems* 33–74.

[3] In a large literature, see e.g. James Meek, 'Why you are first in the great gene race', *The Guardian*, 15 November 2000, p. 4; Nuffield Council on Bioethics, *The Ethics of Patenting DNA* (London, Nuffield Council on Bioethics, 2002); Danish Council of Ethics, *Patenting Human Genes* (Copenhagen, Danish Council on Ethics, 1994); Bartha M. Knoppers, 'Status, sale and patenting of human genetic material: an international survey' (1999) 1 *Nature Reviews Genetics* 23; B. M. Knoppers, M. Hirtle and K. C. Glass, 'Commercialization of genetic research and public policy' (1999) 286 *Science*, 5448, 2277–8; Lopeti Senituli, 'They came for sandalwood, now the b . . . s are after our genes!', paper presented at the conference 'Research ethics, tikanga Maori/indigenous and protocols for working with communities', Wellington, New Zealand, 10–12 June 2004; Donna Dickenson, 'Commodification of human tissue: implications for feminist and development ethics' (2002) 2(1) *Developing World Bioethics* 55–63; Commission on Intellectual Property Rights, *Integrating Intellectual Property Rights and Development Policy* (London, Department for International Development, 2002); Comité Consultatif National d'Ethique, *Umbilical Cord Blood Banks for Autologous Use or for Research* (Report no. 74, Paris, CCNE, 2002); Margaret J. Radin, *Contested Commodities: The Trouble with Trade in Sex, Children, Body Parts and Other Things* (Cambridge, MA, Harvard University Press, 1996); and David Resnik, 'The commodification of human reproductive materials' (1998) 24 *Journal of Medical Ethics* 288–93.

An eBay auction for a healthy human kidney attracted global bids up to US$5.75 billion. The leg bones of the late broadcaster Alistair Cooke were stolen by a criminal ring as his body lay in a New York funeral home, and subsequently sold, like those of an estimated 1,800 others, for processing into dental implants. Advertisements regularly circulate in US college newspapers, offering egg 'donors' amounts varying between US$5,000–$50,000,[4] depending on 'desirability': blond, tall, athletic and musical donors command the higher prices, at considerable risk to themselves. One report documented the taking of seventy eggs at one time from a 'donor' who nearly died in the process;[5] another, the international trade for beauty treatments of fetuses from Ukrainian women paid £100 to have an abortion.[6] The commodification of genetic research, it has been alleged, extends beyond the issues of patenting gene sequences or harvesting DNA, to the way in which the very agenda of research is dictated by corporate requirements.[7] If this is true, the scientific method has itself become a commodity. Even more broadly, both donors and recipients can be seen to become part of the 'phenomenology of exchange'.[8]

As in the old agricultural enclosure movement, 'things that were formerly thought to be uncommodifiable, essentially common or outside the market altogether are being turned into private possessions under a new kind of property regime'.[9] Throughout the world a series of legal cases, statutes and patenting conventions such as the European Biotechnology Directive of 1998, appear to have generated an unstoppable momentum towards the transfer of rights over the body and its component parts from the individual 'owner' to others: for example, the *Moore* case, in which

---

[4] Susan Weidman Schneider, 'Jewish women's eggs: a hot commodity in the IVF marketplace' (2001) 26(3) *Lilith* 22.

[5] Allen Jacobs, James Dwyer and Peter Lee, 'Seventy ova' (2001) 31 *Hastings Center Report* 12–14.

[6] Tom Parfit, 'Beauty salons fuel trade in aborted babies', *Guardian Unlimited*, 17 April 2005, available at www.guardian.co.uk. The report alleged that women were paid extra to have late abortions, since fetuses at an advanced stage of development were thought to have greater restorative powers. In a context where abortion was, until recently, the normal mode of 'contraception', vulnerable women may feel fewer qualms about this procedure; corrupt doctors, it is alleged, are even advising women to have a termination on grounds of fetal abnormality where none exists. An illicit trade between Ukraine and Russia provides the fetuses to Moscow beauty salons, where they are sold for up to £5,000 each.

[7] Dorothy Nelkin, 'Is bioethics for sale?' (2003) 24 *Tocqueville Review* 2, 45–60.

[8] Diane Tober, 'Semen as gift, semen as goods: reproductive workers and the market in altruism' (2001) 7 *Body and Society* 137–60.

[9] James Boyle, 'Fencing off ideas: enclosure and the disappearance of the public domain', Interactivist Info Exchange, available at http://slash.autonomedia.org/analysis, accessed 10 September 2004, p. 5.

an immortal cell line was created from the T-cells of a patient who was held to have no further rights in that cell line.[10]

Most people are surprised and somewhat shocked when they learn that Moore apparently did not 'own' his body. Legal doctrines under both civil and common law systems have left us with something of a vacuum. In fact, we do not own our bodies in law: they are not the subject of property rights in any conventional sense, although traditionally they have been shielded to some extent by what James W. Harris calls 'protected non-property holdings'.[11] Thus while corpses cannot be owned at common law, those charged with their disposal – hospitals, families and public or religious authorities – are restricted by certain duties and endowed with certain powers, although these are not ownership privileges and powers. Once tissue is separated from the living body, however, the common law generally assumes either that it has been abandoned by its original 'owner', or that it is and was always *res nullius*, no one's thing, belonging to no one when removed.[12] Under previous circumstances, the tissue would have been presumed to have been removed because it was diseased, and thus of no further value to the person from whom it was extracted. Civil law systems such as that of France typically view the body as *une chose hors commerce*, or *res extra commercium*: a thing not subject to contract or exchange.[13] Similarly, under French law, tissue removed during a procedure is considered to be abandoned, *res derelictae*. In both cases, contracts in bodily tissue and materials are difficult or impossible to enforce, although for different reasons. In both systems, patients have

[10] *Moore v. Regents of the University of California*, 51 Cal. 3rd 120, 793 P. 2d, 271 Cal. Rptr. 146 (1990). This well-known case concerned a man diagnosed with leukaemia who underwent a splenectomy for therapeutic purposes. He was subsequently asked to return to the hospital several times to donate further tissue samples unrelated to the spleen. It transpired that his unusually active immune cells had been used to produce an immortal cell line with an estimated commercial value of US$3 million. Moore sued to establish proprietrary rights in the cell line and the researchers' and clinicians' failure to obtain his informed consent to the further extractions.

[11] James W. Harris, *Property and Justice* (Oxford, Oxford University Press, 1996), p. 351.

[12] Jean McHale, 'Waste, ownership and bodily products' (2000) 8(2) *Health Care Analysis* 123–35.

[13] For example, an influential and determinative early report of the French Comité Consultatif National d'Ethique (CCNE) (French National Consultative Ethics Committee) states: 'Il faut dresser une digue contre cette merchandisation de la personne, et il n'en est pas d'autre que le principe intangible selon lequel le corps humain est hors commerce.' ('We must set up a bulwark against such commodification of the person, and the most fitting is the intangible principle according to which the human body is beyond commerce.') CCNE, *Recherche biomedicale et respect de la personne humaine* (Paris, DF, 1987), cited in Anne Fagot-Largeault, 'Ownership of the human body: judicial and legislative responses in France' in Henk ten Have and Jos Welie (eds.), *Ownership of the Human Body: Philosophical Considerations on the Use of the Human Body and its Parts in Healthcare* (Dordrecht, Kluwer, 1998), pp. 115–40, at p. 130.

no further property rights in their tissue once an informed consent to its extraction or donation has been given.[14]

But why should it be so widely assumed that we do own our bodies? Why does it matter so much? A large part of what disturbs people about commodification of the body appears to be the way in which it transforms us into objects of property-holding, rather than active human subjects. (For the time being, I will not distinguish between objectification and commodification; chapter 2, however, will tease out some important differences between these two core concepts.) In the French context, this concern is clearly stated in several opinions of the national ethics commission, which has consistently declared that human dignity and subjectivity are incompatible with selling oneself or parts of oneself as objects. 'Trading persons, or parts of persons, or elements of persons in the market place, would turn subjects into objects, that is, subvert the foundations of the social order. Preserving the freedom of subjects involves maintaining (so to speak) all parts and bits of subjects within the realm of persons.'[15] The sociologist Dominique Memmi has characterised the French national ethics committee's response to commodification of the body or genome as grounded in fear of a threat 'to the totality of the subject . . . of an intrusion into what appears to be the most secret and intimate area, that of the body or gene'.[16] In the common law context, the emphasis on human dignity is less pronounced and a libertarian rights-based discourse more frequent.

Although some Anglo-American commentators argue that our rights as moral agents and human subjects actually require us to have the free right of disposal over our bodies,[17] the common law posits that something can be either a person or an object – but not both – and that only objects can be regulated by property-holding. The implication is clear: to the extent that persons' body parts can be regulated by property-holding,

[14] In France, the CCNE Avis on products derived from human materials (no. 9, February 1987) stipulates that products of commercial benefit derived from donated tissues should be sold at a market price which only reflects the researchers' and manufacturers' labour, and that the patient should have no right to any financial benefits. See Fagot-Largeault, 'Ownership', p. 131.

[15] *Ibid.* p. 137. See, in particular, opinion no. 21, 'That the human body should not be used for commercial purposes' (1990) and opinion no. 27, 'That the human genome should not be used for commercial purposes' (1991).

[16] Dominique Memmi, *Les gardiens du corps: dix ans de magistère bioéthique* (Paris, Editions de l'Ecole des Hautes Etudes en Sciences Sociales, 1996), p. 18.

[17] For arguments in favour of removing or modifying legal prohibitions on commodification of human tissue, see e.g., David B. Resnik, 'The commercialization of human stem cells: ethical and policy issues' (2002) 10 *Health Care Analysis* 127–54, and Stephen Wilkinson, 'Commodification arguments for the legal prohibition of organ sale' (2000) 8 *Health Care Analysis* 189–201.

those body parts are objects, or things. If we are embodied persons, then to some extent we become objects too. The question is to what extent.

Bodies, persons and things

This core distinction between persons and things is as much philosophical as legal. It has its origins in Kant:

Man cannot dispose over himself because he is not a thing; he is not his own property; to say that he is would be self-contradictory; for insofar as he is a person he is a Subject in whom the ownership of things can be vested, and if he were his own property he would be a thing over which he could have ownership. But a person cannot be a property and so cannot be a thing which can be owned, for it is impossible to be a person and a thing, the proprietor and the property.[18]

Human tissue and human genetic material, however, fall between the two stools, containing elements of both person and thing, subject and object. It may well be that our discomfort about commodification of human tissue and genetic material reflects a sense that recent developments take us nearer to the object end of the spectrum. In the Kantian formulation, this shift radically undermines our very humanity. The relationship between the body and the person is a constant question which will recur throughout this book, with the insights gained from the intervening chapters summarised and tested in the Afterword; here I merely give some introductory thoughts.

Biotechnology has made the entire notion of the body much more fluid. On the one hand, bodily functions can be replicated or enhanced by objects originally extraneous to the subject, machines such as ventilators and pacemakers, as well as by substances derived from human bodies but through industrial processes, such as factor VIII blood-clotting products. On the other, human biomaterials extracted from the body enter into research and commerce as objects – to a greater extent in more commodified economies such as the USA, but not only there. The second development is the primary focus of my attention, but the first has also drawn feminist comment, for example in Donna Haraway's metaphors about cyborgs.[19] It becomes much more difficult to insist that the body simply *is* the person when tissues from the body are no longer

---

[18] Kant, *Lectures on Ethics* (Indianapolis, Bobbs-Merrill, 1963), p. 4, cited in G. A. Cohen, *Self-Ownership, Freedom and Equality* (Cambridge, Cambridge University Press, 1995), p. 211.

[19] Donna J. Haraway, *Simians, Cyborgs and Women: The Reinvention of Nature* (New York, Routledge, 1991).

physically joined to the person, or when the body is a conglomerate of extraneous tissues and my own. Feminist theory again shows its utility in helping us to frame the current debate over the 'new enclosures' more clearly. Bioethics, by contrast, currently lacks sustained reflection on the relationship between persons and bodies, including body parts and tissues.[20]

New biotechnologies disaggregate the body, robbing it of its organic unity and encouraging the view of body parts as separate components which do not sum to anything more than their compilation.[21] As Maria Marzano-Parisoli has written in her excellent *Penser le corps*, 'In addition to the *natural body* and its parts, there now exists a series of artificially produced bodily elements which make the distinction between *natural body* and *artificial body* much harder to pin down.'[22] The patenting of genetic sequences, considered in chapter 5, provides a clear and, to many, disturbing illustration of the way in which elements extracted from the body take on a separate existence from that of the original subject. Another telling and troublesome example is that of hand and face transplants, in which the bodily identity of the donor is a continual reminder to the recipient of another subject's integration into one's own body.[23]

When body and subject are equated, the body is inviolable because it is identified with the subject, which makes violation not merely philosophically impermissible but jurisprudentially impossible:[24] the body is the substratum of the person, and thus innate to the subject of law. In other words, there can be no distinction between the person as rights-holding subject and the body as the object of rights. If the subject is sovereign, however, there is no necessary logical link between these two propositions. We might want to maintain that the sovereign individual should have the right to dispose of her body as she wishes, and indeed that the right to do so is an important cause for feminists to reclaim: hence the growing literature supporting prostitutes' rights over their own bodies, in

---

[20] Catriona MacKenzie, 'Conceptions of the body and conceptions of autonomy in bioethics', paper presented at the Seventh World International Association of Bioethics conference, Sydney, November 2004.

[21] Jayasna Gupta, 'Postmodern bodies, assisted reproduction and women's agency', paper presented at the Seventh World International Association of Bioethics conference, Sydney, November 2004.

[22] Maria M. Marzano-Parisoli, *Penser le corps* (Paris, Presses Universitaires de France, 2002), p. 118.

[23] Donna Dickenson and Guy Widdershoven, 'Ethical issues in limb transplants' (2001) 15(2) *Bioethics* 115–24; Donna Dickenson and Nadey Hakim, 'Ethical issues in limb allotransplants' (1999) 75 *Postgraduate Medical Journal* 513–15.

[24] Marzano-Parisoli, *Penser le corps*, p. 122.

a neo-liberal style of argument.[25] I do not myself accept that argument, but I do want to draw attention to the illicit slide from the assertion that the body is the subject to the claim that the subject does not have the right to dispose of her body as she sees fit. In the extreme cases of slavery or of the sale of life-sustaining organs, we can see the contradiction between disposing of one's body, in the name of free action as a subject, and the subsequent extinguishing of the subject in whose name this freedom is supposed to operate. A contract of slavery, for example, is logically invalid because it extinguishes the legal existence of one party to the contract. It is therefore consistent in philosophical and legal terms to bar such forms of alienation of the body by sale or other means. The more difficult cases concern disposing of parts of the body which do not threaten the continued existence of the subject.

Again, Kant is often cited as the locus of the assertion that we are barred from using our bodies as mere tools, since that would entail treating ourselves as mere means – although to our own ends rather than those of another subject. While Kant clearly states that we are not authorised to sell any parts of our bodies, he seems to make exceptions for non-vital elements such as hair, although he is uneasy even about that. In other situations, for example in the permissible amputation of a diseased foot, Kant does appear to draw the dualistic distinction between body as object and moral person as subject, so that we are entitled to 'use' the body in such a way as to preserve the person. (I have put 'use' in inverted commas because amputating a diseased foot does not seem to be 'using' the body as a tool in the same way as selling a part of the body, even selling a body part in order to keep body and soul together.)

So although Kant at first denies that the person can be separated from the body, or that the body can be treated as a thing without injuring the person, he makes exceptions for certain parts of the body, particularly those which are not vital to life. One might think that DNA swabs used in genetic and genomic analysis, or tissue slides containing microscopic samples, would be among those modern-day exceptions that could be justified on a Kantian basis. Oddly, however, it seems that these forms of tissue extraction have often occasioned the strongest protest. In chapter 8 I describe a case example from Tonga, where there was deep public resistance to an Australian biotechnology firm's agreement with the government to collect tissue samples for the purpose of genomic research into

---

[25] Julia O'Connell Davidson, *Prostitution, Power and Freedom* (University of Michigan Press, 1999). For an exploration of the assumptions behind this discourse, see my 'Philosophical assumptions and presumptions about trafficking for prostitution' in Christien van den Anker and Jeroen Doemernik (eds.), *Trafficking and Women's Rights* (Basingstoke, Palgrave Macmillan, 2006), pp. 43–53.

diabetes. As the director of the successful protest group put it, 'They came for sandalwood, now the b . . . s are after our genes.'[26]

The feminised body

There is widespread dismay, in both the global South and the wealthy countries, at the notion that by losing a property in our bodies, we lose a part of our individual identity. But why does this phenomenon seem so novel? After all, women's bodies have been subject to various forms of property-holding over many centuries and in many societies. In this book I want to argue that what we are witnessing is fear of *the feminisation of property in the body*. The 'new enclosures' of the genetic commons or of forms of human tissue threaten to extend the objectification and commodification of the body to both sexes. Everyone has a 'female' body now, or, more properly, a feminised body: while men do not have bodies that are biologically female, both male and female bodies are now subject to the objectification that was previously largely confined to women's experience.[27]

That, at least, is the presumption underlying much current discourse and debate over the ethics, law and politics of human tissue, particularly in the areas of genetic patenting and biobanks, as I shall demonstrate in chapters 5 and 6. In those chapters, however, I will also suggest another gender dimension – or perhaps a variant of the same one. Fear of feminisation and the sense of losing a property in the body are most pronounced where both men and women are the 'sources' of tissue, as in genetic patenting and biobanking. The taking of solely female tissue does not provoke such widespread coverage and concern. In other words, objectification and commodification of the body continue to be perceived as more 'normal' for women's bodies; the only difference is that what is objectified and commodified now takes new and disturbing forms, as in the 'harvesting' of ova, the subject of chapter 3, or the private banking of umbilical cord blood, treated in chapter 4. But even though those procedures are more invasive and far riskier than the processes involved in genetic patenting and biobanking, the comparatively small affronts involved in patenting and biobanking technologies cause greater public concern.

---

[26] Senituli, 'They came for sandalwood', p. 1.

[27] Michel Foucault has famously argued that all bodies are now subject to surveillance by modern medicine and cultural proscriptions; my argument differs from Foucault's, however, in that I focus on commodification and objectification, and in that I do not claim that all bodies are equally subject to these processes. Furthermore, my thesis is specifically feminist. While Foucault is widely regarded as the 'father' of 'body politics', this is to ignore the feminist 'mothers' (Lynda Birke, *Feminism and the Biological Body* (Edinburgh, University of Edinburgh Press, 1999), p. 33).

The crux of my claim is that commodification of human tissue and the human genome affects both sexes, and thus appears to feminise men, by threatening to reduce both men and women to the role of objects – the physical matter on which medical interventions, patenting or experimentation takes place, and which serves as the raw material from which added value can be extracted. (This, too, is a feminine role, as feminist theorists such as Donna Haraway and Sandra Harding have pointed out.)[28] Although some bioethicists and sociologists view the body as a *tabula rasa* on which the subject can now inscribe whatever identity he wills,[29] thanks to modern science, here I shall be arguing the opposite position. What is threatening about commodification of the body, judging from a widely accepted discourse, is that it reduces both sexes to the condition of objects. Whereas in many countries the extension of abortion and contraception rights in the 1960s gave women increasing control over their bodies, elevating them to the status of subjects which only men had previously enjoyed, the new enclosures throw the process into reverse. But whereas the new reproductive rights functioned mainly to raise *women* to the level of autonomy men had enjoyed – despite some commentators' view that what happened in the 1960s was that everyone gained new powers over their own bodies[30] – the 'new enclosures' threaten both sexes. They do not threaten both sexes equally: female tissue is more valuable, as I shall illustrate in chapters 3 and 4. But because they also threaten *men*, they provoke a more pointed debate.

In some cases, as I have noted, the feminisation of property in the body takes specific forms that can only apply to women: for example, the developing global trade in human ova.[31] The forms of corporeal commodification which only affect women are under-researched and little noticed, so that part of the task of this book is to draw attention to them. (Indeed,

---

[28] Donna J. Haraway, 'Situated knowledges: the science question in feminism and the privilege of partial perspective' (1988) 14 *Feminist Studies* 3; Sandra Harding, 'Is gender a variable in conceptions of rationality? A survey of issues' in Carol C. Gould (ed.), *Beyond Domination: New Perspectives on Feminism and Philosophy* (Totowa, NJ, Rowman and Allanheld, 1984), pp. 43–63.

[29] Bernard Andrieu, 'La santé biotechnologique du corps-sujet' (2004) 3 *Revue philosophique* 339–44: 'Les transformations biotechnologiques de son corps seront comprises ici comme l'invention d'un corps incarnant le sujet.' ('Biological transformations of one's body will be understood here as the invention of a body that incarnates the subject.' (p. 339), and again on p. 343: 'La matière biologique peut être construite par le sujet lui-même.' ('Biological matter can be constructed by the subject himself.'). This style of analysis rather grandiloquently conflates several different technologies, including preimplantation genetic diagnosis, gene therapy and stem cell lines, assuming that they have all become not merely possible but universal, so that we can all create whatever form of body-objects we as subject-agents may desire.

[30] Memmi, *Les gardiens du corps*, p. 29.

[31] Donna Dickenson, 'The threatened trade in human ova' (2004) 5(2) *Nature Reviews Genetics* 167.

I will spend more time on those issues than on the questions around biobanking and genetic patenting, which already enjoy far more extensive coverage in the literature.) I will also point out in chapter 8 that commodification has particular ramifications for people in the global South, particularly indigenous peoples; it may well be viewed by those peoples as part of disempowering, and arguably feminising, neo-colonialism. Since the 'new enclosures' are global in scale, they require some attempt at a global analysis.[32]

It might seem odd for me to advocate a property approach grounded in feminist reasoning, if property is about objects, and if women's status has hovered uncomfortably between that of a subject and that of an object. However, I shall shortly illustrate how the 'bundle' concept of property concerns relationships, obviously among people, of exclusion and inclusion: common-law jurisprudence typically views property as a set of relationships between persons, not as a thing in itself.[33] This emphasis on property as relationship is entirely consistent with feminist theory, which has frequently foregrounded relationships and relatedness. Chapter 2 has more to say about this contention.

My argument could lead in several directions, and I want to begin by making it clear which roads I have not taken. As Robert Frost says, the road not travelled by can make all the difference. Here are some of the perilous legal and philosophical roads not taken in this book.

1. I certainly do not wish to argue that we should be indifferent to the commodification of the body, or that because women have had to suffer the status of objects of property-holding, men should too. On the contrary, I argue that by and large we should oppose commodification and objectification of the body. By examining the insights offered by feminist theory, which has been sensitive to the myriad ways in which property in female bodies has manifested itself, we may learn more nuanced and historically wise ways of doing so. What appears a new phenomenon, the commodification of human tissue and genetic materials, is, like many other phenomena in bioethics, not really so new as all that. Just because the technologies are new does not mean that the underlying ethical problems and political phenomena are utterly beyond our previous experience. The commodification of the human body has already been compared to the agricultural enclosures of the eighteenth and early nineteenth centuries; feminisation of the body is another comparison,

---

[32] Such an analysis has been undertaken for whole organs by Nancy Scheper-Hughes: see e.g., 'Bodies for sale – whole or in parts' (2002) 7 *Body and Society* 1–8.

[33] Wesley Newcomb Hohfeld, *Fundamental Legal Conceptions as applied in Judicial Reasoning* (New Haven, CT, Yale University Press, 1919). An important exception to this generalisation is Harris's *Property and Justice*.

invoking another set of historical referents, some of which I explored in my earlier *Property, Women and Politics*.[34] If we can understand this history, perhaps we are not doomed to repeat it.

2. Nor do I assert that commodification is always the same for tangible and intangible property, for civil and common law systems and for all types of body tissue or products, in an essentialist manner. Much of the task of this book is to disentangle the historically, medically and culturally specific forms it takes in our present time and in the past. I am concerned throughout to situate objectification and commodification in specific historic and cultural contexts. The inclusion of chapters 7 and 8, on France and Tonga respectively, transcends the usual debate on property in the body, which rarely moves beyond the developed world, and in particular the Anglo-American context.

3. I do not claim at any point that we do actually own our bodies straightforwardly. The arguments presented in my earlier book, *Property, Women and Politics*,[35] distinguished between property in the person, or moral agency, and property in the physical body. The first, I argued, was what Locke meant, not the second, since we do not labour to create our bodies. In chapter 2 of this book, I will say more about my original argument concerning women's property in their reproductive labour, first made in *Property, Women and Politics* and subsequently taken up by a number of other authors.[36] There is no justification in liberal theory for a generalised notion of property in the body, certainly not as routinely assumed in media debate. However, women's reproductive labour in donating enucleated ova for stem cell technologies and umbilical cord blood for banking *does* fit the Lockean argument, as I shall argue in chapters 3 and 4. In chapter 6 I will ask whether the lesser amounts of effort, risk-taking and intentionality involved in donating tissue and DNA samples for genetic patenting and biobanking also confer some lesser set of rights.

Even if we cannot normally be said to own our bodies, that does not mean that we must accept the status of objects: rather, that we can and must find better arguments than overly simplistic liberal ones with which to oppose commodification. I will also develop Hegelian and Marxist

---

[34] Donna Dickenson, *Property, Women and Politics* (Cambridge, Polity Press, 1997).

[35] See especially chapters 3 and 7.

[36] e.g., Laura Brace, *The Politics of Property: Labour, Freedom and Belonging* (Edinburgh, Edinburgh University Press, 2004); Carolyn McLeod and Francoise Baylis, 'For dignity or money: feminists on the commodification of women's reproductive labour' in Bonnie Steinbock (ed.), *The Oxford Handbook of Bioethics* (Oxford, Oxford University Press, 2005); Carole Pateman, 'On critics and contract' in Charles Mills and Carole Pateman, *Contract and Domination* (Cambridge, Polity Press, 2007).

notions concerning contract, mutual recognition and alienation, among others. As I have already noted, liberal and libertarian arguments can cut either way in the commodification debate: the supposed right to control one's own body has been presented as a knock-down argument in favour of allowing free sale of bodily parts.[37] Thus, I emphatically do not take the free market line that we do own our bodies, still less that we should see the sale of our body parts as enhancing our freedom as moral agents. For example, I shall wish to distinguish rights of transfer by donation from rights of sale. Here, I shall be drawing on the accepted characterisation in the common law of property as a bundle of rights, or set of relationships.[38] We can possess none, some or all of the sticks in the bundle.

It will be of enormous importance to both the argument of this book, and to public policy more broadly, that we think long and hard about which rights we want to protect. The proponents of commodification, such as some researchers, universities and biotechnology companies, are prone to assume that once they acquire proprietary rights, those rights are complete and undifferentiated. Although some legal decisions, *Moore* among them, do seem to give aid and comfort to this view, it is incoherent. Property rights can be and should be disaggregated and distinguished: this is the conventional view in jurisprudence, to the extent that some commentators even doubt whether there is such a thing as 'property', as a single coherent concept.[39] (Interestingly, here is another parallel with feminism: some feminist theorists, particularly those of a postmodern persuasion, doubt that there is a single category called 'woman'.)[40]

Those rights that we most need in order to protect ourselves from the enclosure of the body are only partial: just as our ancestors merely demanded rights of use over the commons, rather than powers of complete alienation such as gift or sale, so too can we comfortably make do with a limited number of sticks from the bundle. I will delineate

---

[37] John Harris, for example, presents arguments against allowing the poor to sell their own body parts as a denial of their rights, through the erection of a cartel in bodily products from which the poor are excluded (*Wonderwoman and Superman: The Ethics of Human Biotechnology* (Oxford, Oxford University Press, 1992), p. 132).

[38] A. M. Honoré, 'Ownership', originally published in A. G. Guest (ed.), *Oxford Essays in Jurisprudence* (Oxford, Oxford University Press, 1961), reprinted in A. M. Honoré, *Making Law Bind: Essays Legal and Philosophical* (Oxford, Clarendon Press, 1987), pp. 161–92. The conception of property in civil law is typically more unitary, deriving as it does from the Roman notion of complete *dominium*. See John Christman, *The Myth of Property: Toward an Egalitarian Theory of Ownership* (Oxford, Oxford University Press, 1994), p. 5.

[39] James Penner, *The Idea of Property in Law* (Oxford, Clarendon Press, 1997).

[40] Judith Butler, *Subjects of Desire: Hegelian Reflections on Twentieth-Century France* (New York, Columbia University Press, 1987).

later which sticks those are: they will include certainly protection against unauthorised taking, but we may want to debate rights of conditional gift, income and management over our tissue and gene sequences. Let me begin, however, by explaining the concept of property as a bundle of rights and associated jurisprudential concepts. We need to get these distinctions clear at the outset, particularly since so much current debate on objectification and commodification of the body fails to do so.

It is also essential to delineate exactly which aspects of objectification, which sticks in the property bundle, might be said to have applied to women. In my earlier book I actually argued quite strongly against the prevalent notion in modern feminism that women have typically been nothing other than objects of property, and that therefore the concept of property is inherently anti-feminist. As the legal theorist Carol Rose points out, there has been far more feminist interest in women as objects than as subjects.[41] Yet this is implicitly to accept the sovereignty of the male subject and to consign women to the role of victims, in an essentialist and ahistorical fashion. Ultimately, viewing women's relationship to property purely in the passive leads down a political and theoretical cul-de-sac. We need a more nuanced analysis, and using the concept of property as a bundle of rights can assist us in this task.

Property as a bundle of rights

Honoré's classic list of entitlements and duties involved in the property relationship[42] demonstrates the variety of entitlements and duties into which the concept of property can be disaggregated. The owner of object X may have some or all of the following:
(1) a right to the physical possession of X;
(2) a right to its use;
(3) a right to its management, that is, to determine the ways in which others can use it;
(4) a right to the income that can be derived from its use by others;
(5) a right to its capital value;
(6) a right to security against its being taken by others;
(7) a right to transmit or alienate it to others by gift or bequest;
(8) a right to transmit or alienate it to others by sale;
(9) a permanent right to these other rights, without any limit or term;
(10) a duty to refrain from using X in a way that harms others, that is, liability for harm caused by X.

---

[41] Carol M. Rose, *Property and Persuasion: Essays on the History, Theory and Rhetoric of Ownership* (Boulder, Westview Press, 1994).
[42] Honoré, 'Ownership'.

The notion of property rights as a bundle of relationships – separate 'sticks' in the bundle – helps us to avoid ahistorical forms of essentialism and oversimplification, in analysing the extent to which women and their bodies have been objects or subjects. Similarly, it will also help us to avoid oversimplification and sensationalism in measuring the breadth of commodification of the body more generally, or in terms of my argument, the extent to which both male and female bodies are 'feminised'. In addition it has been put to good practical effect in other contexts than biotechnology: for example, in developing a bundle of 'traditional resource rights' for indigenous communities from those concepts already recognised in international and national law, with the addition of new 'sticks' allowing more effective protections.[43] However, the bundle concept is not immune from criticism within jurisprudence. One influential critique[44] revolves around this question: if the concept of property is so disaggregated as to mean nothing more than a set of relationships, does it retain any core meaning? Is there any whole that is more than the sum of the parts? If the idea of property in law has no independent existence, this argument runs, its applicability is lessened.[45] But why? If anything, the idea's applicability will be greater, because it will be much more flexible.

In relation to tissue, many commentators have mistrusted the property approach because they wrongly perceive property as an all-or-nothing concept. In the *Moore* case, for example, the majority California Supreme Court opinion rejected bestowing a property right in tissue on the subjects of research, partly because the court assumed that such a right would entail all the sticks in the bundle. If Moore were given property rights in his tissue, this argument ran, he (and similarly situated patients) would be in a position to block beneficial medical research: not just because he would enjoy rights (3) (management) and (6) (security against unauthorised taking), but also because he would enjoy all the other rights as well. In particular, if Moore benefited from rights (4), (5) and (8) (to income, capital value and sale proceeds) there would be no incentive for research sponsors or firms to develop the cell line for their own commercial purposes, as well as the benefit of society. Further, it was felt to be inequitable to allow Moore to enjoy income or capital value from his T-cells, when it was only by good fortune that he happened to possess a particularly

---

[43] D. Posey and G. Dutfield, *Beyond Intellectual Property: Towards Traditional Resource Rights for Indigenous Peoples and Local Communities* (Ottawa, International Development Research Centre, 1996).

[44] Thomas Grey, "The disintegration of property' in J. P. Pennock and J. Chapman (eds.), *Nomo XXII: Property* (New York, New York University Press, 1980), pp. 69–85.

[45] Penner, *Idea of Property*.

effective immune system. This last argument from justice has its compelling merits, but it need not be determinative if we disaggregate the rights to income and capital (rights (4) and (5)) from the rights to determine the management of the tissue's use (3) and to enjoy protection from taking by others (8). In fact, these were the needs which seemed to motivate Moore most, and which weighed most heavily with the dissenting judges.

Why shouldn't Moore's initial rights against the unauthorised taking of his tissue have been respected in the final state Supreme Court judgment? As the Court of Appeals had already remarked, the research institution's 'position that plaintiff [Moore] cannot own his tissue, but that they can, is fraught with irony'.[46] In his dissent from the majority opinion, Supreme Court justice Broussard J noted acerbically that if another institution had stolen the Moore cell line from the UCLA Medical Center, where it was held, the Center would doubtless have been regarded as the victim of theft.[47] He favoured a policy effectively permitting Moore rights (3), (6) and (7) (to determine how others use the property, to be protected against unauthorised taking and to transmit the property by gift) but not rights (4), (5) or (8) (income, capital value and sale rights). As Broussard put it, 'It is certainly arguable that as a matter of policy or morality it would be wiser to prohibit any private individual or entity from profiting from the fortuitous value that adheres in a part of a human body and instead to require all valuable excised body parts to be deposited in a public repository which would make such materials freely available to all scientists for the betterment of society as a whole.'[48] (We will return to this alternative policy model in chapter 6, which looks at the notion of the charitable trust as a governance mechanism for tissue biobanks.)

It may well turn out that what we most want to protect from the 'new enclosures' is precisely what was at issue in the *Moore* case: unauthorised taking. The UK Alder Hey scandal, in which dead children's body parts were taken without parents' knowledge or consent by a consultant pathologist, unleashed a torrent of anger which had nothing to do with the parents' desire to profit from their children's tissue and everything to do with unauthorised taking.[49] Much the same reaction arose from indigenous peoples in Fiji and Tonga to genomic research authorised

---

[46] 249 Cal. Rptr. 494, 507 (1988, Court of Appeals).
[47] 271 Cal. Rptr. 146, 168 (1990, Supreme Court).   [48] *Ibid.* at 172.
[49] See the UK Department of Health consultation document resulting from the Alder Hey inquiry, *Human Bodies, Human Choices: The Law on Human Organs and Tissue in England and Wales* (London, DOH, 2002).

by their governments without popular consultation (examined further in chapter 8).[50]

If this is indeed our priority, however, do we need the possible combinations of rights subsumed under the bundle concept of property in order to protect ourselves? It has been argued that we already possess sufficient rights under the criminal law: the Theft Act 1998, for example, was found in the case of R v. *Kelly* to entitle the Royal College of Surgeons and Pathologists to possession of body parts preserved by the college and illicitly purloined by a sculptor.[51] If this were true, it would seem that property is indeed an extraneous or empty concept, affording no more protection than we can already cobble together from other sources. The bundle, in this view, gives us both too much and too little: too much, because what we are really concerned with are the rights proclaiming 'keep off';[52] too little, because there is little separate content to the bundle other than already pre-existing rights under other headings than 'property'.

I think this rejection of the property concept as surplus to requirements is overly optimistic about the strength of our protections from other sources against the 'new enclosures'. So far, the *Kelly* case has only been used – and not used all that often – to protect the rights of researchers and physicians, not patients, since it rewards the application of professional skill and labour to tissue samples, rather than the provision of the original tissue. There are also major inconsistencies within the common law,[53] and between common and civil law jurisdictions, over the preliminary issue of whether individuals own their tissue to a sufficient extent that protection against theft would apply in the first place. It is well established that there is no such right in the French civil system, for example: 'clearly French citizens are not the owners of their bodies'.[54] Within the common law system, it is still debatable whether Moore possessed a property in his tissue.

That does not mean that the researchers or the medical centre necessarily did either. However, in the majority's judgment, the UCLA Medical Center *was* deemed to own the material because of the specialised labour

---

[50] Senituli, 'They came for sandalwood'.

[51] *R v. Kelly* [1998] 3 All ER 741. See also Andrew Grubb, ' "I, me mine": bodies, parts and property' (1998) 3 *Medical Law International* 299–313.

[52] Penner, *Idea of Property*, p. 73: 'The general injunction to "keep off" or "leave alone" the property that is not one's own defines the practice of property much better than a series of specific duties which work to facilitate particular uses of others' property.'

[53] Loane Skene, 'Ownership of human tissue and the law' (2002) 3 *Nature Reviews Genetics* 145–48.

[54] Fagot-Largeault, 'Ownership', p. 137.

and investment which they had put into preparing the cell line. This is why Broussard's parallel with theft from the Center fails: Moore had not put any comparable investment of labour into his tissue. True, he submitted to the original splenectomy in which the tissue was extracted, but he derived sufficient benefit from that once the diseased organ was removed, and thus implicitly abandoned by him. Granted, he was asked to return time and time again to donate further samples of other tissues such as hair, blood and semen; here, the courts did find that he had a case, but only for fraudulent obtaining of consent to these unnecessary further procedures – not a property right. The *Kelly* case represents another similar precedent in favour of researchers and doctors, who were judged to have put sufficient expertise and labour into the extraction and preservation of the body parts to have acquired a right against their unauthorised taking. The question of the rights of those from whom the body parts originally came did not arise.

The right against unauthorised taking, as presently construed in the common law, is not sufficient to protect individual patients and their families, as opposed to researchers and firms, against the 'new enclosures'. We need the strength and flexibility that the broader concept of property can give, construed as a bundle of rights from which we choose those that are most appropriate. Which rights those are will be the subject of further analysis in subsequent chapters; here I have been concerned to introduce the concept, and to defend it against the charge that it is so disaggregated as to be useless.[55]

Property rights, personal rights and the 'gift relationship'

As things stand at present, our main defence against the 'new enclosures' is not the *property rights* model, but informed consent, based on a *personal rights* model. In the *Moore* case, for example, it was held that Moore had not given a properly informed consent to the extraction of further tissue beyond the initial splenectomy, but the argument that he had a property right in his tissue was rejected. The personal rights argument was upheld, the property rights claim dismissed. This common law preference for personal rights rather than property rights over one's body, strongly reiterated in the emphasis on consent in the UK Human Tissue

---

[55] See also J. L. Schroeder, 'Chix nix bundle-o-stix: a feminist critique of the disaggregation of property' (1994) 83 *Michigan Law Review* 239.

Act 2004,[56] is echoed by the centrality of informed consent in French bioethics law, within a civil law jurisdiction.[57]

Why is the protection afforded by informed consent insufficient? In Moore's case the answer is obvious from the outcome: he had no meaningful legal redress. More generally, informed consent gives limited protections because it ignores the imbalance of knowledge in favour of the doctor,[58] normally concerns clinical procedures rather than tissue sampling or DNA extraction, and has little to say about the situation of growing commodification in which we find ourselves.[59] Consent is normally conceived of as consent to the initial procedure, not to 'downstream' uses of the tissue: as a one-off requirement rather than an ongoing set of powers and duties. Together with emphasis on 'the gift relationship' – generally interpreted as meaning that once 'given', tissue is beyond further control by the donor[60] – the doctrine of informed consent may simply be a cover for one-way altruism: from individual donor to tissue banks, research team or corporate entity. Whereas the original purpose of gift, in the anthropological literature,[61] is to establish ongoing relationships of indebtedness and gratitude that bind societies together, the intent of some current guidelines seems to be the exact opposite: to cut off any further claims by the donor and any continuing obligations for the clinician, researcher or biotechnology corporation in receipt of the gift. Where Titmuss saw social solidarity and imagined community as the product of a gift-based blood system in which donors could expect to be recipients

---

[56] For further detail, see Bronwyn Parry, 'The new Human Tissue Bill: categorization and definitional issues and their implications' (2005) 1(1) *Genomics, Society and Policy* 74–85; Kathleen Liddell and Susan Wallace, 'Emerging regulatory issues for stem cell medicine' (2005) 1(1) *Genomics, Society and Policy* 54–73.

[57] Code civil, art. 16.3 al. 2; Code de la santé publique, art. L.1211–2.

[58] What was for many years the main case on informed consent in English law, *Sidaway* v. *Board of Governors of Bethlem Royal Hospital* [1985] 1 All ER 643, established that a patient's consent was still valid even if the doctor fails to disclose essential information such as a serious risk in treatment.

[59] For other arguments, see Ken Mason and Graeme Laurie, 'Consent or property? Dealing with the body and its parts in the shadow of Bristol and Alder Hey' (2001) 9 *Medical Law Review* 710–29.

[60] Although some UK Biobank and the HUGO Ethics Committee reports have taken this view, it is not a necessary corollary of the gift relationship. The Brazilian national health council guidelines give those whose genetic data is stored on research databases the right to withdraw it at any time, despite their initial 'gift' of the genetic material. (Bruno Bays, 'Brazil introduces right to genetic privacy', resolution 340 of 8 July 2004, Science and Development Net, available at www.scidevnet. Accessed 20 September 2004.)

[61] The classical text here is Marcel Mauss's study of gift relations in Polynesian and Native Canadian societies, *The Gift: The Form and Reason for Exchange in Archaic Societies* (2nd edn, London, Routledge, 1990).

some day, or recipients donors,[62] the donor of DNA samples to a typical biobank cannot expect any *quid pro quo* except rather vague promises of future social benefits from research. On a global level, there is even less in the way of ongoing relationship or community between donor and recipient.[63]

In the common law tradition, excised tissue was regarded as either *res nullius*, no one's thing, or as having been abandoned by its original 'owner' (once someone's thing, but now open to all claims). Neither traditional approach gives the living 'donor' any subsequent rights, by virtue of informed consent, over the further uses of the tissue. Although the World Health Organisation's *Guidelines on Ethical Issues in Medical Genetics and Genetic Services* recommend a blanket informed consent from tissue sample donors as 'the most efficient and economical approach', blanket consent is not really 'informed' consent at all.[64] Since the donor has not been informed about what specific future uses will be made of her tissue, she is simply waiving further proprietary rights by signing such a consent form. There is no room to stipulate what might or might not be considered respectful uses of the tissue, whereas a modified property rights approach would permit certain uses to be excluded: use of placental tissue for cosmetics, for example, as occurred when the French firm Mérieux UK was allowed to 'harvest' such tissue from NHS hospitals without mothers' knowledge.

These are primarily practical difficulties; there is also a more conceptual problem in legal terms. Recall that in law something can be either a person or an object but not both, although human tissue and genetic material partake of both categories. Recognising this dual nature represents an advance over the earlier viewpoint that excised tissue was merely waste and that DNA was 'just biological stuff'.[65] Seeing elements of the person in an organ accords with popular perceptions, such as the reactions of bereaved parents in the Alder Hey inquiry concerning the unauthorised taking and retention of tissue and organs from dead children

---

[62] Richard Titmuss, *The Gift Relationship: From Human Blood to Social Policy* (Ann Oakley and J. Ashton (eds.) (2nd edn, London, LSE Books, 1997).

[63] An excellent analysis of the unexpected similarity between commodification and the gift relationship can be found in Catherine Waldby and Robert Mitchell, *Tissue Economies: Blood, Organs and Cell Lines in Late Capitalism* (Durham, NC, Duke University Press, 2006).

[64] Roberto Andorno, 'Population genetic databases: a new challenge to human rights' in Christian Lenk, Nils Hoppe and Roberto Andorno (eds.), *Ethics and Law of Intellectual Property: Current Problems in Politics, Science and Technology* (Aldershot, Ashgate, 2006), pp. 45–73, at p. 58.

[65] Bartha M. Knoppers, 'DNA banking: a retrospective perspective' in J. Burley and J. Harris (eds.), *A Companion to Genethics* (Oxford, Blackwell, 2002), pp. 379–86.

by a hospital pathologist. Even small quantities of someone's tissue may still retain their essence: think of Victorian jewellery, worn by mourners, made from the dead person's hair. The UK Retained Organs Commission, set up in the wake of the Alder Hey scandal, had to confront these issues about personal identity in dealing with the question of whether even tissue blocks and slides retain something of the person. However, the law is not well suited to transcending this dichotomy between persons and things. Up until the present, the law has been reluctant to treat persons in a property framework, which appears at first glance to be more appropriate to objects. Instead, the personal rights framework, including the right of informed consent, has been preferred.

Recent UK policy consultations and documents have continued the traditional pattern of preferring personal rights above a property model, despite survey evidence that the pure consent model is viewed with increasing impatience by a younger generation of patients and research subjects.[66] Thus, for example, the regulatory framework suggested in the UK Retained Organs Commission consultation document of February 2002 relied substantially on an informed consent model, stressing the personal right of the donor or her family to give or withhold consent to further uses of organs and tissues removed from the body, as did the subsequent legislation, the UK Human Tissue Act 2004.[67] While improving informed consent procedures is valuable and important, with considerable backing from other sources such as the Medical Research Council guidelines on tissue storage,[68] consent is not the only possible model in questions of retained organs, tissue banks and other uses of 'human material'.

In contrast to the UK position, the joint German and French national bioethics commissions' opinion on tissue banking, issued in March 2003, says firmly that '[t]he notion of consent needs to be retained', but also adds that we must explore 'the possibility of a return of the benefits of research to the person whose consent made it possible'.[69] This makes an interesting contrast to the ethical basis of the recently established UK Biobank, in which the moral dilemmas are thought to concern informed

---

[66] Medical Research Council, *Public Perceptions of the Collection of Human Biological Samples* (London, MRC, 2000). General practitioners and nurses also believe that patients should retain some degree of ongoing control over donated tissue samples.

[67] Retained Organs Commission, *A Consultation Document on Unclaimed and Unidentifiable Organs and Tissue: A Possible Regulatory Framework* (NHS, February 2002).

[68] Medical Research Council, *Human Tissue and Biological Samples for Use in Research: Operational and Ethical Guidelines* (London, MRC, 2001).

[69] CCNE (Comité Consultatif National d'Ethique) and Nationaler Ethikrat (German National Ethics Council), *Opinion Number 77, Ethical Problems Raised by the Collected Biological Material and Associated Information Data: 'Biobanks', 'Biolibraries'* (Paris, CCNE, 20 March 2003), s. 3. Also available as German National Ethics Council (ed.), *Biobanks for Research* (Berlin, German National Ethics Council, 2004), pp. 101–2.

consent and privacy almost exclusively, with little mention of benefit-sharing and other property-related questions.[70] Although the German and French suggestion concerning return of benefits is phrased in terms of the common good rather than of individual property rights, it does imply tacit acceptance of a modified property rights model. Property rights need not be private, after all: they can be communal, on a Hegelian rather than a Lockean model, and indeed in my earlier book this is precisely what I recommended.[71] The German and French document, stressing this public dimension, clearly has a communal property approach in mind when it says: 'The contents of the bank are the fruit of voluntary donation by those concerned. They cannot from one moment to the next become the property of the researcher or the curator.'[72] A Canadian government commission report also ratified the need for some elements of a property-based approach to be included, because of the precise degree of control that can be given.[73]

Reliance on informed consent alone does not afford the kind of flexible control required by research subjects. If I want to participate in a research study or donate altruistically to UK Biobank, but I also want to prevent having my tissue donation used for particular commercial purposes subsequently, my only real choice is to decline to participate at all. My only alternatives are blanket acceptance or blanket refusal. In this sense 'informed' consent of the sort used by UK Biobank is actually *dis*empowering.[74] If I am going to give my tissue or DNA, ordinary usage suggests that I do retain some sort of interest in what it might be used for afterwards. Indeed, this is the very purpose of gift. in its classic anthropological formulation: to create ongoing interests and relationships between donor and recipient. As Marcel Mauss depicts it, the gift is still in a sense alive – far more so than even he might have realised, in the case of biological tissue.

What imposes obligation in the [gift] received and exchanged, is the fact that the thing received is not inactive. Even when it has been abandoned by the giver, it still possesses something of him. Through it the giver has a hold over the beneficiary . . . to make a gift to someone is to make a present of some part of oneself . . . [and] to accept something from someone is to accept some part of his spiritual essence, his soul.[75]

---

[70] Roger Brownsword, 'Biobank governance – business as usual?', paper presented at a workshop of the EC PropEur project, Tuebingen, 20 January 2005.

[71] *Property, Women and Politics*, ch. 4.

[72] CCNE and Nationaler Ethikrat, *Opinion Number 77*, s. 6.

[73] Canadian Royal Commission on New Reproductive Technologies, *Proceed with Care: Final Report of the Commission on New Reproductive Technologies* (Ottawa, Minister of Government Services Canada, 1993).

[74] Mason and Laurie, 'Consent or property?'.

[75] Mauss, *The Gift*, pp. 11–12, cited in Waldby and Mitchell, *Tissue Economies*, p. 10.

Even on a comparatively trivial level, where part of the donor's body is not concerned, we are not generally best pleased to find that the recipient of a Christmas gift has sold it on to a third party. 'Giving is not mere abandonment of property, involving no interests of the donor . . . One of these interests is the chance to demonstrate altruistic concern for the welfare of others, which is after all the only consideration received in exchange for gift.'[76] How much more, then, may donors of biological materials expect ongoing relationships to be mediated through gift? Such an expectation has already been documented in 'surrogate' mothers, as has the frustration of those hopes by a commercialised system in which the recipient couple views the transaction as purely monetary, while the donor mother is encouraged to think she is giving the greatest gift of all, the gift of life.[77] When such expectations are dashed, cynicism, mistrust and disillusionment are likely to result, which a system of donation by public altruism cannot afford.

Ironically, the dominant model for tissue donation, relying exclusively on 'informed' consent to the donor's binding renunciation of any further rights over the tissue when the 'gift' is made, may also discourage altruism and trust, the very values on which research depends. There is ample evidence that altruism still exists in copious quantities,[78] but also widespread concern that popular attitudes may change if secrecy and scandal continue to dog the issue of tissue taking. A modified property rights model, to make consent *genuinely* informed, would give patients and research subjects confidence and trust that their donation will be used for purposes in which they have some say. Recommending such a property rights approach does not mean accepting commodification of the body: in fact, properly conceived, it is a protection against that.

The organisation of this book

Symmetrically and straightforwardly, this book is divided into four main parts. The first two chapters set out a conceptual framework, eliminating some common confusions and identifying the resources we shall need to analyse the applied issues that follow. Chapters 3 and 4, the first pair of applied sections, look at property in female reproductive tissue; chapters 5 and 6, at commodification of tissue and DNA from both men

---

[76] Penner, *Idea of Property*, p. 90.

[77] Helena Ragone, *Surrogate Motherhood: Conception in the Heart* (Boulder, CO, Westview Press, 1996).

[78] T. Malone, P. J. Catalano, P. J. O'Dwyer and B. Giantonio, 'High rate of consent to bank biologic samples for future research: the Eastern Cooperative Oncology Group experience' (2002) 94 *Journal of the National Cancer Institute* 769–71.

and women. Two 'global' case studies of resistance to commodification follow, evaluating whether France and Tonga offer alternative models to commercial enclosure of the genetic commons. A final chapter – really more of an afterword – brings it all together and evaluates whether the fear of feminisation of all bodies is well founded. Are we dealing with a phantasm or a genuine threat?

Here in chapter 1, I have introduced the personal versus property rights distinction, as the first of several key contrasts enabling us to refine the striking but somewhat simplistic claim with which I began this book: that the apparent effect of tissue and genomic commodification looks to be that we all have 'feminised' bodies now. We have seen that a modified property rights approach can provide important protections against the open, accessible, feminised body. In chapter 2, I begin by elucidating an equally important pair of concepts, objectification and commodification. More broadly, the task of this chapter is to illustrate how feminist critiques of canonical political theory and jurisprudence can provide us with other valuable weapons against the 'new enclosures' in biotechnology. It is important to understand the intricacies of how and why women and their bodies have been both subjects and objects, in order to lessen the moral panic around 'feminisation' of all bodies as purportedly reducing all human subjects to the status of mere objects. In this chapter I will also begin to sketch out some feminist perspectives on the interrelationship between personal and property rights, the limitations of informed consent and contract and the nature of self-ownership. All these are familiar concepts from the debate on ownership of bodily tissues and patenting of the human genome, but they are rarely analysed critically and fully in bioethics and public policy debates. Thus, chapters 1 and 2 build on feminist critiques to lay out the book's conceptual framework.

Chapter 2 also revisits a crucial question which I examined in my earlier book: whether women possess a property right in their reproductive labour. Building on my original argument that they do, in chapters 3 and 4 I then go on to examine the areas in which the new reproductive technologies can be said to commodify women's bodies and to deprive them of that property entitlement. In chapter 3, I examine the use of enucleated ova in stem cell research and the way in which 'the lady vanishes': although ova are crucial in such research, we heard little until very recently about the risks and effort demanded of the women who donated them. Rather, the ethical issues in stem cell research have been seen to centre on the moral status of the embryo. Similarly in chapter 4, on the taking and banking of umbilical cord blood, it has been widely assumed that the cord blood belongs to the baby rather than the mother, that it is merely abandoned tissue that would otherwise be wasted, and that the potential benefit to the baby of banking the blood is considerable. All these assumptions are debatable, and so I debate them. In both chapters we see a dual phenomenon: property in female tissue is increasingly valuable, increasingly at risk of commodification, but we hear much less about that than we do about other areas in biotechnology where commodification threatens both sexes.

Those are the areas considered in chapters 5 and 6: genetic patenting and tissue or genomic biobanks. In chapter 5, I look at the gendered politics of genetic patenting, examining in particular the question of whether human DNA is a subject or a thing, and the requirement in patent law of the inventive step. Chapter 6 begins with the example of the Icelandic database as an instance of presumed consent, and therefore of the potential reduction of all bodies to feminised status. But what rights should donors to biobanks have? After all, the effort they put into contribution is relatively trivial. In an important instance of the interplay between theory and practice, I devote further theoretical analysis here to the issue of labour as conferring a property right, offering an alternative model of governance in the shape of the charitable biotrust.

In chapters 7 and 8, I examine two case studies of resistance to commodification: France and Tonga. Although one might imagine that France would subscribe to Western values favouring an instrumental approach to the body, in fact the two examples both demonstrate a view of the body as *tapu* or sacred, in contradistinction to the body as tool. In its bioethics laws of 1994 and 2004, in the opinions of its national ethics committee, and in its refusal to ratify the 1998 EC Biotechnology Directive, France has consistently rallied behind the doctrine of non-commodification of the body, as a bioethical equivalent of *le drapeau tricolore*. Tonga resisted Western firms' attempts to access the genome of its population, even when offered benefit-sharing arrangements. The distinction between the body as sacred and the body as a tool[79] may merely mask use of the supposedly sacrosanct body for instrumental purposes.

While it is widely feared that all bodies are becoming 'feminised', there are new demands on the female body. The traditional expectation of altruism from women may now be extended to include egg donation for the provision of stem cells or the donation of umbilical cord blood for 'spare parts kits' for their babies, produced at considerable profit to private cord blood banks. Here women undergo what may be an unnecessarily prolonged labour, allowing extraction of cord blood most efficiently, for what is as yet an unproved benefit to the next generation. Contrariwise, it has been suggested that we are witnessing a new form of the social contract,

---

[79] Memmi, *Les gardiens du corps*, p. 20.

in which young women will be expected to sacrifice parts of their bodies in order to extend life for older family members.[80] All bodies are at risk from commodification, but women's bodies are most at risk. Not only are they richer in 'raw materials' than men's bodies; women are also more routinely expected to allow access to their bodies. Only by remaining alert to the incessant inventiveness of biotechnological commodification can we protect all bodies, male and female, in the way they deserve.

[80] Ingrid Schneider and Claudia Schumann, 'Stem cells, therapeutic cloning, embryo research: women as raw material suppliers for science and industry' in Svea Luise Herrmann and Margaretha Kurmann (eds.), *Reproductive Medicine and Genetic Engineering: Women between Self-Determination and Societal Standardisation*, proceedings of a conference held in Berlin 15–17 November 2001 (Reprokult, 2002), pp. 70–9. See also Ann McGovern, 'Sharing our body and blood: organ donation and feminist critiques of sacrifice' (2003) 28(1) *Journal of Medicine and Philosophy* 89–114.

2 Property, Objectification and Commodification

This chapter's job is to suggest some preliminary insights from the objectification and commodification of women's bodies, in such a way as to help us to better understand whether all bodies are being made into objects and commodities by the new biotechnologies. I have argued that there is a parallel between the historical ways in which women's bodies have been made objects and the 'new enclosures' in bioethics and biotechnology. A comprehensive history or typology of women's objectification and commodification is impossible in a single chapter; nor do I view the task before me as exclusively historical. Rather, the concepts that will help us to analyse and combat objectification and commodification of the body in both sexes come not only from practice, but also from theory. By viewing the 'new enclosures' through the prism of women's social entitlements and feminist theory, we will gain important insights into the interrelationship between personal and property rights, the extent to which agency can survive objectification of the body, the limitations of informed consent and the nature of self-ownership. These all have ramifications for property in human tissue and the human genome, and later chapters will draw on them. Very few commentators on bioethics or biolaw have traced the historical roots of modern attitudes about biotechnology and property in the body to canonical political theorists and the historical circumstances in which they wrote. That, I hope, is a novel achievement of this chapter.

In attempting this task, I shall develop further the original theory of property set forth in my earlier book, *Property, Women and Politics*. The model I proposed there relied on critical insights from canonical political theory, feminist theory, law and historical practice. My goal was to transcend the passive view of women and their bodies as merely objects, while still accepting, with Simone de Beauvoir, that 'what marks the specificity of woman's situation is that while she, like any other human being, is an autonomous freedom, she discovers and chooses herself in a world where men force her to assume herself as the Other; they claim to fix her as

26

an object'.[1] But although the many ways in which women's bodies had been made objects were originally an important target for feminism, I felt that it was imperative to move beyond the conventional feminist view that women were *merely* objects. As I wrote:

> Why should feminists be content to accept that women can have no other relation to property than as its *objects*? In political theory and jurisprudence, property is generally linked to being a *subject* . . . Both nineteenth-century and second-wave feminists made good polemical use of the notion of women as objects, and it was strategically important that they did. But ultimately, I think, viewing women's relationship to property purely in the passive leads down a political and theoretical cul-de-sac.[2]

Although the distinction between subjects and objects of property-holding was crucial to that book and to this one, much feminist theory has been sceptical about the straightforwardness of the subject-object distinction. That makes a useful reminder at the start of my task. As Catharine MacKinnon writes, 'Having been objectified as sexual beings while stigmatized as ruled by subjective passions, women reject the distinction between knowing subject and known object.'[3] Another task of this chapter, then, is to explore the subtleties of the subject-object distinction: that will help us, in later chapters, to move beyond the simplistic treatment of human bodies, both male and female, as simply the 'known objects' of the 'knowing subjects' behind commodification of human tissue and the human genome.

If the subject-object distinction is complex, however, it is also self-reinforcing. In political theory, law and historical practice, there is a dialectical relationship between women's propertylessness and their lack of full subject status. It is a truism, but an instructive one, to note that women now and in the past typically hold and held less property than men, and that in many instances they have been more like the objects of property-holding. What is less often noted is the relationship between that fact and women's agency. As I remarked in *Property, Women and Politics*,

---

[1] Simone de Beauvoir, *Le deuxième sexe* (Paris: Gallimard, 1986), cited in Michèle le Dœuff, *Hipparchia's Choice An Essay Concerning Women, Philosophy, etc.* (Trista Selous (tr.), Oxford, Blackwell, 1991), pp. 55–56.

[2] *Property, Women and Politics*, p. 2, original emphasis.

[3] Catharine A. MacKinnon, *Toward a Feminist Theory of the State* (Cambridge, MA, Harvard University Press, 1989), p. 120. For feminist critiques of agency and embodiment, see, among others, Christine Battersby, *The Phenomenal Woman: Feminist Metaphysics and the Patterns of Identity* (Cambridge, Polity Press, 1997); Rosi Braidotti, *Nomadic Subjects: Embodiment and Sexual Difference in Contemporary Feminist Theory* (New York, Columbia University Press, 1994); and Iris Marion Young, *On Female Body Experience: 'Throwing like a Girl' and Other Essays* (Oxford, Oxford University Press, 2005).

'It is because they [women] are propertyless that they are not construed as political subjects; it is because they are not accorded the status of subject that they hold little or no property'.[4]

This insight affords an instructive parallel with the 'new enclosures'. In chapter 1, I rejected the conventional position in medical ethics and medical law which holds that informed consent is sufficient to guarantee full agency and autonomy to those who 'donate' tissue or DNA samples. There I argued for property rights *as well as* personal rights. Without some form of property rights in the material taken from our bodies, our personal rights are inevitably less than complete. It is because we are propertyless in our own bodies, according to legal doctrines such as abandonment or *res nullius*, that we are vulnerable, as something akin to objects, to the 'new enclosures'. Personal rights such as informed consent are necessary but not sufficient, on their own, to put that right.

We have one advantage, however: whereas in feminist theory, and in political theory more generally, property has often been a largely neglected concept,[5] in bioethics and biolaw there is an enormous and continually expanding literature on the subject. Furthermore, in the notion of property as a bundle of rights, as explained in chapter 1, we possess a well-enunciated, flexible and sophisticated concept that can help us to identify the most pressing and also the most practical objectives concerning property rights in the body.

Before beginning in earnest, I need to make my use of objectification and commodification clearer. I shall use 'objectification' in a broad rather than an excessively literal sense, although not as comprehensively as does Martha Nussbaum, who presents objectification as a plurality of denials imposed on human subjects: denials of their agency, autonomy, uniqueness and dignity.[6] Similarly, Nancy Scheper-Hughes argues for an enlarged conception of commodification to include 'all capitalized economic relations between humans in which human bodies are the token

---

[4] *Property, Women and Politics*, p. 6.

[5] Carol M. Rose, *Property and Persuasion: Essays on the History, Theory and Rhetoric of Ownership* (Boulder, Westview Press, 1994), pp. 1–2. Rose rightly points out that this theoretical neglect sits oddly with the political resurgence of neo-liberal models of politics. A notable exception is the influential model of property offered by Stephen R. Munzer in his many works, including *A Theory of Property* (Cambridge, Cambridge University Press, 1990), especially ch. 3, 'Persons and their bodies', pp. 37–58; 'An uneasy case against property rights in human body parts' (1994) 11(2) *Social Philosophy and Policy* 259–86; 'The special case of property rights in umbilical cord blood for transplantation' (1999) 51 *Rutgers Law Review* 493–568; and his edited collection, *New Essays in the Legal and Political Theory of Property* (Cambridge, Cambridge University Press, 2002), which includes his chapter, 'Property as social relations' (pp. 36–75).

[6] Martha Nussbaum, 'Objectification' (1995) 24(4) *Philosophy and Public Affairs* 249–91.

of economic exchanges that are often masked as something else – love, pleasure, altruism, kindness'.[7] Both definitions are too broad for my purposes, but they do draw our attention to unexpected forms of objectification and commodification.

Objects and commodities are not the same, and neither are objectification and commodification, although they are linked. Physical objects of property-holding may or may not have fungible value like commodities: although personal memorabilia are objects which can be owned, their value is generally seen as merely sentimental.[8] (Margaret Radin, however, points out that the Chicago school of economics assigned monetary prices to anything or any person that people value, with authors such as Becker and Posner applying an economic analysis to children, marriage and family life,[9] thus obliterating the conventional distinction between objectification and commodification.)

My understanding of *commodities* is consistent with Marx's position that commodities should be seen as possessing *both use and exchange* value.[10] *Objectification*, by contrast, only entails the attribution *of use value*, the process by which something external to ourselves is made to satisfy human needs and wants. Only objects separate from the self can be alienated and objectified in this fashion.[11] I noted in chapter 1 that modern biotechnology muddies the clear distinction between things external to our bodily selves and those intrinsic to us, so that mechanical ventilators or pacemakers are incorporated from outside into our bodies, and parts of our bodies such as tissue samples or DNA swabs may be disaggregated and separated from us. The notion of 'external' is problematised and problematic in modern bioethics and biolaw, and with that come difficulties that Marx did not have to confront about what is alienable and what is inalienable from the subject.

Although some analysts contend that Marx viewed commodification as wrong in itself, favouring universal non-commodification, others assert

---

[7] Nancy Scheper-Hughes, 'Bodies for sale – whole or in parts' (2002) 7 *Body and Society* 1–8, 2.

[8] My thanks to Carolyn McLeod for this example and for her helpful comments on an early draft of this chapter. See also her article 'Means and partial means: the full range of the objectification of women' (2003) 28 *Canadian Journal of Philosophy* 219–44.

[9] Gary S. Becker, *A Treatise on the Family* (enlarged edition, 1991) and Richard A. Posner, *Economic Analysis of Law* (4th edn, 1992), cited in Margaret J. Radin, *Contested Commodities: The Trouble with Trade in Sex, Children, Body Parts and Other Things* (Cambridge, MA, Harvard University Press, 1996), p. xii.

[10] Karl Marx, *Capital* (Samuel Moore and Edward Aveling (tr.), Frederick Engels (ed.), Moscow, Progress, 1954, original edn, 1867), p. 48.

[11] Radin, in *Contested Commodities* (p. 34), traces the origin of this firm distinction to Kant and Hegel, but clearly it continued to influence Marx.

that neither objectification nor commodification is intrinsically malign in Marx or anywhere else.[12] What is wrong is the objectification or commodification of that which should be treated as having value in itself, irrespective of what use might be made of it. As Carolyn McLeod and Francoise Baylis note:

> the act of commodification can be morally permissible or impermissible depending upon: i) whether the thing commodified has intrinsic value that is incompatible with it being either fully or even partially commodified; ii) whether moral constraints exist on the alienability of the thing from persons; or iii) whether the consequences of making the thing alienable and of commodifying it are favorable.[13]

To avoid the abuses of full-blown consequentialism, I would prefer to replace the final 'or' by 'and'. Even where the consequences of making a thing alienable and commodifying it are favourable, a Kantian perspective would require us to avoid *commodification* of that which has most intrinsic value in itself: the human subject as a member of the Kingdom of Ends. I have already noted in chapter 1, however, that Kant recognises the right to use the body in such a way as to preserve one's life, for example by amputating a diseased limb. Clearly, commodification is not involved in that example, although it might be argued that the limb is objectified both by being made something external, and by being used to satisfy the most basic of human needs, staying alive. Nevertheless, Kant is willing to tolerate this extent of objectification.

Blood is likewise objectified in any system of donation, as soon as it leaves the body and becomes something which can be tested, measured or transferred; but in a system of free donation it is not monetarily commodified (although as we saw in the previous chapter, it is still an object of exchange insofar as gift may be expected to occasion counter-gift).[14] Nor is the individual donating the blood necessarily objectified by the mere fact of giving blood. We shall see in chapter 7 that the French system of gratuitous blood donation rests on the notions of common ownership of the *patrimoine* and social solidarity, so that the blood donor demonstrates agency and citizenship by her action: the attributes of a subject rather than an object. Much the same can be said of the portrait of the UK system as delineated by Titmuss, although very little of that altruistic system

---

[12] Carolyn McLeod and Francoise Baylis, 'Feminists on the inalienability of human embryos' (2006) 21 *Hypatia* 1–14.

[13] *Ibid.*

[14] John Frow, 'Gift and commodity' in his *Time and Commodity Culture: Essays in Cultural Theory and Postmodernity* (Oxford, Clarendon Press, 1997).

now remains, except for the fact that donors are not paid.[15] Something is going on in a true gift relationship, at the communal level, which resembles the Kantian exemption for individuals: it is morally permissible, and indeed good, to objectify part of one's body in order to satisfy other individuals' needs to stay alive. If done freely, this is the laudable action of a subject, although enforced 'donation' would clearly reduce the 'donor' to the status of an object. (The difficult case is someone who sells her blood simply to keep body and soul together: in one sense, that is to reduce oneself to the level of an object, but insofar as ought implies can, it might even be thought permissible to sell one's blood to stay alive, if there is no other choice.)

Since objectification is a more extensive category than commodification, the range of ways in which people can be treated as objects is also greater than the variety of modes in which they can be regarded as commodified, despite the inventiveness of modern biotechnology and late capitalism in finding ever-new ways to commodify things and people alike. Many of the historical forms of women's objectification do not demonstrate commodification as such. This is one of the first lessons that feminist thought and theory can suggest for a nuanced analysis of objectification and commodification in modern bioethics. Not all forms of objectification in modern biotechnology commodify individuals or their body parts, although they may still be ethically debatable. Essentially, such practices will be wrong if they objectify that which should be treated as having value in itself, regardless of its use potential: if they reduce subjects to objects in some essential sense. What that sense is remains to be seen in the concrete contexts which I shall examine in later chapters.

The second useful aspect of a historical survey is to suggest how objectification and commodification differ for men and women. Although it is broadly true that the extent of objectification is normally greater for women, there may also be a degree of objectification for men in the historical systems examined in this chapter. Generally, however, we will find that women are more heavily objectified. If extrapolated to present-day biotechnology, this difference undermines any simplistic claim that men and women are alike subject to objectification and commodification in the new biotechnologies. I do not claim that they are *equally* vulnerable, or that the new forms of objectification and commodification are always

[15] Richard Titmuss, *The Gift Relationship: From Human Blood to Social Policy* (Ann Oakley and J. Ashton (eds.), 2nd edn, London, LSE Books, 1997). Catherine Waldby and Robert Mitchell, *Tissue Economies: Blood, Organs and Cell Lines in Late Capitalism* (Durham, NC, Duke University Press, 2006), ch. 1, delineate how far from the gift ideal the UK 'blood economy' has travelled.

the same for both men and women. In chapters 3 and 4, I demonstrate ways in which female tissue has greater 'biovalue' than male tissue, with the result that female bodies are more likely to be the objects of commodification. But it is also true, and importantly true, that some aspects of objectification which were previously limited to women's historical experience are now being extended to biologically male bodies as well: that is the meaning of 'feminisation' as I use it.

The objectification of women's bodies: lessons from classical Athens

From the Athenian *polis*, we have inherited, along with essentials of our democratic system and democratic theory, a particularly objectified history of women's relationship to property. Although it is a misconception to think of Athenian women as effectively slaves, their property entitlements were considerably fewer than those of other Greek women, such as those in Sparta or Crete, and also fewer than those of Egyptian women of the same epoch.[16] I noted in *Property, Women and Politics* that during the period when liberal democratic theory was developing, England and colonial America likewise operated particularly oppressive systems of property entitlements for women. It is certainly unfortunate that those political theories and particular legal systems which we consider our historical forebears had particularly punitive property regimes for women.

Not only did women lack entitlements to property in the systems that have most influenced our own democracy: in important aspects they were treated as the objects of property, even if not fully commodified in a monetary sense. The first important insight imparted by a look at women's history is that the law's insistence on drawing a thick black line between persons and objects is untenable. Even when they were not slaves, women's status has frequently hovered between subject and object. It is too easy for the law in a modern society to say that the firm distinction between persons and things remains intact, once slavery no longer exists. Women's history suggests that half of humanity has found and still finds it difficult to attain full subjectivity, even when 'free'.

For example, an Athenian woman was subject to right (7) in Honoré's classification, the right to transmit or alienate property to others by bequest or gift: she could be given in marriage by her father as her lord, and then, if widowed, bequeathed to her husband's brother. Aristotle's

---

[16] For further detail, see *Property, Women and Politics*, p. 51 *et seq.*

will[17] provides for the gift of his daughter (who is conspicuously anonymous, unlike the males party to the will) to Nicanor, or, if Nicanor dies first, to Theophrastus, if he will have her. Theophrastus, as a full human subject, is allowed to say no, but she is not, although she is not a slave. She may not choose her own husband; nor may she choose whether to marry at all.

An Athenian woman was not party to her own marriage contract: that was a transaction between her father as her present *kyrios* (lord) and her husband-to-be as her future one. Although modern commentators have sometimes been shocked by the lack of freedom of choice in Plato's proposals for eugenically dictated marriages in *The Republic*, this is to ignore the fact that no Athenian woman had a free choice of whom to marry, or indeed whether to marry.[18] What we see in the outrage of such commentators is a similar phenomenon to the feminisation of the body by biotechnology in late capitalism: the assault on freedom is only noticed when it begins to apply to men.

Property in classical Athens, although not in Sparta or other city-states, belonged primarily (although not exclusively) to the household rather than to the individual, and to the *kyrios* as head of the household. The husband's only legal obligation to the wife was to maintain her so long as he kept her dowry, although that could be confiscated to meet his debts. In that case she might seek a divorce, but a childless divorced woman in Athens had no claim to maintenance in any household. Effectively she had no property entitlements whatsoever. A married Athenian woman did not even have title to her clothes, and certainly could not own land, the more secure and prestigious form of property (although there are records of women owning land in Sparta, Delphi, Gortyn, Thessaly and Megara). Full legal persons can possess proprietary rights in things, but the Athenian woman was neither a full legal person nor a thing.

As in the Athenian legal system, so in classical Athenian political theory women's property entitlements were limited, and their status ambivalently posed between subjects and objects of property-holding. Plato, despite his well-known proposals for a certain degree of equality between male and female guardians in the *Republic*, actually refers quite blatantly to women as private property: in the same work, Socrates discusses the 'right acquisition and use of children and women' and 'the law concerning

---

[17] From Diogenes Laertius, *Lives of the Eminent Philosophers*, V, 11–16, reproduced in Mary F. Lefkowitz and Maureen Fant (eds.), *Women in Greece and Rome* (Sarasota, FL, Samuel Stevens, 1977), pp. 19–21.

[18] This point is made by Susan Moller Okin, *Women in Western Political Thought* (London, Virago, 1980), p. 34.

the possession and rearing of the women and children'.[19] Similarly, in the *Laws* he typifies the state second only to the Republic in ideal qualities as one in which 'women and children and houses remain private, and all these things are established as the private property of individuals'.[20] Although Plato does not mean commodified private property, women were certainly objectified in his system.

The prevalent Athenian property model appears to influence the way in which women's activity in sustaining the household is not recognised by Aristotle, even though he claims that the point of property and of all economic activity is precisely to maintain the household or *oikos*. Although Aristotle denies that women are slaves or objects of property – 'nature has distinguished between the female and the slave'[21] – neither does he recognise them as full subjects. In Aristotle, women's economic activity is reduced to safeguarding the household property which men have created; their labour adds no value, since 'the art of household management is not identical with the art of getting wealth, for the one uses the material which the other provides'.[22] In reality, of course, the Athenian woman's labours in spinning, weaving, food processing and animal husbandry all created a product and added value to what was by nature mere substance. We shall see in chapters 3 and 4 that an attitude not so very different from Aristotle's has prevailed in the stem cell technologies and in the banking of umbilical cord blood, where women's labour is not recognised as adding value to 'natural' resources.

In Aristotle, it is women's intermediate nature between full subject and something more akin to an object, although not a chattel slave, that makes their labour of lesser value. 'A husband and father . . . rules over wife and children, both free, but the rule differs',[23] for rule over sons is temporary, but wives can never attain the status of self-ruled or rulers. Yet, conversely, it is also the gendered nature of property acquisition which justifies men's rule over women in the family, and, more particularly, the way in which women's labour is not perceived to add wealth to the *oikos*. As the Danish political scientist Mogens Hansen writes, however, 'it was the work of the women even more than that of the slaves that provided the male citizens of Athens with their opportunity to run the political

---

[19] Plato, *Republic* (Paul Shorey (tr.)) in *The Collected Dialogues of Plato including the Letters* (Edith Hamilton and Huntington Cairns (eds.), New York, Pantheon Books, 1961), 451c and 453d.

[20] Plato, *Laws* (Paul Shorey (tr.)) in *The Collected Dialogues of Plato including the Letters* (Edith Hamilton and Huntington Cairns (eds.), New York, Pantheon Books, 1961), 807b.

[21] Aristotle, *Politics* (Benjamin Jowett (tr.)) in *The Basic Works of Aristotle* (Richard McKeon (ed.), New York, Random House, 1941), 1252b1.

[22] Aristotle, *Politics*, 1236a10.   [23] Aristotle, *Politics*, 1259a39.

institutions'.[24] Notwithstanding the fact that Athenian women brought dowries into their marriages, Aristotle considers wives to be 'bought' – although more indirectly than slaves – through sharing in the husband's supposedly greater economic contribution to the household, and in the children, who in this view are created predominantly by the male's active, energising, soul-creating power.[25] Thus, an element of commodification does enter in, albeit indirectly.

Here, in Aristotle's blindness to the value of women's reproductive labour, construed as not only as birth and child-rearing but also as reproducing the next generation through labour in the household, we see the beginnings of a phenomenon that can be traced through the history of Western political theory and law and into modern biotechnology, as I will demonstrate in later chapters. Without women's reproductive labour in producing ova for the stem cell technologies and cord blood for private profit-making banks, these technologies would not exist. Yet women's role in modern biotechnology is viewed in the same way Aristotle saw it 2,500 years ago: as a mere receptacle or conduit for the energising, value-creating male principle. This claim will be developed at further length in chapters 3 and 4; all I do here is to trace its historical provenance.

Women's propertylessness in their own tissue and reproductive labour is one lesson from Athens; another relates to the connection between holding property and having political rights, particularly having the right to govern others. Although this link is more clearly established in liberal political theory, which I shall consider in the next section of this chapter, it is also present in the Athenian model. As I wrote in *Property, Women and Politics*, 'It was property in the private household which gave the master a place in the outside world . . . the flow is from economic agency to political personhood.'[26] In classical Athens, citizenship was defined in terms of the means of life, such as a farm. Women were excluded from political life because they did not own the means of independent living, or the property in their own bodies. 'Without autonomy over their own bodies and actions, they could not be given the right of political control over those who did own themselves, freeborn men.'[27] Only those who unequivocally 'own' themselves have wider political and legal rights: they are 'the lords and owners of their faces', as Shakespeare put it.

If we do not unequivocally own our own bodies, does that imperil our personal rights such as informed consent? If this proposition were true,

[24] Mogens Herman Hansen, *The Athenian Democracy in the Age of Demosthenes: Structures, Principles and Ideology* (Oxford: Blackwell, 1991), p. 318.

[25] Aristotle, *The Generation of Animals* (William Ogle (tr.)) in *The Basic Works of Aristotle* (Richard McKeon (ed.), New York, Random House, 1941), 731b30.

[26] *Property, Women and Politics*, p. 60.   [27] *Ibid.*

it would lend even greater urgency to the need to develop a bundle of property rights in our bodies; rather than co-existing on equal terms with personal rights, property rights would then underpin them, in such a way that personal rights would be derivative and secondary. The gist of this argument would be something like this: if we do not have a property in our own bodies, we cannot have such a thing as personal rights. Thus, the choice sketched in chapter 1 between the personal and the property rights model would be a false dichotomy. Without the property rights model, the personal rights framework would collapse. The trust placed in personal rights such as informed consent by consultative commissions, professional bodies and law-makers dealing with property in the body would then be doubly misguided. Not only would such institutions be at fault for failing to recognise the need for property rights as an *adjunct* to personal rights, they would have wrongly assumed that personal rights can stand on their own, without a *foundation* in property rights.

Liberal political theory: property in the body and property in the person

We have seen that Aristotle distinguishes between women and slaves, yet denies women the full privileges associated in modern times with 'self-ownership'. It may well appear contradictory that a person who is not a chattel slave, and whose body is therefore not simply the object of property, should not own herself or her own actions, including those that produce use value. In liberal theory, self-ownership is logically prior to other rights: hence the argument, stated briefly above, that if we do not have a property in our own bodies, we cannot have any other entitlements. But is self-ownership literally a form of property entitlement? And must it necessarily be true that if I am not a slave, I must own myself? James W. Harris has identified the illicit jump from the first proposition to the second as the crucial mistake made by liberal theory, and carried over from it into Marxist thought. Even if I am not a slave, that does not mean that I own my body. No one then owns my body, not even I myself, and self-ownership then becomes a nonsensical concept.[28]

If self-ownership is supposed to be similar to property rights, then it consists in a set of relations of exclusion or control concerning a particular object or objects. Are these merely negative rights of non-interference? – like protection against theft, for example.[29] Or does self-ownership imply

---

[28] James W. Harris, *Property and Justice* (Oxford, Oxford University Press, 1996), p. 189.

[29] Penner, for example, construes a property entitlement as being like a gate rather than a wall: the owner has the right to decide who will be admitted and not excluded. (James Penner, *The Idea of Property in Law* (Oxford, Clarendon Press, 1997), p. 87).

all the rights in the property bundle? – full powers to determine all uses of the 'object'. And what would that 'object' be? Is it ownership of the physical body? We have already seen in chapter 1, and at the start of this chapter, that there is something strange about this idea, not least because it objectifies the body. Objects of property, typically, 'are only contingently ours . . . [and] might just as well be someone else's'.[30] How can this possibly be true of my own body?

If we are our bodies, if we are embodied subjects, then it is nonsensical to assert that we *own* our bodies; we simply *are* our bodies. As Kant says, 'Man cannot dispose over himself because he is not a thing; he is not his own property; to say that he is would be self-contradictory; for insofar as he is a person he is a Subject in whom the ownership of things can be vested, and if he were his own property he would be a thing over which he could have ownership.'[31] This is a strong strain not only in Kant but also in feminist theory, which has generally distrusted what it sees as 'masculine' mind-body dualism, whether Cartesian or religious in origin. Feminists have alleged that wherever there is a rigid division between body and subject, or soul, or intellect, or reason, the body has tended to be identified with women and given an inferior status, as being merely animal or natural.[32] Thus, feminism is generally sympathetic to the identification of body and subject, rather than to the self-ownership model in which the subject is seen as some disembodied force possessing the body – indeed, objectifying and alienating it.[33]

All these considerations might appear at first to rule out any contribution from liberal or neo-liberal thought to the debate on the 'new enclosures'. The strongest voices arguing for commodification of human tissue have typically been neo-liberal;[34] if their argument is rooted in a fallacy about the right to sell one's body because one owns it, what use is liberal

---

[30] Penner, *Idea of Property*, p. 112.

[31] Kant, *Lectures on Ethics* (Indianapolis, Bobbs-Merrill, 1963), p. 4, cited in G. A. Cohen, *Self-Ownership, Freedom and Equality* (Cambridge, Cambridge University Press, 1995), p. 211, and in chapter 1. For critiques and counter-critiques of the Kantian position, see Nicole Gerrand, 'The misuse of Kant in the debate about a market in human body parts' (1999) 16(1) *Journal of Applied Philosophy* 59–67, and Jean-Christophe Merle, 'A Kantian argument for a duty to donate one's own organs: a reply to Nicole Gerrand' (2000) 17(1) *Journal of Applied Philosophy* 93–101.

[32] Moira Gatens, *Feminism and Philosophy: Perspectives on Difference and Equality* (Cambridge, Polity Press, 1991).

[33] See e.g., Jackie Leach Scully, 'Normative ethics and non-normative embodiment', paper presented at the Feminist Approaches to Bioethics conference, Sydney, November 2004.

[34] David Resnik, 'The commercialization of human stem cells: ethical and policy issues' (2002) 10 *Health Care Analysis* 127–54 and 'Regulating the market for human eggs' (2001) 15(1) *Bioethics* 1–26; Richard Arneson, 'Commodification and commercial surrogacy' (1992) 21(2) *Philosophy and Public Affairs* 132–64.

thought? However, the claim that we *cannot* own our bodies is actually more consistent with Locke's position, and neo-liberals who claim a Lockean basis for the argument that we own our bodies unreservedly are misinterpreting proper Lockean liberalism rather badly. Self-ownership in the sense of ownership of the physical body is not the crux of his argument: rather, the claim that I own my actions, and therefore the resources or wealth produced by my actions. It is not necessary to assert that I own my physical body in order to stake a claim in the results produced by my agency.

Chapters 3 and 4 will argue that in the case of women's reproductive labour and work in producing tissue such as enucleated ova for nonreproductive purposes, effort, intentionality and agency ground individual property in that tissue, on a Lockean basis. In the instances of genetic patenting and biobanks, discussed in chapters 5 and 6, there is less extensive labour, intentionality and agency involved, but still enough so that a Lockean labour-desert argument can justify a communal property for donors, to be administered by a form of charitable trust on their behalf. Lockean liberalism does have an important contribution to make to the philosophical and legal resources we need to defend ourselves from the 'new enclosures', particularly for protecting women.

The right to property in Locke's *Second Treatise on Civil Government* is founded, famously, on the 'mixing of labour' with resources: when we do so, we acquire property rights in the results. (I realise this is a vastly oversimplified account, but here I do not wish to focus on the structure of the argument for acquisition in itself: for more detail see *Property, Women and Politics*, ch. 3.) Our right to the resultant wealth depends in turn on our prior rights in our own selves. The question I want to examine here is the nature of those selves and rights.

This issue is important in the context of objectification and commodification because many people seem to assume that if we do not own our bodies straightforwardly (and we do not in law) then we do not own our selves, and are less than full subjects. Again, this is also to assume a bright line between persons and things, which we have already seen to be an inaccurate assumption regarding women's status. The present discussion concerns another component of that misleading dichotomy: between full subjects, who own their bodies straightforwardly, and things, which are the objects of ownership. But it is not necessary to believe that full subjects own their bodies like things in order to believe that they have certain rights, selected from the 'bundle', in relation to their bodies.

Now although the conventional belief that we do own our bodies implicitly rests on Lockean foundations, in fact Locke never says that we have a property in our physical *bodies*: rather that we have a property in our *persons*. He is careful to distinguish between persons and bodies, and between the labour of our bodies and our bodies themselves, when he says that 'Every man has a property in his own person; this nobody has any right to but himself. The labour of his body and the work of his hands we may say are properly his.'[35] We have a title to that with which we have 'mixed our labour' because our labour is the expression of our agency and status as persons, not because the raw materials have touched our bodies. The connection is not literally between our bodies and the hoe, flute or pen, but between our skills and the fruit, music or poem that flow from the labour for which we use those tools. Jeremy Waldron makes this distinction very ably: 'Humans, then, do not have creators' rights over their bodies. But they can be regarded in this strong sense as the creators of their own actions (and *a fortiori* of their work and labour).'[36]

Further – and this is crucial for property in tissue, body parts or DNA – we do not have a property in that which we have *not* laboured to create. We do not own our bodies merely because 'we' (whoever that disembodied 'we' may be) inhabit them. In Locke's view, we do not own our bodies at all: God does, because He alone created them. The final proof that rights in what one has created flow from subjecthood or agency rather than from possession of a physical body must be God's own disembodiment.

Absent or present Locke's belief in God, the conclusion remains the same: we have not laboured to create our own bodies. Those who argue, on a purportedly Lockean basis, that we do have complete and full-blooded ownership rights in our bodies actually ignore this distinction in Locke between property in the moral person, which I equate with self-ownership, and property in the physical body. The liberal basis of a right to property is thus intimately linked to self-ownership; it derives from the connection between our value-creating labour and our agency, although not from our ownership of our physical bodies.[37] That labour is an expression of our agency and not of our bodies as such; it derives its values from that agency, but it is done through the medium of our bodies. This interpretation is consistent with the view of the subject as embodied, and with the desire to avoid the objectification or commodification

---

[35] John Locke, *The Second Treatise on Civil Government* (1689), cited in G. A. Cohen, *Self-Ownership, Freedom and Equality* (Cambridge, Cambridge University Press, 1995), p. 209. See also my further elaboration of the claim that Locke distinguishes between property in the person and property in goods: *Property, Women and Politics*, p. 78.

[36] Jeremy Waldron, *The Right to Private Property* (Oxford, Clarendon Press, 1988), p. 179.

[37] John Christman, in *The Myth of Property: Toward an Egalitarian Theory of Ownership* (Oxford, Oxford University Press, 1994), argues that Locke would not actually have subscribed to the notion of self-ownership, because we do not own our bodies. However, he does not distinguish between property in the body *per se* and property in labour.

of the body, which opens up as a possibility once we admit the notion that bodies can be owned by subjects.

Returning to the question posed in chapter 1, concerning why the 'new enclosures' cause us so much distress, we now need to consider whether we could conceivably retain our self-ownership, even if we do not have a property in our own bodies as such. Conversely, what distresses us about the supposed loss of property in our physical tissue, body parts or DNA may be simply an erroneous impression that we have thereby lost our agency, our subjecthood: that we have become the objects of property-holding. We have already seen that under both civil and common law, property in the body is at best a weak concept, or even an oxymoron. Yet both systems, using different vocabularies, make a great deal out of self-ownership, in the guise of individual freedoms in the common law system and of human dignity in the civil system.

Can we then be said to own ourselves in another sense? – in terms of owning our moral persons rather than our physical bodies. This Lock-ean interpretation is surprisingly similar to that made by Paul Ricœur between the two senses in which something can be said to belong to me.[38] In the first sense, I own a physical object like a book, car or house; in the second, closer to that of owning the moral person, 'what belongs to me is more appropriately understood through the notion of consti-tution, as constitutive of who I am'.[39] Ricœur asserts that we should understand our bodies as belonging to us in this second sense. 'They are "ours" because they are expressive of our agency . . . Our bodies belong to us in the sense that we are embodied in them, we express our agency and intentions through them, and we experience the world from the perspective of our particular embodied points of view.'[40] Although Ricœur and commentators on him generally restrict the sphere of prop-erty or ownership to the first set of relationships, which would exclude the self from the realm of property, I do not see why this has to be so. An embodied self, in my view, can still be conceived of in terms of some of the property relationships in Honoré's formulation, and indeed Catriona MacKenzie, in commenting on Ricœur, does something like this when she argues that the rights to bodily non-interference and bodily self-determination should be grounded in Ricœur's constitutive sense of belonging.[41]

---

[38] Paul Ricœur, *Oneself as Another* (Kathleen Blamey (tr.), University of Chicago Press, 1992), especially the Fifth Study, 'Personal identity and narrative identity,' cited in Catri-ona MacKenzie, 'Conceptions of the body and conceptions of autonomy in bioethics,' paper presented at the Seventh World International Association of Bioethics conference, Sydney, November 2004, p. 8.
[39] *Ibid.*   [40] *Ibid.*   [41] *Ibid.*

If redefined as a question about who has the right to control 'ourselves and our powers',[42] then self-ownership appears to be less about the physical body as the object of relations of exclusion and control. Property is about the relations among persons in regard to objects; this alternative formulation conceives of 'ourselves and our powers' as such an object, but not necessarily as a physical object. There is no reason why property has to be about tangible objects, of course; copyright and patent are forms of property relations, intellectual property, concerning intangible things. Indeed, one could go further: defined as control over 'ourselves and our powers', self-ownership does not even require the potentially self-contradictory notion of a self that is being owned by a self. The self need not be a tangible or even an intangible thing, in this formulation, any more than personal reputation, public persona or good name, which are actionable goods in intellectual property law. The right to sell the use of one's name or image has evolved into a full property right in US courts, although on close examination it is far from clear exactly what is being protected in such cases.[43] This insight may be useful in addressing our concern about whether our physical bodies are being so thoroughly appropriated in the 'new enclosures' that we have lost a crucial component of our selfhood. The question remains whether others are attempting to undermine our selfhood, to control ourselves and our powers, in such a way that our self-ownership, defined as moral agency, is threatened. In later chapters, particularly in the examples of Fiji and Tonga in chapter 8, I shall examine this contention at further length.

It might be said, however, that this reformulation stretches the notion of self-ownership to an unacceptable degree of looseness. The principle lacks concrete content, if defined neither in terms of particular powers of control nor of a tangible or intangible object of control. This objection would be similar to that detailed in the previous chapter, about the vague content of the property bundle and of the very notion of property as lacking in determinative content.[44] Here, as there, this looseness seems to me to be productive and flexible, rather than damning. It is up to us

[42] As does Cohen, in *Self-Ownership*, p. 210.

[43] E. Richard Gold, *Body Parts: Property Rights and the Ownership of Human Biological Materials* (Washington, DC, Georgetown University Press, 1996), p. 89.

[44] See Penner, *The Idea of Property*, and Richard Arneson, 'Lockean self-ownership: towards a demolition' (1991) 39 *Political Studies* 54, cited in Cohen, *Self-Ownership*, p. 213. For further discussions of self-ownership, see, *inter alia*, Daniel Attas, 'Freedom and self-ownership' (2000) 26 *Social Theory and Practice* 1–23; George Brenkert, 'Self-ownership, freedom and autonomy' (1998) 2 *Journal of Ethics* 27–55; Alan Ryan, 'Self-ownership, autonomy and property rights' (1994) 11 *Social Philosophy and Policy* 341; Christman, *The Myth of Property*; and Robert S. Taylor, 'A Kantian defense of self-ownership' (2004) 12(1) *Journal of Political Philosophy* 65–78.

to define which sticks in the bundle, or which powers of control, we need most urgently, in order to protect ourselves against the 'new enclosures'. The concept of self-ownership, if extended to the further liberal premise that everyone enjoys full self-ownership compatible with such powers' enjoyment by others,[45] does in fact dictate that certain rights and powers of control are fundamental.

The liberal notion of self-ownership, if distinguished from ownership of the physical body and linked to the delineation of particular forms of control, thus illustrates how property rights do underpin personal rights. However, even on the looser formulation of self-ownership employed above, women were not thought to own themselves unreservedly in Lockean liberal theory. Although Locke speculates about the possibility of divorce and of married women holding property, he never questions the natural basis of conjugal power: only how far the husband's rights over the wife should extend. Some commentators have claimed that the actual worsening of women's political and property rights under the legal system of coverture[46] during the high tide of liberalism was no coincidence, but a direct and intentional result of liberal thought. Although liberalism laid the foundations for human rights and democratic political participation, these rights were not extended to women; odder still, democratic liberals did not seem to notice that their construction of such notions as 'universal suffrage' meant 'male suffrage'. Women's democratic political rights were only granted anywhere between 150 and 200 years after men's suffrage in most democracies. Was this an oversight, an unresolved contradiction, or a natural outgrowth of liberalism itself? If self-ownership really is universal – if everyone enjoys self-ownership – how did this anomaly arise, and why did it go unnoticed? This is not merely some arcane question whose relevance has disappeared with genuinely universal suffrage. We shall see in chapters 3 and 4 that in the new biotechnologies, too, women's rights of ownership over their own tissue have not been recognised. The same phenomenon – counting women out – is occurring in new guises.

Conventional writers on canonical political theory have typically either ignored women's exclusion from the political realm or mentioned it only

---

[45] Cohen, *Self-Ownership*, p. 213. I disagree with Cohen's subsequent argument, however, to the effect that 'to own oneself is to enjoy with respect to oneself all those rights which a slaveowner has over a complete chattel slave' (p. 214). Here Cohen fails to separate out the sticks of the property bundle: there are other models of ownership than chattel slavery, employing different 'mixes' of 'sticks'. In fact, Cohen has failed to distinguish between ownership of the body and ownership of labour.

[46] For a more detailed discussion of the restrictions imposed on women under coverture, see *Property, Women and Politics*, pp. 79–91.

in passing, as an oversight that time would put right.[47] Those liberals generally considered more feminist than Locke, such as Harriet Taylor and John Stuart Mill, did address women's simultaneous subjection and objectification, but thought women's inferior position was the last vestige of barbarism in politics. More recent feminist critics, such as Carole Pateman,[48] instead present liberalism as obstacle rather than solution. This viewpoint has important ramifications for property in human tissue, where at present a neo-liberal framework of regulation rules, to the extent that any framework rules at all. If this feminist viewpoint is correct, the semblance of contract (given, for example, by signing a consent form to unknown further uses of one's tissue) parallels the semblance of legitimacy given by the social contract in contractarian liberalism. Both are to be distrusted. Each merely legitimises what is in fact an assault on self-ownership, rather than an expression of it.

Here, then, is another concept from recent feminist theory which can help us to understand and resist the appropriation of bodies in modern biotechnology, particularly where female bodies are concerned, but also where all bodies are 'feminised'. The notion of the sexual contract might conceivably encompass surrogate motherhood, oocyte sale and other uses of female bodies which are justified by their proponents as being like any other economic transaction. Where women's bodies are concerned, however, the 'normal contractual manner' does not necessarily apply. Women's bodies are assumed to be 'open access' to such an extent that even when material such as ova for the stem cell technologies is taken from them in risky and laborious processes, no one notices what is going on. There are profounder reasons why transactions concerning the use of women's bodies, even if distinguished from the sale of women's bodies, cannot simply be assumed to be the same as any other economic transaction. To the extent that all bodies are now being treated like women's bodies, feminist theory alerts us to distrust the arguments in favour of contract in the body.

A feminist analysis such as Pateman's should warn us against the use of oversimplified, knock-down neo-liberal arguments about choice, consent and contract where female bodies are concerned, or indeed potentially of all bodies. Once the woman's supposed initial consent to the sexual or marriage contract has been given, all other rights are extinguished. This is the parallel to be drawn from Pateman's critique of self-ownership

---

47 For example, John Dunn, 'Consent in the political theory of John Locke' in his *Political Obligation in its Historical Context* (Oxford, Oxford University Press, 1980); Alan Ryan, 'Locke, labour and the purposes of God' in his *Property and Political Theory* (Oxford, Blackwell, 1984).
48 Carole Pateman, *The Sexual Contract* (Cambridge, Polity Press, 1988).

under contractarian liberalism, and a good illustration of the way in which feminist theory can afford unexpected insights into the ways in which the new enclosures threaten to limit the free agency and self-ownership of both men and women. As I remarked in chapter 1, a rather bastardised version of the personal rights model would have us believe that initial consent to tissue extraction extinguishes all other powers of control over the subsequent uses of the tissue. This widely accepted but legally dubious claim has direct relevance to patenting, considered in chapter 5, and to biobanks, in chapter 6.

That is indeed a useful warning against uncritical acceptance of neo-liberalism in the governance regimes of the new biotechnologies, but it is not necessarily a categorical argument against the use of contract, provided the contract can be made genuinely mutual. Contract has been used effectively by vulnerable groups to protect their rights in genetic material and tissue: I would not want to jettison so useful a weapon, but rather reformulate it to include new models such as benefit-sharing and the charitable biotrust. Similarly, in my critique of Pateman in *Property, Women and Politics*, I argued that 'What makes the sexual contract an instrument of domination is not that it is a contract, but that it is sexual.'[49] Contract itself is neutral, I argued, or even implicitly egalitarian. While the sexual contract is gendered – made between men as subjects, concerning women as objects – liberal contractarianism points logically towards equal self-ownership for both sexes.

In its dislike for Lockean liberal concepts such as property and contract, feminist theory has not always been careful to keep the concepts separate from the society in which they arose,[50] but there are many aspects of contractarian liberalism which outstrip their legal and political background. The rights of first comers in Locke are also tempered by the proviso of 'enough and as good' left for late comers. This 'Lockean proviso' requires the first person appropriating part of a common resource to leave 'enough and as good' for others, and to avoid waste.[51] That notion could be made more powerful than the law has so far done, restricting the rights of researchers, biotechnology firms and patent-holders rather than affording them unrestricted dominion over the genetic commons.[52] Similarly, protest groups in the global South have used their own traditional notions of commons to denounce what they perceive as neo-colonialist

---

[49] *Property, Women and Politics*, p. 67.
[50] This is part of my critique of Pateman, in *Property, Women and Politics*, p. 71 *et seq.*
[51] Locke, *Second Treatise*, s. 31 and 33.
[52] This path is followed by Seana Valentine Shiffrin, in her 'Lockean arguments for private intellectual property' in Stephen R. Munzer (ed.), *New Essays in the Legal and Political Theory of Property* (Cambridge, Cambridge University Press, 2002), pp. 138–67.

biotechnology firms; the example of Tonga, in chapter 8, will illustrate how effective that protest can be.

These and other campaigners against the 'new enclosures' could also rely much more on the requirement in contract that both parties must derive a benefit or 'consideration', in the parlance of contract law:[53] contracts in which only one party benefits are legally void. When donors are asked to surrender not only their tissue but also all further say over its use in the future, even if later commercial uses contravene the altruistic purpose for which the donation has been made, it can be argued that the sole consideration for which they donated – altruistic satisfaction – has been negated, and that the 'contract' is invalid. Although the language of gift is often used to mask what is really going on, it is certainly arguable that in fact a contract has been set up between the donor and the recipient biobank, research organisation or hospital. Gifts are retractable, whereas the whole intention of such consent forms is to put paid to any future claims from the donors if the tissue turns out to be valuable. Although English law does not recognise a general doctrine of unequal bargaining power or 'unconscionability' in contract, it does accept three grounds of procedural unfairness which would have a similar effect, in the case of consent forms of this type:

(1) dealings between sophisticated and less sophisticated parties, or between parties in a relationship of trust and dependency;
(2) cases in which one party has effectively surrendered her judgement to another; and
(3) instances in which one party is not fully aware of the meaning of terms or implications of the contract.[54]

Any one of these three conditions may be enough to set aside a contract; all three can be said to apply when patients, in a relationship of trust with a doctor, surrender their judgement about what the best use of their tissue would be to the presumably altruistic researcher, and fail to understand the potential commercial value, finality or other implications of the contract. Thus, contract law can be an important weapon in resisting the 'new enclosures', and the absence of any such consideration might well invalidate the donation protocol in the case of ova extraction or a private cord blood contract.

With the key distinction between property in the body and property in the person borne in mind, liberal political theory can provide us with important concepts, including contract, with which to reclaim the body from the new enclosures, particularly in relation to female reproductive

[53] Stephen A. Smith, *Contract Theory* (Oxford, Oxford University Press, 2004), p. 215.
[54] Smith, *Contract Theory*, pp. 348–52.

tissue. However, I reject the liberal attempt to subsume all social relations to the contractual, including, in terms of the property bundle, the sale of body tissue on a contractual basis. In this respect I agree with the distrust of contract evinced in much feminism.[55] What feminist theory does is to make us wary of contract used as a knock-down argument, to alert us to hidden power imbalances in contractual relations.

In the next section, however, I shall also argue that although there are very useful aspects of contractarian liberalism, its emphasis on individual property rights is less reliable a concept than Hegel's developmental, public model of property. Liberal arguments are not the be-all and end-all, and indeed their innate tendency to reduce social relations to transactions between individuals often blinds those writing in the liberal tradition to the wider social ramifications and background of what appear to be contracts between individuals. This is a besetting sin of much of the Anglo-American literature on the supposed free right to sell our body tissues: the reduction of everything to an individual transaction and the ignoring of relationship.[56] Civil law frameworks, and Continental theorists, are less prone to these 'Anglo-Saxon attitudes', as I shall elaborate in chapter 7 on France. In particular, Hegelian theory denies that we exist apart from our embodied selves, an insight which it shares with feminist approaches and with resistance from indigenous peoples and the environmental movement to the 'new enclosures'.

Contract, property and mutual recognition in Hegel

We have seen that the limitations of liberal thought relevant to the 'new enclosures', as seen through a feminist lens, include the following shortcomings.

1. Liberalism tends to take consent at face value, whereas feminist theorists such as Pateman are suspicious of the way in which an apparent initial consent, such as in the 'marriage contract', can justify relations of subordination in relation to the body. This mistrust can be instructive

---

[55] See e.g., Patricia J. Williams, 'On being the object of property' in D. Kelly Weisberg (ed.), *Feminist Legal Theory: Foundations* (Philadelphia, Temple University Press, 1992), pp. 594–602.

[56] David Resnik, in 'The commodification of human reproductive materials' (1998) 24 *Journal of Medical Ethics* 288–93, suggests that 'bodies that do not contain persons, such as anencephalic newborns, bodies in a persistent vegetative state (PVS), or cadavers, could be commodified without violating the dignity or worth of persons' (p. 389). He seems quite unaware of the effect on parents of anencephalic newborns, or relatives of persons in a persistent vegetative state: in short, of relationships extending beyond the patient as a single individual.

for policy formulation on property in tissue, which has been too ready to take consent as the best or indeed only form of protection.

2. In liberal thought, particularly in modern neo-liberalism, society is contract 'all the way down'. This tendency is particularly troublesome because of its connection to the first problem: if contracts are not necessarily made between equals, the danger of subordination is reinforced if contract is the main model of relations between individuals or collectives. Similarly, and relevantly to point (1), we cannot assume that 'gifts' of tissue or other forms of alienation of tissue, including contracts of either gift or sale, are necessarily made between equals.

3. Although the social contract is ostensibly drawn up between individuals, in fact it is made in a context of prior relationships among groups, including the family. Male individuals act as heads of families, which predate the social contract, even in modern liberal theorists (for example, in the first edition of Rawls's *Theory of Justice*).[57] Relationships among collectivities, and the ways in which power structures relationships within collectivities, are largely ignored by liberalism. This shortcoming has important ramifications for property in the body or in the human genome, not only in relation to women, but also for societies which view social life not in terms of individuals but in terms of collectives. Individual informed consent is insufficient or even meaningless for many indigenous peoples who are at risk from the global commodification of human tissue and the human genome.[58] This limitation will be further explored in chapter 8, on Tongan and Maori cultures' resistance to international biotechnology firms.

4. The notion of self-ownership is central to liberalism, but it is by no means certain that women have been included in this core concept. Instead, in Pateman's analysis, liberalism actually requires the 'ownership' of women by men in the sexual contract. Furthermore, 'self-ownership' oversimplifies our real relation to our bodies, whether male or female. We shall see in chapter 5 that self-ownership as a shibboleth lies behind much of the 'moral panic' over the patenting of the human genome.

5. The corollary of the above limitation is that women are not held to have the same sort of property in their own labour that men do. Even if women's bodies are not literally the property of men, and even if we distinguish property in one's body from property in one's labour, women's reproductive labour is not unequivocally their own. In terms of

[57] John Rawls, *A Theory of Justice* (Cambridge, MA, Harvard University Press, 1971).
[58] See also my article 'Human tissue and global ethics' (2005) 1(1) *Genomics, Society and Policy* 41–53.

commodification of the body, this will turn out to have important ramifications, which I explore further in chapters 3 and 4. Essentially, the
argument there is that the labour which women put into processes such
as oocyte and cord blood extraction is not recognised, nor counted as
adding value to commodified products such as stem cell lines, because
women's reproductive labour is not recognised in other contexts either.
Liberal theory is not alone in this blindness – we have just seen a similar
lack of awareness in Aristotle – but it is more at fault for failing to extend
its own inner logic sufficiently.

These restrictions in liberal thought carry instructive parallels for commodification of the body, which I shall draw out in succeeding chapters.
They also demonstrate some of the subtleties of objectification, and of
the tricky relationship between self-ownership and ownership of the body.
Hegelian and Marxist thought helps us to move beyond some of these
limitations, although neither Hegelianism nor Marxism transcends them
altogether.

The focus in the Hegelian model of property is on the experiential process of identity formation and recognition of others' subjectivities, and
the Hegelian notion that 'everyone must have property' does not mean
that everyone must hold private wealth. Relationship, rather than appropriation, is the question. Property, in Hegel, is not merely about relations of possession and control, but rather about the broader dynamics
of social recognition. Because of this emphasis on relationship, feminists
have been intrigued by Hegel, despite his ambivalent attitudes towards
women's place in the home or in the world, with the largest body of feminist work centring on *The Phenomenology of Spirit*.[59] Feminists' interest,
including Beauvoir's own work, has revolved around the meanings of Subject and Object in Hegel's master-servant dialectic. There has been less
interest among feminists in Hegel's writings on property. My own view
is that there are three potentially liberating elements in Hegel's political
writings which tie up with crucial feminist concerns, and also with our
concerns in bioethics about the 'new enclosures':

(1) the justification of property in terms of self-development, social
    recognition and public good(s);
(2) the importance of embodiment in self-development; and
(3) the connected thoughts that contract reflects relationship, but that
    nevertheless not all relationships boil down to contract.

---

[59] G.W. F. Hegel, *Phenomenology of Spirit* (A. V. Miller (tr.), Oxford, Oxford University
Press, 1977); Judith Butler, *Subjects of Desire: Hegelian Reflections on Twentieth-Century
France* (New York, Columbia University Press, 1987); Luce Irigaray, *Le temps de la
différence: pour une résvolution pacifique* (Paris: Livre de Poche, 1989); Susan M. Easton,
'Hegel and feminism' in David Lamb (ed.), *Hegel and Modern Philosophy* (London,
Croom Helm, 1987).

Although Hegel's *Philosophy of Right* is concerned with the development of the subject, it begins with property and contract, which appear to belong to the realm of objects. Only by engaging with the world of objects can we become full subjects. 'The Hegelian subject always has to go outside itself to know what is inside; by seeing itself reflected in the world it discovers relations constitutive of itself.'[60] Unlike in liberal theory, the high road to *individual* autonomy and self-awareness is through the recognition of *others* who also possess self-consciousness, who also own themselves – to put the matter in terms more familiar to liberal thought. Our individuality is not given but created, through active relationship with our environment, which of course includes other subjects. It 'translates' itself into reality 'through the use of its own activity and some external means',[61] of which the first is property.

Perhaps more accurately, property is the first venue of interaction with the world, followed, in the *Philosophy of Right*, by contract, the family, civil society and then, only then, the state. Whereas in liberal contractarianism, disconnected individuals in the state of nature form the state in order to assure the security of their property and lives, in Hegelian thought the state is the final and highest stage of mutual recognition. Property is not guaranteed by the state apparatus subsequent to its formation by the social contract; rather, the order of events is reversed, so that property is a lower but still essential stage in the process of mutual recognition that eventually culminates in the state. Rights, including the bundle of claim-rights, privileges, powers and immunities[62] which constitute property, are consequent to society rather than prior to it. As I noted in *Property, Women and Politics*:

Now this is not necessarily an argument for *private* property; it might be enough to participate in the creation and control of some collective enterprise. Individuality does not itself require limitless individually owned property.[63]

What ramifications might this aspect of Hegelian thought have for resistance to private corporations' commercialisation of the body? The appeal of a societally rather than individually centred model of property is that it suggests *collective* mechanisms for governance of the new biotechnologies, vesting the controls that constitute property relations in genuinely communal bodies. I shall develop one such model in chapter 6: the charitable 'biotrust'. Thus, the Hegelian approach to property and

---

[60] Kathy E. Ferguson, *The Man Question: Visions of Subjectivity in Feminist Theory* (Berkeley and Oxford, University of California Press, 1993), p. 41.

[61] Hegel, *Philosophy of Right*, p. 9.

[62] W. N. Hohfield, *Fundamental Legal Conceptions as applied in Judicial Reasoning* (New Haven, CT, Yale University Press, 1919).

[63] *Property, Women and Politics*, p. 97.

contract is neither liberal nor utilitarian. The usual consequentialist arguments for private ownership[64] foreground either the superior efficiency
of private-property systems or the security which private property provides for the projects important to us. Instead, Hegel sees the stages
represented by property and contract as emblematic of the individual's
self-development.[65]

So far I have mainly discussed the first of the useful elements which
Hegelianism adds to the more limited analysis of liberalism, that is, the
justification of property and contract as stages in self-development; now
I want to move on to the second way in which it is more sympathetic
to both feminist thought and the arguments against commodification of
the body. Here I am concerned with the importance of embodiment in
Hegel's thought.

The debate around patenting of the human genome or the commercial
use of human tissue often comes down to opposing viewpoints about
whether these developments threaten human dignity.[66] But why should
the taking of bits of tissue threaten our essential selves in any way? –
any more than having our hair cut does (with the possible exception of
Samson and Delilah). If there is a Cartesian separation between mind
and body, and if the self is identified primarily with the mind, there is no
reason why our essential subjectivity should be harmed by the loss of body
tissue. The argument might then boil down to which parts of our body
do actually contain our personalities, in a way that shorn locks of hair
supposedly do not. If we can separate our personalities from a particular
body part, in the simple biological sense that we can survive without that

---

[64] For example, John Christman, in *The Myth of Property*, proposes a consequentialist justification of property rights and distributive justice, setting the well-off person's reliance
interests in certain levels of income or security from property against the needs of the
less well-off for security against propertylessness. Arguments in favour of patenting usually hinge on consequentialist arguments: that the patenting system produces desirable
outcomes such as higher productivity for researchers, availability of beneficial therapies to society or greater national wealth. Increasingly, arguments *against* patenting the
human genome or its sequences are also being made on a consequentialist basis. The
argument that patents actually tend to stifle research is put forward by Lori B. Andrews
in 'Genes and patent policy: rethinking intellectual property rights' (2002) 3 *Nature
Reviews Genetics* 803–8.

[65] One limitation of Hegel's own thought, however, is that the individual who imposes his
will on the world in this fashion is primarily a male individual in Hegel, and that the
process of development is curtailed for women (Kathy E. Ferguson, *The Man Question:
Visions of Subjectivity in Feminist Theory* (Berkeley and Oxford, University of California
Press, 1993)).

[66] For a sceptical argument about the vague content of the notion of human dignity, see John
Harris and John Sulston, 'Genetic Equity' (2004) 5 *Nature Reviews Genetics* 796–800.
The 'dignitarian' approach is defended by Roger Brownsword in 'Biobank governance'.
Dignity as a rationale against commodification is discussed at greater length in chapter 5,
where it arises in the context of genetic patenting.

tissue, then this part might rightfully be the subject of property rights.[67] On this argument, cut hair, fingernails, DNA samples, oocytes and even single kidneys could be the subject of property rights, but hearts, livers and brains could not. The living body as a whole could not be alienated in any form, by gift or sale, and neither could any part of the body necessary to sustain life.

This seems a rather crass formulation, however, and one that fails to provide as firm a guarantee as we might like. If, say, through the ostensible wonders of stem cell research, biotechnology eventually learns to produce and implant fully functional and tissue-compatible brains, or hearts or livers, then we would have to say that there is no theoretical objection to selling brains, or hearts or livers. Because this style of argument is naturalistic, depending on what can be done to tell us what *should* be done, it is vulnerable to transformations in what *can* be done. On a more metaphysical basis, it also depends on a strict division between the self and the body, or parts of the body: a bifurcation which Hegel rejects, as has much feminist thought. In Hegel, my only real existence is as an embodied will; that embodiment is indissoluble and unified. While Hegel's own thought is limited by his belief that the anatomical differences between the sexes have a supposedly 'rational' basis, his position on embodiment, as seen through a feminist lens, nevertheless provides important insights for commodification of the body.

The third productive aspect of Hegel, for feminist thought and resistance to commodification of the body, is the insight that society is not 'contract all the way down'. Instead, contract is merely a necessary but preliminary stage among many, in terms of social relations and mutual recognition. Contract reflects relationships, but not all relationships can or should be reduced to contractual ones. As a simultaneously symbolic and practical mechanism of recognition of other wills, contract is neither a realm of subordination and domination over women, nor of fraternal bonding among men – the meanings assigned it in liberal theory, according to Pateman. Rather, it is a limited but significant progress from self-absorption:

A person by distinguishing himself from himself relates himself to another person, and it is only as owners that these two persons really exist for each other. Their implicit identity is realized through the transference of property from one to the other in conformity with a common will and without detriment to the rights of others. This is *contract*.[68]

[67] This is the 'separability thesis' put forward by Penner, *The Idea of Property*, p. 111.

[68] G. W. F. Hegel, *Hegel's Philosophy of Right* (T. M. Knox (tr.), Oxford, Oxford University Press, 1967), 40, original emphasis.

Contract is not merely the instrumental means by which property is protected, as in liberal thought: rather, it has value in itself, as the symbol of the common will and mutual recognition of both parties. In relation to tissue or DNA donors, for example, a form of contract may be useful in forcing researchers to respect the donor as an equal, as a subject – which consent does not necessarily do. It is often argued that once we admit property and contract models into the discourse surrounding the body, we must see all relationships between donors and recipients of tissue as contractual, and also as diminishing trust or social solidarity.[69] This attitude underpins the French emphasis on gift and reluctance to employ property rights as a model, although some recent French academic writing does accept a modified notion of contract.[70] If we employ a Hegelian model, however, we may circumvent both this limitation and the tendency of liberalism to identify property as private.

Furthermore, the way in which Hegel deals with a central paradox of contract casts a clearer light on the ongoing duties of the recipient of a gift, which is highly relevant to the donation of tissue or genetic data. Although contract symbolises the recognition of my entitlements, normally when I alienate something to you through a contract, I apparently cease to have entitlements in it. This paradox holds whether I sell or give away the object of the contract, that is, regardless of the manner of its alienation. As Hegel puts it, 'Contract is the process in which there is revealed and mediated the contradiction that I am and remain the independent owner of something from which I exclude the will of another, only in so far as in identifying my will with the will of another, I cease to be an owner.'[71] His answer to this contradiction of his own creation reminds us, as he says, that property is not mere physical possession, but rather 'the social recognition that something belongs to me'.[72] This is why Hegel can make this rather surprising statement:

In a contract my purpose is both to acquire property and to surrender it. Contract is real when the action of both parties is complete, i.e. when both surrender and both acquire property, and when both remain property owners even in the act of surrender.[73]

---

[69] A prime example is the 2002 UK Department of Health consultation document *Human Bodies, Human Choices*, with its continued emphasis on the gift relationship (Department of Health, *Human Bodies, Human Choices: The Law on Human Organs and Tissue in England and Wales* (London, DOH, 2002)).

[70] Draft works by Florence Bellivier and Christine Noiville, 'The commercialisation of human biomaterials: what are the rights of donors of biological materials?' and 'La circulation du vivant humain: modèle de la propriété ou du contrat?', papers presented at seminar at Faculté de Droit, Universite de Paris-I, October 2004.

[71] Hegel, *Philosophy of Right*, 72.

[72] William E. Connolly, *Political Theory and Modernity* (Oxford, Blackwell, 1988), p. 117.

[73] Hegel, *Philosophy of Right*, 76A.

If this is so, then the natural tendency of contract, as opposed to the one-off nature of informed consent, is to require *ongoing* recognition of the donor by the recipient. I have already suggested a simple metaphor about the continued interest donors have in the use of their gifts: the rudeness of selling something one has received for Christmas. Now it begins to look as if this commonsense metaphor has some serious philosophical content, in Hegel. In a Hegelian contract both partners are equals. Their nature as equals requires the ongoing recognition of each other's rights even after the transfer or alienation of the object which the contract concerns. That object is less important than the mutual recognition itself.

My task in later chapters will be to tease out what that recognition might imply in practical terms, and where its rightful limits lie. Before that, however, I want to look at one last concept from my feminist analysis of property in the body: property in reproductive labour. Although there is a Hegelian link here – a failure of mutual recognition – the canonical theorist who has the most to say about this concept is, of course, Marx.

Marx, Delphy and Arendt: alienation and women's reproductive labour

It is well known that Marx and Engels believed that the solution to women's oppression was to bring them out of the archaic isolation of the home and into productive employment. We might say that modern biotechnology has achieved this transition in a way that Marx and Engels could never have foreseen. Women's labour in producing oocytes for private IVF clinics and the stem cell technologies has brought the most intimate, 'archaic' biological functions into the marketplace.

I say this with tongue firmly in cheek, of course, because this form of women's reproductive labour is actually a further site of oppression. It is not that women are not paid for these functions, which I would oppose as a form of commodification; it is rather that their labour goes almost entirely unnoticed. The 'cloning wars' concern the moral status of the embryo; few bring the question of women's exploitation into the debate concerning therapeutic cloning or stem cell therapies.[74] Women's labour in pregnancy and childbirth is likewise ignored when 'surrogate'

---

[74] The Nuffield Council on Bioethics concluded that stem cell therapies were acceptable on ethical grounds because 'the removal and cultivation of cells from a donated embryo does not indicate lack of respect for the embryo'. The ethical debate was felt to stop there, apparently, without discussion of whether extraction of ova for use as enucleated eggs in the production of stem cell lines indicates lack of respect for the woman (Nuffield Council on Bioethics, *Stem Cell Therapy: The Ethical Issues, A Discussion Paper* (London, Nuffield Council on Bioethics, 2000)).

motherhood is depicted as merely renting out their wombs, turning these women into a 'biological *lumpenproletariat*'.[75]

Why is women's labour so routinely ignored in the new biotechnologies? In Marx, the alienated worker's labour is always in fact the symbol of his oppression, not of his freedom, although under capitalism he is not a slave. In the capitalist system, writes Marx, labour is none the less external and forced, even though the labourer is not physically compelled to work, as the slave is.[76] But at least Marx credits the worker with a property in his own labour, which is more than women have in relation to the new reproductive technologies.

Feminist theorists might point out that this is not in fact an anomaly. From Mary Wollstonecraft onward, feminists have extended the notion that women's labour is forced and external into the domestic realm, including the creation of that most intimate 'product', children. The effect of the new biotechnologies is to take that propertylessness in the labour of reproduction back to stages before the birth of children: to the production of ova for the stem cell technologies, for example. At the same time, childbirth itself is now valued not just for the sake of the child as 'product', but also for the harvesting of an additional product, umbilical cord blood. Both cord blood and ova for the stem cell technologies have commercial value, but that value does not accrue to the women who produce them. Indeed, in the case of cord blood, the mother actually pays the cord blood bank for the privilege of storing her blood, which in fact is rarely recognised *as* hers in either the academic literature or the contract with the blood bank.

A Marxist feminist analysis of the new reproductive technologies might present them as the apotheosis of the way in which capitalism degrades women's labour. Under the conditions of IVF, for instance, the circumstances under which women perform the task of reproducing the species

---

[75] The idea of the 'biological *lumpenproletariat*' originates in Dorothy Nelkin's *Dangerous Diagnostics: The Social Power of Biological Information* (Chicago, University of Chicago Press, 1994), but Nelkin does not apply it to women: rather to those who are unable to get work or insurance because of unfavourable genetic profiles. My usage of it here is influenced by Jennifer Merchant's *synthèse* submitted for her *habilitation à diriger les recherches*; I served on the panel for her HDV in December 2004, and am grateful to her for this application of the concept. On the commodification of surrogacy, see Radin, *Contested Commodities*, pp. 134–53; Elizabeth Anderson, 'Is women's labor a commodity?' (1990) 19 *Philosophy and Public Affairs* 71–92; Arneson, 'Commodification and commercial surrogacy'; and *Property, Women and Politics*, ch. 7.

[76] Karl Marx, *Grundrisse: Foundations of the Critique of Political Economy* (Martin Nicolas (tr.), New York, Vintage Books, 1973), p. 611. See also the comparison of Marx's position on male labourers compared to the situation of women workers in *Property, Women and Politics*, pp. 123–4.

become more and more external and less 'natural'. Just as the Marxist feminist Ann Ferguson asks whether contemporary high-technology childbirth is a form of alienated labour,[77] so might one ask whether even higher technology processes such as superovulation and 'egg harvesting' also fit this Marxist mould.[78]

Although the processes of commodification have doubtless accelerated under late capitalism, however, it is a mistake to think that women's alienation from their own reproductive labour is limited to the modern period. The short survey of Athenian property systems at the start of this chapter demonstrates that much. The question, then, is whether the Marxist concept of alienation can still be useful, even if it is not an 'unnatural' condition, as it is to Marx, who believes that the worker always 'naturally' and rightfully has a property in the labour of his person. In particular, the Marxist concept of alienation is limited in relation to the new reproductive technologies by Marx's own belief that women's reproductive labour lies outside the realm of productive work. What women do, in giving life, is, to Marx, like what the earth does: it is natural, not social, and it cannot confer added value. Perhaps those who fail to see how much added value women impart in the new reproductive technologies are secret Marxists: at any rate, they seem to share the same blind spot.

Pressing the Marxist distinction between labour and work further, Hannah Arendt writes: 'The mark of all laboring is that it leaves nothing behind': it is mere futile repetition of the effort necessary to sustain life, even though life itself depends upon it.[79] Arendt contrasts the *animal laborans* with *homo faber*, who transcends the endless cycle of grim necessity through creative and productive work. 'Unlike the productivity of work, which adds new objects to the human artifice, the productivity of labor power produces objects only incidentally and is primarily concerned with the means of its own reproduction . . . it never "produces" anything but life.'[80] In this analysis, women's labour in childbirth might epitomise the round of endless reproduction of life, the curse of Eve, rather than creative, value-adding work. But even if that much is granted, what women do in labouring for the new reproductive technologies is clearly productive work, not 'merely' reproductive labour. 'New objects to the human artifice' – stem cell technologies, the apotheosis of scientific progress

---

[77] Ann Ferguson, *Sexual Democracy: Women, Oppression and Revolution* (Boulder, CO, Westview Press, 1991).

[78] For a more extended discussion of this point, see my 'Property and women's alienation from their own reproductive labour' (2001) 15(3) *Bioethics* 203–17.

[79] Hannah Arendt, *The Human Condition* (2nd edn, Chicago, University of Chicago Press, 1998), p. 87.

[80] Arendt, *The Human Condition*, p. 88.

to many commentators – depend on the work and value generated by women's contribution of extracted ova.

The French feminist Christine Delphy has added to classical Marxism an explanation of why women are not seen to own their reproductive labour, and why their labour can be properly regarded as alienated. In what she calls 'domestic relations of production', women produce value but receive no share in it. Indeed, in conventional Marxism, domestic work which supposedly produces no exchange value, such as cooking for one's family, is actually regarded as consumption and not as production at all. To call women's domestic labour consumption rather than production, Delphy says, ignores the question of why what women produce is not seen as adding value, even when products such as food would have exchange value if purchased in the marketplace. (We encountered a similar question in relation to the Athenian household, illustrating once more that women's propertylessness in their labour is not confined to capitalism.) Thus, as Delphy writes:

[F]ar from it being the nature of the work performed by women which explains their [women's] relationship to production, it is their relations of production which explain why their work is excluded from the realm of value. It is women as economic agents who are excluded from the (exchange) market, not what they produce.[81]

In what Waldby and Mitchell call the 'tissue economies' of late capitalism,[82] we are now witnessing the extraction of surplus value from women's reproductive labour, or the extrapolation from women's propertylessness under the domestic mode of production even when the production is no longer domestic. The products of women's bodies are commodified, gaining tremendously in value, but women's contribution to that use-value is not recognised in the marketplace because it is viewed under the same rubric as 'home production'. What women do in providing reproductive tissue for the new biotechnologies is implicitly viewed as no different from the 'natural', non-market processes of pregnancy and childbirth. Yet there is nothing remotely 'natural' about the processes of ovarian stimulation and egg extraction, as I shall demonstrate in the next chapter.

By preserving women's domestic labour as the unpolluted realm free of market forces, writes the feminist historian Leonore Davidoff, early capitalism conducted a 'struggle to keep unlimited calculation from creeping

---

[81] Christine Delphy, *Close to Home: A Materialist Analysis of Women's Oppression* (D. Leonard (tr. and ed.), London, Hutchinson with the Explorations in Feminism Collective, 1984).

[82] Catherine Waldby and Robert Mitchell, *Tissue Economies: Blood, Organs and Cell Lines in Late Capitalism* (Durham, NC, Duke University Press, 2006).

into every sphere of life'.[83] In late capitalism we see the same process at work, using a feminist Marxist analysis: by refusing to recognise that women's reproductive labour in fact produces material of tremendous value in the marketplace. The commodification of women's reproductive tissue, ironically, can proceed unfettered so long as we refuse to recognise women's reproductive labour as being capable of commodification. Bioethicists have rightly been concerned to preserve some space free of commodification, but this is not the way to do it. In the succeeding chapters, I now want to ask what *is* the right way to do it.

[83] Leonore Davidoff, 'The rationalisation of housework' in *Worlds Between: Historical Perspectives on Gender and Class* (Cambridge, Polity Press, 1995), p. 83.

3   The Lady Vanishes: What's Missing from the Stem Cell Debate

In most public discussion of the ethical issues in stem cell research, only the status of the embryo seems to count. Yet because ova are crucial to stem cell research, particularly in somatic cell nuclear transfer, there are also important regulatory issues concerning protection of women from whom ova are taken.[1] Rarely are these issues aired: hence the title of this chapter, 'The lady vanishes'. In most commentaries and debates, the women from whom the ova are taken have virtually disappeared from view.

In the extraction of ova for IVF therapy, a more commodified system already prevails than in any other form of tissue donation, even in the highly commercialised tissue economy of the USA.[2] Many recent reports have documented a burgeoning trade in human ova for IVF, with eggs being extracted from Eastern European women and sold on to infertile couples in Britain, Germany, Israel and other wealthier countries.[3] Young Ukrainian women, for example, may be flown to clinics in Cyprus, or even as far as Belize, to have their eggs extracted. The price paid to these

---

[1] Soren Holm, 'Going to the roots of the stem cell controversy' (2002) 16(6) *Bioethics* 493–507; Donna Dickenson, 'Commodification of human tissue: implications for feminist and developmental ethics' (2002) 2(1) *Developing World Bioethics* 55–63. I have not provided a detailed explanation of the increasingly well-known biology involved in stem cell research; instead I have concentrated on the physiology of the less well-known risks involved in oocyte donation. For a more detailed explanation of stem cell techniques, see Holm, 'Going to the roots', 494–6.

[2] Jeffrey Kahn, 'Can we broker eggs without making omelets?' (2001) 1(4) *American Journal of Bioethics* 14–15. Payment for solid organs is illegal under the US federal National Organ Transplant Act, but ova are not covered by this provision. (In October 2006, the state of California did pass legislation making it illegal to pay for eggs used in research.)

[3] Antony Barnett and Helen Smith, 'Cruel cost of the human egg trade', *Observer*, 30 April 2006, pp. 6–7; European Commission Health and Consumer Protection Directorate-General, *Report on the Regulation of Reproductive Cell Donation in the European Union* (Brussels, European Commission, 2006). Women interviewed in these studies readily and regretfully saw their 'donations' as selling their bodies. As one Ukrainian woman put it, 'I feel like I sold part of my body . . . I don't want anybody to know; for me it's unpleasant that I have sold a part of myself. That I have sold myself for money.' ('Svetlana', in Barnett and Smith, 'Cruel cost', p. 6.)

women is typically between US$200 and US$300 per cycle, whereas clients are charged between £7,900 and £11,000, allowing the private clinics to make a healthy profit even if they have to pay for the odd air fare or two. That commercialised and globalised network of clinics is ready and available for 'producing' ova to be used in stem cell research rather than in IVF therapy. Although there are few indications as yet that ova are being bought and sold internationally for research purposes, there has been until recently such widespread silence about the need for ova in IVF that an illicit exchange could easily develop without monitoring.

Even apart from such global networks of ova supply, blatant abuses have already emerged within single research teams. The ostensible stem cell pioneer Dr Hwang Woo Suk used over 2,200 eggs from 129 women (some of them his own junior researchers, others paid 'donors') in what was later revealed to be fraudulent research.[4] When Hwang announced a supposed new technology involving cloned blastocysts,[5] followed by a later announcement of ostensibly patient-specific embryonic stem cells derived through human somatic cell nuclear transfer,[6] the media debate predictably revolved around the implications for human cloning and the status of the embryo. Almost no attention was paid to the number and identity of the ovum donors. Under pressure from feminist activists, however, the truth finally began to emerge about the scale and style of Hwang's use of ova. Qualms about the unethical nature of the ova 'sourcing' led to the resignation of Hwang's collaborator, Gerald Schatten, in November 2005, precipitating the revelation later that year that Hwang's claims in both papers were fraudulent.

Many of Hwang's fellow researchers resent his waste of so many ova and fear that his disgrace will put new donors off donating.[7] If so, then the 'lady' may well 'vanish' underground, into an illicit trade in ova for research. The threat of this abuse has impelled the UK Human Fertilisation and Embryology Authority to call a public consultation beginning in September 2006, on the issue of whether women should be allowed

---

[4] Gary Younge, 'Embryo scientist quits team over ethics fear', *Guardian*, 14 November 2005, p. 19; Jonathan Watts and Ian Semple, 'Cloning fraud hits search for stem cell cures', *Guardian*, 24 December 2005; James Randerson, 'Rise and fall of clone king who doctored stem-cell research', *Guardian*, 24 December 2005; Ian Sample, 'Stem cell pioneer accused of faking all his research. apart from the cloned dog', *Guardian*, 11 January 2006, p. 11.

[5] Hwang Woo Suk et al., 'Evidence of a pluripotent human embryonic stem cell line derived from a cloned blastocyst' (2004) *Science* online, 13 February. Accessed 1 March 2004 at www.science.com.

[6] Hwang Woo Suk et al., 'Patient-specific embryonic stem cells derived from human SCNT blastocysts' (2005) 306 *Science* 1777–83.

[7] Robert Steinbrook, 'Egg donation and human embryonic stem-cell research' (2006) 354 *New England Journal of Medicine* 324–6.

to donate ova for research; similar debates and hearings have recently taken place in the USA. At last the issue of ova 'donation' is emerging tentatively into public debate; yet it is still widely assumed that if the need for embryos disappeared in the stem cell technologies, they would be ethically unobjectionable.

Several such 'embryo-lite' techniques have recently been mooted.[8] The first involves genetically manipulating a nucleus from an adult cell, inactivating certain genes, before inserting it into an enucleated ovum. Because the genetically manipulated nucleus would lack certain essential parts, proponents of the technique argue, no embryo would result and hence no ethical issues arise. This is a sort of New Scholasticism: how many angels can fit on the head of a pin? How many genes need to be switched off if something formally called an embryo is not to result? More importantly, however, this method still requires an ovum, just like conventional stem cell technologies. So does the second sort of technical fix, producing a 'parthenote' (an unfertilised egg induced to begin dividing) and the third, recovering cells from a non-viable embryo and then injecting their nuclei into enucleated ova. All that these inventive methods have in common, in fact, is that they are blind to the ethical issues involved in 'harvesting' and 'sourcing' ova. (Such terms themselves indicate how far along the path to objectification and commodification we have already proceeded.)

Indeed, some of the proposed 'solutions' would place an increased burden on women who supply ova, because they will almost certainly require *more* ova. A fourth proposed technique, 'altered nuclear transfer', involves deliberately inserting into the enucleated ovum a somatic cell nucleus which has been programmed to be defective in key developmental genes required to continue to the embryo stage. Since the nuclear division would stop before an embryo could develop, proponents of this untested technique claim that no ethical issues would arise. They ignore, of course, the fact that the failure rate for ova used in somatic cell nuclear transfer is already high, as in the abject case of Dr Hwang. Presumably the wastage rate of ova would be even higher with the 'altered nuclear transfer' technique; where are these vast quantities of human ova to come from? One might be forgiven for thinking that some participants in the stem cell debates really do assume they just grow on trees, if they think about them at all.

---

[8] Thomas Murray, 'Will new ways of creating stem cells dodge the objections?' (2005) 35(1) *Hastings Center Report* 8–9; Bonnie Steinbock, 'Alternative sources of stem cells' (2005) 35(4) *Hastings Center Report* 24–26; President's Council on Bioethics, *Alternative Sources of Human Pluripotent Stem Cells* (Washington, DC, President's Council on Bioethics, 2005).

Although stem cell banks such as that recently established in the United Kingdom may aim at reducing the need for individual research teams to generate their own stem cell lines, and thereby the use of human tissues and embryos, there will continue to be a requirement for ova available to be enucleated. If stem cell therapies are ever successfully developed, the immune rejection problem is likely to mean that a given stem cell-based therapy for a particular disorder will need to be developed in a variety of lines differentiated by haplotype matches. Thus, the pressures on supply of ova to be enucleated may well lessen with the establishment of public and private stem cell banks, but by no means will they disappear entirely, particularly not when the demands for ova from other research than stem cells are considered.[9]

For example, the UK Human Fertilisation and Embryology Authority recently authorised a new form of research into the mitochondrial disorder producing muscular dystrophy. The researchers extract ova from women at risk of passing muscular dystrophy on to their children through their own mitochondrial DNA, transfer the genetic content of the fertilised ova to enucleated healthy eggs taken from other women, and leave the defective mitochondria from the first ova behind. As usual, the only questions thought to arise in the procedure have concerned the status of the embryo, not the two sets of women from whom ova were to be taken. An appeal committee overturned the HFEA's initial rejection of the application once it became clear that the genetic structure of the embryo would not be changed.[10] This approval will clearly generate further pressures on the supply of ova, yet another source of 'demand' for eggs from research technologies. The medical historian Ruth Richardson asserts that the supply of bodies for dissection could never be satisfied. Demand always outstripped supply, as soon as demand was legitimised: 'Once the need was recognized, a supply was obtained; and once a supply was obtained, it always fell short of demand.'[11] What was once true of cadavers for dissection, I would suggest, will soon be true of ova for stem cell technologies and other forms of research.

In this chapter I begin by exploring the risks to women from ovum 'donation', together with the extent of labour required of women in producing ova for the stem cell technologies. I then go on to establish the

---

[9] Ruth R. Faden *et al.*, 'Public stem cell banks: considerations of justice in stem cell research and therapy' (2003) 33(6) *Hastings Center Report* 13–27; H. Bok, K. E. Schill and R. Faden, 'Justice, ethnicity and stem-cell banks' (2004) 364 *Lancet* 118–21.

[10] Ian Sample, 'Human embryo from two mothers gets go-ahead', *Guardian*, 9 September 2005, p. 1.

[11] Ruth Richardson, 'Fearful symmetry,' in Stuart Younger *et al.* (eds.), *Death, Dissection and the Destitute* (Chicago, University of Chicago Press, 2001).

sorts of rights women might be said to have in those ova, on a Lockean basis, and to explore the kind of Hegelian mutual recognition through contract which women might want to seek in relation to donated ova.

The ensuing section deals with the Marxist concepts of alienation, exploitation and seizure of surplus value raised in the stem cell technologies. Here I build on the original theoretical position concerning commodification of women's reproductive labour which I developed in earlier articles. My approach differs from that of such influential writers on commodification as Elizabeth Anderson[12] and Margaret Radin,[13] in that I focus on the way in which women's labour is excluded from markets in tissue.[14] While most commentators concentrate on tissue *per se*, I am more interested in the labour that goes into producing that tissue, and in the ways in which women's reproductive labour is either reduced to the level of a natural function or ignored altogether. Here, I have used Christine Delphy's notion of 'the domestic mode of production', introduced in the previous chapter: it is women as agents who are excluded from the exchange market, not what they produce. Stem cells provide a telling new application of this claim, although they require me to modify Delphy's argument. Ova available for enucleation are rarely recognised as necessary components in the biotechnology market; where they are, women, as the agents who produce them, are either excluded from the exchange market or subjected to exploitation in the process of 'production'.

I end the chapter by considering the way in which the example of stem cells demonstrates how genetic content is privileged over the 'mere' receptacle of the ovum. This insight both looks back to classical political theory and looks ahead to the privileging of genetic content, and the masculine principle, which I will identify in chapter 5, on genomic patenting.

What are the risks?

On the one hand, the recalcitrance of opponents of embryonic stem cell technologies is generally grounded in the twin assertions that the embryo is either a human being or a potential human being, and that it is wrong to destroy an existing or potential human being in order to produce stem cell lines. Proponents' justifications of stem cell research are more varied,

---

[12] Elizabeth Anderson, *Value in Ethics and Economics* (Cambridge, MA, Harvard University Press, 1993).

[13] Margaret J. Radin, *Contested Commodities: The Trouble with Trade in Sex, Children, Body Parts and Other Things* (Cambridge, MA, Harvard University Press, 1996).

[14] Susan Dodds, 'Women, commodification and embryonic stem cell research' in James Humber and Robert F. Almeder (eds.), *Biomedical Ethics Reviews: Stem Cell Research* (Totowa, NJ, Humana Press, 2003), pp. 149–75.

but not varied enough to escape the charge of obsession with the status of the embryo. What unites the two warring sides in the stem cell wars is that women are equally invisible to both.

The revealing title of an article by Gilbert Meilaender illustrates the presumption that respect for the embryo is the only relevant question: 'The point of a ban, or, how to think about stem cell research.' 'How to think about stem cell research' does not, it seems, require thinking about its effect on the women from whom oocytes are taken. Although Meilaender tries to provide a more nuanced examination of the proposition that it is wrong to destroy an existing or potential human being, he shares with other opponents of stem cell research a concentration on harms to the embryo. Taking the notion of respect for embryos seriously, Meilaender claims, may mean that the counter-weight of relieving suffering through scientific progress is 'a real but not supreme imperative'.[15] No mention is made of the suffering inflicted on women who donate ova; that simply doesn't enter the utilitarian calculus. Although Meilaender explicitly sets out to widen the debate beyond 'a seemingly endless argument about the embryo's status',[16] he does not broaden it all that far. Apparently there is nothing else to think about in relation to stem cell research than respect for the embryo: is it or is it not an absolute imperative, when consequentialist arguments favouring relief of suffering are weighed against it?

Proponents of the technologies, such as David Resnik, also typically fail to distinguish between their impact on men and their impact on women. In his modified pro-market view favouring largely unregulated commodification of stem cells, Resnik asserts that 'the potential for exploitation that arises in ES [embryonic stem] cells is much less than the potential for exploitation in organ donation because the risk and potential loss to donors in [sic] much less. Selling gametes is not like selling kidneys.'[17] Clearly, Resnik thinks of 'gametes' as sperm. Selling ova is in fact very much more like selling kidneys than like selling sperm, in terms of potential loss: ova are finite in number, like kidneys and unlike sperm, and ova extraction is a surgical procedure, like the removal of a kidney and unlike masturbation to produce semen.

In fact, the removal of ova is arguably *more* risky than the excision of a kidney. The surgical procedure is only the third and last of three risk-laden stages: shutting down the woman's own ovaries, stimulating

[15] Gilbert Meilaender 'The point of a ban, or, how to think about stem cell research' (2001) 31 *Hastings Center Report* 9–15, at 13.

[16] *Ibid.*

[17] David Resnik, 'The commercialization of human stem cells: ethical and policy issues' (2002) 10 *Health Care Analysis* 127–54, at 147.

them to produce multiple follicles rather than the single follicle usually produced in a cycle, and then – only then – extraction of the resulting ova. The usual drug in the first process is leuprolide acetate, which has been reported as causing symptoms ranging from arthralgia (severe non-inflammatory joint pain) to dyspnoea (difficulty in breathing), and also including chest pain, nausea, depression, dimness of vision, loss of pituitary function, hypertension, tachycardia (rapid beating of the heart), asthma, generalised oedema and abnormal liver function.[18] Irreversible losses of bone density, up to 7.3 per cent of total bone, have also been reported.[19]

In the second stage, hyperstimulating the ovaries may produce cysts, enlargement of the ovaries and severe fluid retention, with a potentially fatal outcome. Other complications of ovarian hyperstimulation syndrome (OHSS) include increased risk of clotting disorders, kidney damage and ovarian twisting. Even in the absence of full-blown OHSS, ovarian stimulation in general has been linked in trials to pulmonary embolism, stroke, arterial occlusion and other life-threatening risks.[20] The incidence of this syndrome ranges between 0.5 and 5 per cent of cases.[21] Some commentators term these risks 'minor',[22] which seems debatable, particularly in light of the potential risk of death.

Large or small, the risk is iatrogenic, and it may well be asked whether it is part of the duties of a doctor to impose such risks on women who derive no clinical benefit from the procedure, unlike women undergoing egg extraction during IVF. Although doctors may have believed at one point that women donating eggs did not suffer the complications to which patients undergoing IVF were exposed, a recent review of 1,000 cycles of egg donation found that not to be true.[23] There is no evidence-based excuse, or indeed any other excuse, for imposing such risks without therapeutic benefit, often in the absence of a fully informed consent. Particularly in the commercialised US environment, women selling eggs are often

---

[18] Judy Norsigian, 'Egg donation for IVF and stem cell research: Time to weigh the risks to women's health' in Boston Women's Health Collective (ed.), *Our Bodies Ourselves* (2005), ch. 25, accessed 22 April 2005 at www.ourbodiesourselves./orgbook/companion.

[19] K. Lazar, 'Wonder drug for men alleged to cause harm in women' *Boston Herald*, 22 August 1999.

[20] Norsigian, 'Egg donation', p. 2.

[21] A. Delavigne and S. Rozenberg, 'Epidemiology and prevention of ovarian hyperstimulation syndrome (OHSS): a review' (2002) 8 *Human Reproduction Update* 559–77.

[22] Younge, 'Embryo scientist quits team over ethics fear'.

[23] M. V. Sauer, R. J. Paulson and R. A. Lobo, 'Rare occurrence of ovarian hyperstimulation syndrome in oocyte donors' (1996) 52 *International Journal of Gynecology and Obstetrics* 259–62; M. V. Sauer, 'Defining the incidence of serious complications experienced by oocyte donors: a review of 1,000 cases' (2001) 184 *American Journal of Obstetrics and Gynecology* 277–8.

insufficiently informed about the risks: when questioned by a researcher posing as a potential egg seller, one clinic shrugged off the risks as 'irritability, a little water retention, so you gain a couple pounds'.[24] Another denied that there could possibly be any risk, 'because they aren't doing anything invasive. All they're doing is taking eggs out.'[25]

Even if risk information is given, it can still be said that egg cell removal breaks with the medical mandate to heal.[26] Mark Sauer, professor of obstetrics and gynecology at Columbia, has written: 'What is certain is that physicians are sworn to "do no harm". Donors are as much our patients as the recipients we so eagerly serve.'[27] That is also the position recently taken in a statement from the Royal College of Obstetricians and Gynaecologists Ethics Committee: in response to a consultation on whether egg donors should be paid, the committee insisted that the prior question was whether egg donation should take place at all, where there is no benefit to the donor.[28] In California, a proposed senate bill required assisted reproductive technology physicians to disclose the potential risks of oocyte donation, although the final weakened version of the bill set no other limitations on the procedure.[29] Such moves by professional and legislative bodies are somewhat encouraging, but it remains to be seen how widespread they will become.

A 'technical fix' may be sought instead: for example, new techniques of *in vitro* maturation, by which extra egg follicles are removed before ovulation and matured outside the women's body. Even if those techniques were reliable, however, women undergoing egg extraction for use in stem cell technologies would still be subject to a surgical procedure – the equivalent of Resnik's kidney excision – and possibly to other long-term risks, such as earlier menopause, all for no therapeutic benefit to themselves. They are effectively being used merely as means to another's end, in contravention of the Kantian categorical imperative (never to use

---

[24] Andrea D. Gurmankin, 'Risk information provided to prospective oocyte donors in a preliminary phone call' (2001) 1(4) *American Journal of Bioethics* 3–13, at 7.

[25] Gurmankin, 'Risk information', p. 9.

[26] Ingrid Schneider and Claudia Schumann, 'Stem cells, therapeutic cloning, embryo research: women as raw material suppliers for science and industry' in S. L. Herrmann and M. Kurmann (eds.), *Reproductive Medicine and Genetic Engineering: Women between Self-Determination and Societal Standardisation*, proceedings of a conference held in Berlin, 15–17 November 2001 (Reprokult, 2002) pp. 70–9.

[27] Mark V. Sauer, 'Egg donor solicitation: problems exist, but do abuses?' (2001) 1(4) *American Journal of Bioethics* 1–2, at 2.

[28] Royal College of Obstetricians and Gynaecologists Ethics Committee, unpublished opinion on HFEA consultation document, *The Regulation of Donor-Assisted Conception* (RCOG, 2005).

[29] Senate Bill 1630, s. 1702[b]1[D], proposed in February 2000, summarised in Judith F. Daar, 'Regulating the fiction of informed consent in ART medicine' (2001) 1(4) *American Journal of Bioethics* 19–20.

another solely as a means) and of the medical duty of *primum non nocere* (first do no harm), irrespective of whether consent has been obtained. Although paid 'donation' of ova for the production of embryonic stem cell lines has been reported in the USA,[30] in the United Kingdom and the rest of Europe the official position has more often been that the ova used should be 'surplus' from IVF, but that becomes less and less tenable: most clinics report shortages, not surpluses.[31] In order to create a 'surplus', some clinicians may even be tempted to induce even riskier regimes of ovarian stimulation, again failing in the primary duty of non-maleficence. Regimes of ovarian stimulation at over twice the recommended rate have already been documented in one Ukrainian IVF clinic.[32]

In egg extraction for use in stem cell technologies, there is even more of a temptation for clinicians to extract multiple eggs than in IVF, and even less ethical basis for doing so. Multiple egg extraction has become the norm for IVF because it increases the chances of success; if only one egg is extracted per cycle, fertilisation is less likely. Asking a woman undergoing IVF to submit to intensive ovarian stimulation for multiple egg extraction does at least lessen the likelihood that she will have to return for treatment again and again. But by some sleight-of-hand akin to that in which women become invisible in stem cell technologies, multiple egg extraction has also become the norm in the 'harvesting' of ova for stem cell technologies. Few commentators on the Korean blastocyst claim acknowledged the existence of the ova 'donors', let alone noticed that an average of twice as many eggs were being extracted from each woman as would have been the norm in an IVF clinic. The clinical rationale for ovarian hyperstimulation in the IVF case cannot possibly have applied to these women. They were exposed to risk for no medical benefit.

The commodification of ova has already resulted in unacceptably high rates of eggs being extracted for sale to IVF clinics – up to seventy in one cycle.[33] We have very little idea of the long-term risks of accelerated menopause, fragile bones and other harms to health which may result, but we can be sure that the short-term risks of OHSS are considerable. In the case of extraction for stem cell research, they are not offset by any clinical benefit to the women. Although some women may genuinely wish

---

[30] S. E. Lanzendorf *et al.*, 'Use of human gametes obtained from anonymous donors for the production of human embryonic stem cell lines' (2001) 76 *Fertility and Society* 132–7.

[31] United Kingdom Parliament, House of Commons, Select Committee on Science and Technology Fifth Report, accessed 20 April 2005 at www.publications,parliament.uk/pa/cm200405.

[32] Barnett and Smith, 'Cruel cost of the human egg trade', p. 6.

[33] Allen Jacobs, James Dwyer and Peter Lee, 'Seventy ova' (2001) 31 *Hastings Center Report* 12–14.

to volunteer in order to help scientific progress, and although we do allow volunteers in phase I trials deliberately to impose risks on themselves, we require a higher standard in that case, as well as an entire apparatus of randomised clinical trials and meta-analyses in evidence-based medicine. Furthermore, we generally impose higher standards for fully informed consent in research than in treatment.[34] Finally, we require the approval of a local research ethics committee.

That standard of monitoring rarely seems to apply in egg extraction, for the simple reason that few commentators have noticed that the process is going on at all. They are even less likely to notice when it is going on with vulnerable women in Eastern Europe or the Third World, who are pleasantly invisible to sight. Because enucleated ova contain no genetic material (except perhaps for traces of maternal mitochondrial DNA), the racial or ethnic background of the women donors does not matter. As I have argued elsewhere,[35] this phenomenon is an invitation to wholesale exploitation of women in the global South.

Women's property in ova: a Lockean basis

For some years I have been arguing what I believe to be a novel position: that the most legitimate property in the body is that which women possess in their extracted reproductive tissue, specifically in tissue products of their reproductive labour. However, I do not believe that there is any such thing as a generalised right to dispose of one's body or body parts; I am certainly not a laissez-faire, free-market libertarian. My argument is grounded in my interpretation of what Locke really said, and in a Hegelian notion of contract as mutual recognition. Essentially, however, this is my own argument rather than that of any canonical theorist; other feminist theorists have recently begun to develop it further.[36] The phenomenon of the vanishing lady should itself vanish from the stem cell debate, if my interpretation is true.

As I argued in chapter 2, a correct interpretation of Locke would entail the premiss that we do not normally own our bodies, because we have not laboured to create them. This interpretation is consistent with the view of the subject as embodied, and with the desire to avoid the objectification

---

[34] Jonathan Montgomery, *Health Care Law* (Oxford, Oxford University Press, 1997), p. 344.

[35] Donna Dickenson, 'The threatened trade in human ova' (2004) 5(2) *Nature Reviews Genetics* 167.

[36] Dodds, 'Women, commodification and embryonic stem cell research'; Carolyn McLeod and Francoise Baylis, 'For dignity or money: feminists on the inalienability of human embryos' (2006) 21(1) *Hypatia* 1–14; Laura Brace, *The Politics of Property: Labour, Freedom and Belonging* (Edinburgh, Edinburgh University Press, 2004).

or commodification of the body, which opens up as a possibility once we admit the notion that bodies can be owned by subjects. However, women do labour to create ova used in the stem cell technologies. We have seen in the preceding section that these ova do not just come out of nowhere: they are extracted, in multiple and unnatural quantities, through laborious and risky procedures. Put more properly in the active rather than the passive voice, women labour to produce extracted ova, in the purposeful manner characterising the sort of labour which grounds property rights in Locke. The intricacies of the stem cell technologies should make it clear that what women do in producing extracted ova is not simply 'natural'. Because what women do in pregnancy and childbirth has been likened to what the earth does by many theorists, including those like Marx who should have known better, it has been easy to ignore their reproductive labour: to make the lady vanish.

What a woman does in giving life, to Marx, is natural, not social; constitutive of an object, rather than a subject; part of the 'material substratum' that is not subject to social analysis.[37] To Marx, what gives labour its transformative power is intentionality and control. Pregnancy and childbirth, in his view, lack those qualities. But it takes a great deal of intentionality and control to undergo the threefold processes of ova donation; of course it is labour, and hard labour at that. Women have a genuine Lockean property in the labour of ova extraction, and likewise in that which they have laboured to create. It is clear this is not just what nature does, clear that value is created through their labours, and clear that ova are a commodity with exchange value, even if the women who produce them do not receive their full market value, as in the case of the Ukrainian women.

Women's labour in 'surrogate' motherhood does not give them full-blooded property rights over the child, but does demand that we recognise a limited set of property and contract rights sufficient to protect 'surrogates' from exploitation, such as protections against contracting couples who default if the 'surrogate' bears a disabled child. This argument, first rehearsed in *Property, Women and Politics*, has been misinterpreted by some critics, who wrongly assume I am trying to claim what I explicitly reject: that the woman's labour in pregnancy and childbirth gives something akin to a slave-owner's rights over the child. In the case of ova extracted for the stem cell technologies, however, that confusion clearly cannot arise, since no child is created. Stem cells, in fact, constitute an ideal example with which to clinch my argument, which would also apply to the commodification of aborted fetal tissue, where I have previously

---

[37] Catharine A. MacKinnon, *Toward a Feminist Theory of the State* (Cambridge, MA, Harvard University Press, 1989), p. 11.

argued that women likewise possess a property right, conceived alternatively as a privilege, power or immunity.[38] Then, I predicted that we would risk tumbling down some increasingly slippery slopes without a firm notion that women and women alone own their labour in producing reproductive tissue. The phenomenon of the vanishing lady in the stem cell wars is proof of that prediction. However, I was also sceptical even then of regarding women's rights in aborted fetal tissue as unqualified and complete property rights, and the same applies to my position on ova. Although some commentators generally sympathetic to feminism have argued in favour of allowing women to enjoy unqualified property rights in their bodily tissue,[39] I am more inclined to limit those rights in order to prevent the untrammelled commodification of practically everything. My approach is more typical of most feminist responses, I think, particularly outside the USA.[40]

Having established that women's property in their extracted ova can justifiably be regarded as conferring a Lockean property right, I will now briefly delimit what sort of right that might be, before going on to discuss how such a right could be secured through a Hegelian model of contract. Recall that in Honoré's classic formulation of the 'bundle' of rights in property, the owner of object X may have some or all of the following:

(1) a right to the physical possession of X;
(2) a right to its use;
(3) a right to its management, that is, to determine the ways in which others can use it;
(4) a right to the income that can be derived from its use by others;
(5) a right to its capital value;
(6) a right to security against its being taken by others;
(7) a right to transmit or alienate it to others by gift or bequest;
(8) a right to transmit or alienate it to others by sale;
(9) a permanent right to these other rights, without any limit or term;
(10) a duty to refrain from using X in a way that harms others, that is, liability for harm caused by X.

Which of these rights do I want to bestow on women who provide ova for the stem cell technologies? Those rights that we most need in

---

[38] *Property, Women and Politics*, pp. 166–170.
[39] Ruth Macklin, 'What is wrong with commodification?' in C. R. Cohen (ed.), *New Ways of Making Babies: The Case of Egg Donation* (Bloomington: Indiana University Press, 1996), pp. 106–21; K. Momberger, 'Breeder at Law' (2002) 11 *Columbia Journal of Gender and Law* 127–74.
[40] Dodds, 'Women, commodification and embryonic stem cell research'; McLeod and Baylis, 'Feminists on inalienability'; Schneider and Schumann, 'Stem cells, therapeutic cloning, embryo research'.

order to protect women from 'vanishing' in the stem cell debates must include protection against unauthorised taking, certainly – right (6). By 'unauthorised' taking, I also mean taking without fully informed consent or the imposition of regimes of ovarian hyperstimulation that go well beyond what is clinically advisable. It has been extensively documented that women selling their ova are not told the full facts, and not just in clinics exploiting Eastern European women, or in the case of Hwang Woo Suk.[41] Informed consent is a necessary protection, if not a sufficient one.

Right (3), to determine management of the tissue, is also crucial, although highly contentious. If we wish to allow genuine ova donation for altruistic reasons, which many want to allow, then we must respect the quite noble self-sacrifice which ova donors exhibit by not trivialising or commercialising the purposes to which their donation is put. Donors should have the right at the time of donation to refuse particular uses to which they object, and a right to be recontacted at periodic intervals about further downstream uses which were not known at the time of donation. If informed consent is to be genuine, a 'blanket' consent to all uses is impermissible, because it is not genuinely informed. This argument has been raised in the context of biobanks,[42] and indeed I will discuss it at further length in chapter 6, as well as in the next section of this chapter.

I am much less convinced that women need the right to the capital value of their ova or the right to sell those ova, rights (5) and (8). To avoid commodification, I would prefer to restrict the right to transmit or alienate to right (7), gift. I am well aware, however, that the 'gift relationship' is increasingly used to exclude tissue 'donors' from any further say in how their tissue is used, once they have consented to the initial tissue donation.[43] So right (7) must be exercised in conjunction with right (3), not as a substitute for it. Altruism already tends to be mandatory for women: one commentator has even predicted 'a new contract between the sexes and the generations, where young, fertile women are expected to provide the material resources for the treatment of the old and the sick' through provision of ova for therapeutic cloning.[44] Yet I do not want to rule out the right to transmit by gift altogether: altruism remains an important value, provided that it is not expected of women alone.

---

[41] Gurmankin, 'Risk information provided to prospective oocyte donors', pertaining to US donors; Barnett and Smith, 'Cruel cost of the human egg trade', on Eastern European women.

[42] Roberto Andorno, 'Population genetic databases: a new challenge to human rights' in C. Lenk, N. Hoppe and R. Adorno (eds.), *Ethics and Law of Intellectual Property: Current Problems in Politics, Science and Technology* (Aldershot, Ashgate, 2006), pp. 45–73.

[43] Catherine Waldby and Robert Mitchell, *Tissue Economies: Blood, Organs and Cell Lines in Late Capitalism* (Durham, NC, Duke University Press, 2006).

[44] Schneider and Schumann, 'Stem cells, therapeutic cloning, embryo research', p. 76.

Hegel, contract and stem cells

All the rights and duties summarised in the 'bundle' model of property can be seen as forms of relationship between two parties, and thus as linked to a Hegelian model of contract as mutual recognition. As I noted in chapter 2, the focus in the Hegelian model of property is on the experiential process of identity formation and recognition of others' subjectivities, with the emphasis on relationship rather than appropriation. Property, in Hegel, is not merely about relations of possession and control, but rather about the broader dynamics of social recognition. Contract in Hegel is a first stage of progress from the self-absorption of the immature subject into the social domain. By recognising women's labour in producing stem cells as conferring a Lockean property right, and adding the Hegelian contract analogy involving contract as mutual recognition, we would move two steps beyond the immature, rigid and discriminatory debate now dominating the stem cell discourse.

Furthermore, the way in which Hegel deals with a central paradox of contract casts a clearer light on the ongoing duties of the *recipient* of a gift, such as oocytes. Although contract symbolises the recognition of my entitlements, normally when I alienate something to you through a contract, I apparently cease to have entitlements in it. (This paradox holds whether I sell or give away the object of the contract, that is, regardless of the manner of its alienation.) As Hegel puts it, however, 'Contract is the process in which there is revealed and mediated the contradiction that I am and remain the independent owner of something from which I exclude the will of another, only in so far as in identifying my will with the will of another, I cease to be an owner.'[45] His answer to this contradiction of his own creation reminds us that property is not mere physical possession, but rather 'the social recognition that something belongs to me'.[46] It is this social recognition of women's property in their oocytes which is notably absent in the stem cell debates.

The nature as equals of partners in a contract requires the ongoing recognition of each other's rights, even after the transfer or alienation of the object which the contract concerns. That object is less important than the mutual recognition itself. Because contract interpreted on a Hegelian basis is primarily about ongoing mutual recognition, it should not be viewed as a one-off event, but neither should the rights of the 'donors' necessarily be regarded as all-embracing. The use of contract in protecting

---

[45] G. W. F. Hegel, *Philosophy of Right* (T. M. Knox (tr.), Oxford, Oxford University Press, 1967), s. 72.
[46] William E. Connolly, *Political Theory and Modernity* (Oxford, Blackwell, 1988), p. 117.

women ovum 'donors' for the stem cell technologies should be limited to the rights delineated in the previous section: security against unauthorised taking, donation rather than sale, and management of 'downstream' uses of the ova, so that women are able at any time to withdraw consent to a use which they find ethically objectionable. This is itself a major concession, one which even a comparatively enlightened guideline-setters such as the Human Genome Organization has been unwilling to recognise.[47]

It may be objected that the relationship between medical researchers and ovum donors is not literally contractual. In many cases it is, of course: where oocyte donors are paid, the transaction looks perfectly commercial and contractual. Where women who donate occytes receive no benefit, in the form of either payment or treatment services, it may well seem that the conditions for a contract do not exist: normally, a contract must involve a benefit or 'consideration' for both parties. On the other hand, it appears that many researchers do view the donation as a contractually binding transfer. Hence the 'second consent' box on Medical Research Council-approved forms for tissue donors in the United Kingdom, stipulating that the signatory understands that she possesses no further rights in any developments arising out of the donation. Whatever this is, it is certainly not an informed consent in the usual sense of a consent to the procedure itself; its purpose is not to protect the clinician from a possible battery action, but to preserve the commercial interests of researchers and their funders from later claims such as those launched by Moore. I think it is better understood as part of a contract in which something of potential value is being transferred for a price below its market value, or for no price at all. Effectively, the unrestricted second consent to all further uses of the tissue, now prevalent in consent forms, is already a contract, but one weighted entirely in the interests of the recipient of the tissue.[48] Applying contract law to oocyte donation would also have the advantage of clarifying the position regarding fraud, where one party fails to share pertinent information concerning risks with another.[49]

The model 'contract' for oocyte providers should not include an unfettered right for researchers, private firms and commercial funders to profit from the sale of their tissue, to hold complete rights over its capital value and to dictate all 'downstream' uses of the tissue. All the sticks in the property bundle need not be held by the recipients of reproductive

---

[47] HUGO (Human Genome Organisation) Ethics Council, *Statement on Benefit-Sharing*, Vancouver, 9 April 2000.

[48] Catherine Waldby, Contribution to 'Biopolitics, bioethics and biotechnology' panel, International Association of Bioethics Seventh Conference, Sydney, 9 November 2004.

[49] Jessica W. Berg, 'Risky business: evaluating oocyte donation' (2001) 1 (4) *American Journal of Bioethics* 18–19.

tissue, if we employ a disaggregated concept of property which permits more complex and differentiated rights and powers available to be claimed by both parties to a 'contract'. Even the isolated rights that I favour (protection against taking and rights to donate and control management of the tissue) would be a significant advance on current practice, ensuring that women's interests do not vanish altogether. We do not need to award such rights to oocyte providers as the right to profit from the sale of one's tissue; indeed, we should not, for reasons I discussed earlier. The point of contract as limited protection and as mutual recognition for women is precisely to avoid complete commodification of female reproductive tissue, rather than to enhance it. Contracts along these deliberately limited lines for the use of women's ova in the production of stem cell lines would probably be upheld by the courts, since a contract weighted entirely in the interests of one person is invalid in law. Current practice in ova 'donation' is arguably so unbalanced as to be legally void, if ever tested.

The limited model of contract that I advocate is philosophically coherent as well as practically sound. It is consistent both with the interpretation of property in most jurisprudence as differentiated forms of relationship to objects, and with a Hegelian approach emphasising the developmental, identity-creating benefits of property. The Hegelian model does not view property as merely instrumental to the pursuit of ends that have already been decided, in Lockean fashion.[50] Rather, it suggests that the relationship between me and what I own is indeed a bond of relationship rather than of appropriation, and it is thus eminently appropriate for women's reproductive tissue, itself the locus of relationship with future generations.[51] In addition, the Hegelian outlook incorporates a view of contract as a bond between myself and others, the first stage in a process of engagement with the existence of other moral subjects. The model of contract in ova that I am proposing here also chimes with much feminist theory's emphasis on relationship. However, it still requires the input of a feminist Marxist model emphasising women's alienation from their own labour.

Women's alienation from their own reproductive labour

I began this chapter by remarking how odd it is that women's contribution in producing ova for the stem cell technologies continues to go largely unrecognised. What explains this strange anomaly? Lynda Birke

---

[50] Alan Ryan, *Property and Political Theory* (Oxford, Blackwell, 1984).
[51] Donna Dickenson, 'Procuring gametes for research and therapy: the case for unisex altruism' (1997) 23 *Journal of Medical Ethics* 93–5.

has argued that life is increasingly seen as manipulable by scientists, with the result that women's role in giving life is increasingly ignored.[52] In particular, the new genetics, together with the popularity of the 'selfish gene' hypothesis, has led to a widespread but scientifically misguided perception that it is genes which carry the life force. But while I find this a plausible hypothesis, helping to explain why the genetic content in stem cell technologies is privileged over the enucleated ovum, it seems to me that women's role in giving life has been ignored for a very long time, well before the advent of modern science. Our society's blindness to what women do in giving life is merely manifested in a new form, when their role in creating an immortal stem cell line can be so blithely passed over.

In *Property, Women and Politics* and later writings,[53] I have offered an alternative mode of conceptualising this strangeness, in terms of women's propertylessness in their own reproductive labour. So long as the undeniable efforts that women put into extraction of ova continue to be ignored, that propertylessness goes on. It differs in kind and implications from the situation of the worker in Marx, who owns nothing but his labour, but does at least have a property in that. By contrast, the ovum donor's 'sweat equity' in her labour is rarely acknowledged. However, the Marxist concept of alienation can be productively applied here, even though Marx himself limits application of alienation to 'productive' rather than 'reproductive' labour. In fact, what women do in the stem cell technologies can be characterised as both productive and reproductive: productive in that it creates a product of exchangeable value, stem cell lines, in which there is already a market;[54] reproductive in that the environment where it is performed is typically the IVF clinic rather than the factory, and that the 'raw material' consists of ova within the woman's body. (It is important to note that ova, once extracted from the body, are a product rather than a raw material, even if an intermediate product in the stem cell technologies.[55] Labour by the woman is required to turn the raw material into the

---

[52] Lynda Birke, *Feminism and the Biological Body* (Edinburgh, University of Edinburgh Press, 1999), p. 168.

[53] Particularly 'Property and women's alienation from their own reproductive labour' (2001) 15(3) *Bioethics* 203–17.

[54] Dodds, 'Women, commodification and embryonic stem cell research', p. 156. However, Dodds does not view this contradiction in capitalism as applying only to women, instead regarding all workers as simultaneously possessing their labour power and as being alienated from it. I prefer Pateman's rendition: it is only male workers in Marx who do unequivocally possess their labour power, even if that is all they possess. This interpretation is more consistent with Marx's own inconsistency over what Delphy terms domestic relations of production, that is, the status of reproductive labour.

[55] Dodds, in an otherwise excellent discussion, demonstrates some confusion on this point (at p. 164 *et seq.*). There is a similar ambivalence in Schneider and Schumann, 'Stem cells, therapeutic cloning, embryo research'.

intermediate product, as I have amply demonstrated in the first section of this chapter.)

What is shown by the instance of ova used in the stem cell technologies is that there is no firm divide, as Marx thought there was, between the use-values produced through social means of 'production' and the absence of use-values in 'reproduction'. Conventional Marxists presuppose that when the activities of reproducing the labour force (in which, for the moment, I am including biological reproduction)[56] take place in the home, they add no value; they are classified as consumption rather than production. Women's work in the home, including the labours of pregnancy and childbirth, are thus excluded from the realm of value. Yet if these services had to be purchased in the market, they would possess a fungible value. As the French feminist Marxist Christine Delphy has written, this obvious contradiction is best explained not by the nature of the work performed, but by the gender of the agent performing it. It is worth repeating her crucial insight, which I first introduced in chapter 2:

[F]ar from it being the nature of the work performed by women which explains their relationship to production, it is their relations of production which explain why their work is excluded from the realm of value. It is women as economic agents who are excluded from the (exchange) market, not what they produce.[57]

Something of this assumption seems to have carried over into the biotechnology market place, where what women produce, ova for enucleation in the stem cell technologies, is clearly not excluded from the exchange market, but their role in producing it continues to be minimised. My primary concern, however, is not with the injustice of women being excluded from the exchange market; as I have stated from the very beginning of this book, I oppose the commodification of human tissue, including ova. Nor am I concerned to quantify the respective contributions of researchers and ovum donors in adding value to the stem cell technologies; I go no further than noting that both the researchers' and the women's labour is essential, although only the researchers' contribution is conventionally recognised.[58]

Indeed, Susan Dodds argues that this blinkered outlook, 'the lack of an appropriate means for recognizing the contribution of women's bodily capacities in the commodification of the resources they provide to stem

---

[56] As Dodds points out, Marx does distinguish reproduction of the species from reproduction of the conditions of social production (*Capital* (S. Moore and E. Aueling (tr.), F. Engels (ed.), Moscow, Progress, 1954, original edn 1867), pp. 167, 170).

[57] Christine Delphy, *Close to Home: A Materialist Analysis of Women's Oppression* (D. Leonard (tr. and ed.), London, Hutchinson with the Explorations in Feminism Collective, 1984), p. 60.

[58] As, for example, in the *Moore* judgment.

cell research', 'exemplifies an inherent contradiction of capitalist com-modification'.[59] It is certainly intrinsic to capitalist commodification, I would agree – whether or not it is irremediable, as 'inherent' tends to imply. The Marxist concept of alienation is useful in the context of com-modification of human tissue, because it is closely linked to the manner in which capitalism is potentially capable of objectifying and commodifying almost everything. As I have noted, however, Marx himself did not apply it to labour within the home, which he did not view as a site of capitalist oppression. To Marx it was the capitalist system which produced alien-ation, in which 'labour always appears as repulsive, always as external forced labour', and not labour as 'freedom and happiness'.[60]

From the earliest days of the Woman Question, however, feminists have extended the logic of alienation into the home, insisting that wives' domestic labour is actually external and forced, including the creation of that most intimate 'product', children. Carole Pateman's notion of the sexual contract is the most sophisticated of many feminist critiques which have viewed women's labour as inherently external and forced, and which in addition rightly draws our attention to the way in which women, unlike workers in Marx, are not viewed as possessing a prop-erty in that labour.[61] If reproductive labour in the home can be viewed as alienated, then certainly alienation can apply to reproductive labour undertaken outside the home, and to a situation where there need be no inverted commas around 'product'. Although children are neither prop-erty nor truly a product, stem cells are both. When women labour to produce the intermediate product used in the stem cell technologies, ova available for enucleation, there can be no question that their labour is neither natural nor performed in a realm extraneous to capitalism. Their reproductive labour has entered into the very heart of one of the most thriving applications of capitalism in modern biotechnology, and they are liable to oppression in that site.

In producing ova for the stem cell technologies, women undeniably perform work; furthermore, they perform work which is 'external' to the worker and 'not part of their nature', both characteristics defining alienation in Marx's terms.[62] The commodification and objectification of well-nigh everything under capitalism extends to the worker's subjectivity in Marx, so that the workman's labours actually undermine his nature as

---

[59] Dodds, 'Women, commodification and embryonic stem cell research', p. 149.
[60] Karl Marx, *Grundrisse: Foundations of the Critique of Political Economy* (Martin Nicolas (tr.), New York, Vintage Books, 1973), p. 611.
[61] Carole Pateman, *The Sexual Contract* (Cambridge, Polity Press, 1988), p. 134.
[62] Karl Marx, *Early Writings* (T. B. Bottomore (tr. and ed.), New York, McGraw-Hill, 1963), p. 123.

an autonomous agent, rather than contributing to his self-development. In the case of women's donation of ova, the altruism and dedication displayed by women who undergo the risky and laborious processes detailed in this chapter likewise go unrecognised at best, and at worst threaten to reduce them to 'egg machines', making themselves objects when they should be subjects.[63] Finally, alienated relationships typically deny the reality of mutual interdependence:[64] of employer and worker under capitalism, for example. In the stem cell technologies we likewise witness a denial of the essential contribution made by donors of ova to be enucleated, and the genuine interdependence of researchers and donors.

As I remarked in chapter 2, 'The effect of the new biotechnologies is merely to take [women's] propertylessness in the labour of reproduction back to stages before the birth of children: to the production of oocytes, for example . . . Just as the Marxist feminist Ann Ferguson asks whether contemporary high-technology childbirth is a form of alienated labour,[65] so might one ask whether even higher-technology processes such as superovulation and 'egg harvesting' also fit this Marxist mould.'[66] Now that we have seen in more detail exactly what is involved in the processes of 'egg harvesting', and how surprisingly close to the Marxist notion of alienation they come, I think the answer has to be 'yes'.

Just as the solution in Marx is not just to pay workers a bit more while retaining all the trappings of capitalism, so the answer to women's alienation from their own reproductive labour does not lie in paid egg donation, however high the price. Rather, in my view, the injustice lies in the lack of recognition of what women do in producing ova for the stem cell technologies. This is a form of alienation of women from their own labour, and thus in a broad sense a form of exploitation, but even though the surplus value created by women's labour is seized by the biotechnology capitalist, the injustice does not lie in the disparity between the market value of their ova and what they are paid, if they are paid at all.[67] Instead, the sources of the injustice are threefold: the commodification of

---

[63] This insight applies whether or not women are paid, since typically their altruism is elicited even in a paid system. See Andrea M. Braverman, 'Exploring ovum donors' motivations and needs' (2001) 1(4) *American Journal of Bioethics* 16–17; M. Patrick, A. L. Smith, W. R. Meyer and A. Bashford, 'Anonymous oocyte donation: a follow-up questionnaire' (2001) 75 *Fertility and Sterility* 1034–6.

[64] Alison Jaggar, *Feminist Politics and Human Nature*, (Totowa, NJ, Rowman and Allanheld, 1983), p. 216

[65] Ann Ferguson, *Sexual Democracy: Women, Oppression and Revolution* (Boulder, CO, Westview Press, 1991).

[66] For a more extended discussion of this point, see Dickenson, 'Property and women's alienation'.

[67] Dodds, in 'Women, commodification and embryonic stem cell research', wrongly focuses on this disparity as the source of the injustice, in my view.

what should not be commodified, the performance of procedures which contravene the duty of 'first do no harm' and the co-opting of women's altruism into the process.

As I have written before, 'If donors believe they are demonstrating altruism, but biotechnology firms and researchers use the discourse of commodity and profit, we have not "incomplete commodification" but complete commodification with a human face.'[68] The solution is not to engage in scholastic disputations over how much women should be paid,[69] but to use the tools provided by the notion of property in jurisprudence and the remedies of contract law which I suggested in the previous section. The injustice can thus be partly put right by recognising a property right in women's labour in ovum donation, provided that the right is limited to the 'sticks' in the property bundle which I have delineated elsewhere, particularly the right to determine management of the tissue's use (right (3) in Honoré's classification) and protection against unauthorised taking (right (6)).[70] This is the core of my argument.[71]

It may be thought that my analysis would prevent ova from ever being extracted for the stem cell technologies, to the enormous detriment of possibly beneficial research. Although the benefits of stem cell research have incontrovertibly been exaggerated, that remains a serious objection. I do not wish to prevent all instances of ovum extraction, in a thoroughly Luddite fashion, but rather to alter the 'burden of proof', so that it is no longer simply assumed that ova will be readily available. Where the duty of 'first do no harm' is not threatened, where women retain control over 'downstream' uses of their ova, and where they are protected against unauthorised taking through some form of contract, progress will have been made. However, even the contract approach still has its limitations.

The woman as receptacle and the limitations of contract

The impetus of Hegel's argument is about the mutual recognition embodied in contract. A contract alone, however, will not protect 'donors' of ova to be enucleated unless their equal role in creating the stem cell line

---

[68] Dickenson, 'Property and women's alienation', p. 212.

[69] As per the recent HFEA 'SEED' consultation and many US sources, e.g. Gregory Stock, 'Eggs for sale: How much is too much?' (2001) 1(4) *American Journal of Bioethics* 26–27.

[70] What is specifically required in the UK context is for the finding in *R* v. *Kelly* [1998] 3 All ER 741 to be extended to the labour which women put into ovum donation.

[71] My argument in the stem cell context is somewhat similar to Stephen Munzer's more generalised view that our property rights in our tissue are primarily powers (to transfer, waive and exclude others) rather than claim-rights (to possess, use and receive income), except that I also want to include the claim-right of managing further uses to which the tissue is put. See Stephen R. Munzer, *A Theory of Property* (Cambridge, Cambridge University Press, 1990), pp. 41–56.

is recognised in that contract. Hence the need to incorporate the Marxist concept of alienation, extended beyond Marx's own formulation into women's alienation from their reproductive labour. This caveat already applies to 'contract motherhood': even in jurisdictions where contracts between 'surrogate mothers' and commissioning parents are valid, contract alone is not enough where the woman's role is merely viewed as that of a sort of receptacle.

In the infamous *Baby M* 'surrogacy' case, the court effectively held that genetic fatherhood was privileged over gestational motherhood, by finding that the genetic father already had sole rights over the child, and that his contract with the 'surrogate' mother merely covered her willingness to be impregnated and carry 'his' baby to term.[72] In particular, it was the man's genetic contribution that was determinative: even though the 'surrogate' was both the genetic and the gestational mother, the baby still 'belonged' to the father. In the stem cell debates, we can see a similar prejudice in favour of genetic content, within a deeply gendered discourse. Although in somatic cell nuclear transfer enucleated ova are as essential to creating the new life of the stem cell line as is the genetic content, the genetic material transferred is afforded a privileged position over the mere 'substance' of the enucleated ovum. The fact of enucleation is significant: the essence of the woman is lost, so that only the shell of the ultimate female object, the egg, remains.

This view is consistent with ancient metaphors presenting women's reproductive role as merely housing the active male element in generation: as Aeschylus writes in the *Eumenides*, 'A stranger she preserves a stranger's seed.' Such a limited understanding of women's role in reproduction is likewise found in Aristotle, who views woman as a mere receptacle for the active, energising, soul-creating power of the male.[73] She is merely passive, manipulable, open to a higher force. In the stem cell technologies, the receptacle is not the woman or her womb, rather the enucleated ovum; yet the implied metaphor is similar. The genetic material injected into the enucleated ovum is seen as the guiding force or intelligence producing the stem cell line.

A contract such as that in the *Baby M* case failed to protect the birth mother in a socio-legal context inherited from the common-law system of coverture, where the father's genetic parenthood is privileged over the mother's gestational role – even when the 'surrogate' was both the genetic and the gestational mother. Motherhood conveyed few rights compared to fatherhood in the 'marriage contract' under the law of coverture, and

---

[72] *In the matter of Baby M*, 217 N. J. Supr. 313 (1987), 109 N. J. 396 (1988).

[73] Aristotle, *The Generation of Animals* (W. Ogle (tr.)) in *The Basic Works of Aristotle* (R. McKeon (ed.), New York, Random House, 1941), 731b30.

we are a very long way from having abolished all traces of coverture. Contracts in women's reproductive tissue are automatically different from other forms of contract, because women's bodies have long been assumed to be open and available. That is the brunt of Carole Pateman's notion of the sexual contract, which can indeed be made to encompass the stem cell technologies, as well as surrogate motherhood, private cord blood banking, and other uses of female bodies which are justified by their proponents as being like any other economic transaction. Pateman's model is also valuable for its insight that once an initial consent has been given, for example to the marriage 'contract', all further rights are extinguished. This is also at present the effect of consent to further uses of donated tissue.

Where women's bodies are concerned, the 'normal contractual manner' does not necessarily apply. There are profounder reasons why transactions concerning the use of women's bodies, even if distinguished from the sale of women's bodies, cannot simply be assumed to be the same as any other economic transaction. A feminist analysis such as Pateman's should warn us against the use of oversimplified, knock-down, neo-liberal arguments about choice, consent and contract where female bodies are concerned – or indeed potentially all bodies. As I asserted in the opening pages of this book, all bodies now risk the sorts of objectification and commodification to which women's bodies have previously been particularly vulnerable.

The answer to that problem, however, lies in extending the logic of contract to make it genuinely beneficial to women, in forcing its liberal defenders to recognise that contract has been used in such a one-sided fashion in the new reproductive technologies as not to be genuine at all. The problem is not that the sexual contract is a contract, but that it is sexual. Similarly, in relation to the stem cell technologies, the problem is not necessarily the inherent limitations of contract as such, but the surrounding cultural beliefs concerning women's role in reproduction more broadly and in ovum donation in particular. The view of the woman as receptacle is one such belief.

In the case of 'contract' or 'surrogate' motherhood, gestational mothers can be protected by a contract providing remedies for the 'surrogate' if she miscarries, produces a child of the 'wrong' sex, or conceives more children than the contracting couple will accept.[74] However, I emphatically

---

[74] For an example of the last eventuality, see Donna Dickenson, 'Genetic research and the economic paradigm' ('Einwilligung, Kommodifizierung und Vortelsausgleich in der Genforschung') in L. Honnefelder et al. (eds.), Das Genetische Wissen und die Zukunft des Menschen (Berlin, De Gruyter, 2003), pp. 139–51.

disagree with those liberal feminists who insist that gestational mothers must adhere to strict contract observance, requiring them to deliver rather than keep their babies, if women's autonomy is to be taken seriously.[75] What this sort of analysis ignores is the power imbalance between the 'surrogate' and the contracting couple, who are typically of a higher socio-economic status.[76] The role of contract here, I would argue, should be to protect the rights of the weaker party. In a system such as the United Kingdom's, where 'surrogacy' arrangements are void at law, few protections exist for the weaker party, typically the 'surrogate'. Restrictions on absolute freedom of contract are recognised in other branches of law, such as employment protection or landlord and tenant law.[77] The choice is not between complete absence of contract and complete freedom of contract: we can make contract suit our feminist purposes, just as other constituencies such as trades unions have historically made it serve theirs. Our task may be more difficult in a globalised era of neo-liberalisation, I grant, but we should use whatever weapons are available to us.

It may be objected that just as no contracting couple would want to enter a surrogacy arrangement on the terms I have proposed, so no research team or commercial biotechnology company would want to invest in a stem cell line which could be nullified at a later date by an ovum donor exercising her right to refuse consent to a particular use. I find myself strangely unbothered by this possibility. The terms of the power imbalance between women who 'donate' ova and commercial biotechnology companies, stem cell banks and funded research teams are now so great that any power shift towards the 'suppliers' of tissue must be welcome. We are a very long way from the situation in which the 'supplier' calls the shots: the existence of the 'supplier' is barely even recognised. In any case, it should not be beyond human wit to devise contractual or consent mechanisms that afford ovum donors some rights of later refusal: as we have seen, the French and German national ethics committees have already made concrete recommendations. Since the commercial stakes are immensely valuable, presumably researchers and biotechnology companies would still want to invest in stem cell research, even if the protections afforded to ova donors were somewhat less minuscule than they are at present.

[75] Macklin, 'What is wrong with commodification?'; Momberger, 'Breeder at law'.
[76] Helena Ragone, *Surrogate Motherhood: Conception in the Heart* (Boulder, CO, Westview Press, 1996).
[77] Joan Mahoney, 'An Essay on Surrogacy and Feminist Thought' in Larry Gostin (ed.), *Surrogate Motherhood: Politics and Privacy* (Bloomington, Indiana University Press, 1990), pp. 183–97.

Personal rights, such as consent, can no longer be distinguished from property rights; ova donation represents a radical change in the political economy of human tissue. What has not changed is the unbalanced power relationship between donors and recipients of tissue; or, perhaps more correctly, what has changed is that the imbalance has worsened, in the case of ova donors to the stem cell technologies. If the lady is not to vanish altogether, she needs protections such as contract, but a form of contract limited to the protections she most needs, and aimed at ensuring that women's contribution to the stem cell technologies is actually recognised. Without recognition of women's property in the labour of ova donation, not only are women estranged from their reproductive labour; the terms in which the stem cell debate is conducted are deceptive and disingenuous. As Tom Sawyer discovered to his advantage in the tale of the picket fence, the cleverest way to exploit someone's labour is to pretend they are not working at all.

It has been said that stem cell research threatens to encourage a view of the natural world as an artefact: 'to see the entire natural world, the human body along with it, as having the status only of material to be manipulated'.[78] By creating immortal stem cell lines touted as having the pluripotent potential to reverse degradation and decay, we may see ourselves as remoulding the biological universe. Government science policies have long tended to 'privilege the promissory',[79] and stem cell research technology is the promissory technology *par excellence*. Potentially it turns the whole natural world into an object for human utility: a highly symbolic form of the new biotechnological enclosures. Although the practical demand for ova in the stem cell technologies affects women's bodies particularly fiercely, on a more figurative level the stem cell technologies may be said to illustrate my thesis that all bodies are increasingly at risk of becoming objectified. In chapter 5, I examine the application of that hypothesis to the patenting of the human genome. First, however, I turn to another example of the way in which women's production of valuable tissue is not recognised: the case of umbilical cord blood.

---

[78] Paul Lauritzen, 'Stem cells, biotechnology and human rights: implications for a posthuman future' (2005) 35(2) *Hastings Center Report* 25–33, at 25.
[79] I am grateful to Paul Oldham of the University of Lancaster for this term.

4 Umbilical Cord Blood Banks: Seizing Surplus Value

> Christmas shopping for the unborn baby has never been easy. However, stem cell technology may have brought what is possibly this year's most original gift. For a mere £1,250, it is possible to harvest stem cells from the umbilical cord at birth and store them frozen for up to 25 years. 'Stem cells are not just for life – they're for Christmas', said Shamshad Ahmed, managing director of Smart Cells International, a company offering stem cell gift certificates as a new line this year. He has sold the idea to fifty customers so far – mainly grandparents who want their descendants to have access to stem cells' healing powers in the event of illness or injury.[1]

Private umbilical cord blood banks like Smart Cells International offer benevolent grandparents and parents a 'most original gift', tinged with the glamour of the stem cell technologies. Umbilical cord blood banking plays on parents' natural wish to do everything possible for their child, even if the 'healing powers' of stem cells are so far largely theoretical. If there is a possible enormous benefit to be gained, and no risk of harm, then a Pascal's Wager strategy would still dictate in favour of cord blood banking, however speculative and distant that benefit might be. Just as Pascal counselled doubters to wager on the existence of God because the benefit to be gained is eternal bliss, no matter how shaky the grounds for belief might appear, so parents might regard banking cord blood as a good investment because the potential return is of such enormous value, however inchoate the stem cell technologies' promises of cure might be at present. As one parent said, 'I think it's quite clear that this technology is moving very quickly, and for not a huge amount of money, in fact quite a small amount of money, it's a good punt.'[2]

---

[1] John Carvel, 'With love at Christmas: a set of stem cells,' *Guardian*, 6 December 2005, p. 7.

[2] Interview for the programme 'Catalyst' with the father of a child on whose behalf blood had been banked with Cryocite, Australian Broadcasting Service Television, 25 September 2004, quoted in Catherine Waldby and Robert Mitchell, *Tissue Economies: Blood, Organs and Cell Lines in Late Capitalism* (Durham, NC, Duke University Press, 2006), p. 129.

Cord blood banking for children's use as adults, in this view, 'allows them to live in a double biological time. The body will age and change, lose its self-renewing power and succumb to illnesses of various kinds. The banked fragment, frozen and preserved from deterioration . . . can literally remake a crucial part of the account holder's body: the blood system.'[3] Like the stem cell technologies, umbilical cord blood banking partakes of the myth of the infinitely regenerative body, 'the dream that every biological loss can be repaired',[4] which we see on a more trivial and increasingly acceptable level in cosmetic surgery. In the US context, the bioethics commentator George Annas attributes the success of private cord blood banks to the frugal Puritan desire to avoid waste, the US love affair with technology, the collective denial of death and the widespread notion that it is individual parents rather than society who are responsible for their families' welfare.[5] These attitudes, however, are no more confined to the USA than is the commodification of umbilical cord blood. In the United Kingdom, the private cord blood bank Cryo-Care (UK) Ltd, whose parent firm is based in Belgium, distributes advertising leaflets with the arguably misleading title 'Stem cell technology preserving the life of your child', playing up cord blood as a natural form of healing while simultaneously extolling the wonders of science.

The French National Ethics Committee has denounced private cord blood banks – which 'disguise a mercantile project using assistance to children as a screen'[6] – and a European Commission advisory group, the European Group on Ethics, has issued a similar report in favour of public rather than private banks.[7] Yet commercial cord blood banks are also on the rise throughout Europe. Often there is no bright line between their activities and those of their public counterparts. For example, the director of the non-profit Düsseldorf CB Bank is a scientific advisor and member of the board of directors of the profit-making firm Kourion Therapeutics AG, which estimates that the total cell therapy market in Germany will exceed US$30 billion by the end of this decade. Kourion, in turn, was recently taken over by the US firm Viacell, parent company of the Viacord private cord blood bank.[8]

---

[3] *Ibid.* p. 125.   [4] *Ibid.* p. 120.

[5] Report of a presentation by George Annas, in Rebecca Haley, Liana Harvath and Jeremy Sugarman, 'Ethical issues in cord blood banking: summary of a workshop' (1998) 38 *Transfusion* 867–73, at 869.

[6] CCNE (Comité Consultatif National d'Ethique), *Umbilical Cord Blood Banks for Autologous Use or Research*, opinion number 74 (Paris, CCNE, 2002).

[7] European Group on Ethics and New Technologies (EGE), *Opinion on the Ethical Aspects of Umbilical Cord Blood Banking*, opinion number 19, IP/04/364 (Brussels, EGE, 2004).

[8] Jennifer Gunning, 'Umbilical cord blood banking: a surprisingly controversial issue', unpublished report for Cardiff Centre for Ethics, Law and Science (CCELS, no date).

Taking out a cord blood 'account' for one's child is also consistent with the rise in peripheral blood donations to oneself. With increasing distrust of public blood banks following the HIV and BSE scares of the 1980s and 1990s, many people are now storing up blood before a procedure by 'giving' to themselves. Autologous donation of this sort has passed from a procedure practised occasionally for patients with very rare blood types to a practice involving between 6 and 9 per cent of all donations within the European Union.[9] That figure can be expected to rise: a Eurobarometer survey found that 25 per cent of those surveyed would refuse to accept anything but their own blood.[10]

Cord blood banking is touted as both a biological and an ethical miracle cure. 'What if the umbilical cord blood stem cells we usually discard with the placenta could replace controversial embryonic stem cells in therapy?' ask the authors of an article entitled 'Lifeline in an ethical quagmire'.[11] On the tried-but-not-true assumption that the only ethical issues about stem cells concern the moral status of the embryo, this argument suggests that the plasticity of embryonic stem cells is very nearly matched by that of haematopoietic (blood-making) cells found in the umbilical cord. 'This observation raises the exciting possibility of replacing human ES (embryonic stem) cells for tissue and cell therapeutics with umbilical cord hematopoietic stem cells that are normally discarded with the placenta after delivery',[12] without any of the ethical bother of embryonic stem cell lines.

The short answer to the question 'what if umbilical cord blood stem cells could replace embryonic stem cells in therapy?' is that women would then be asked to do two dangerous things rather than one. Not only would some women continue to undergo the risky processes of ovarian stimulation and egg extraction documented in the previous chapter, if enucleated ova continue to be required in the stem cell technologies. Other women, mothers in childbirth, would also come under increasing pressure to allow the extraction of umbilical cord blood, even though the process may well increase the length and risks of the third stage of labour. These risks may not be as serious as those involved in egg 'harvesting'; nor is the process likely to become the subject of the worldwide trade we are beginning to see in ova. However, if extraction of umbilical cord blood did ever become the clinical norm, many more women would be affected than is the case with ova collection.

[9] Waldby and Mitchell, *Tissue Economies*, p. 55.   [10] *Ibid.*

[11] Ian Rogers and Robert F. Casper, 'Lifeline in an ethical quagmire: umbilical cord blood as an alternative to embryonic stem cells' (2004) 2(2) *Sexuality, Reproduction and Menopause* 64–70.

[12] Rogers and Casper, 'Lifeline in an ethical quagmire', 64.

What links these two chapters, then, is the way in which 'the lady vanishes' in both instances: it is widely assumed that neither the stem cell technologies nor the extraction of umbilical cord blood pose any ethical issues about harms to women, but they do. Furthermore, in both cases women's property in their own reproductive labour is widely ignored, or presented simply as a natural function, even though there is nothing natural about either technique. Finally, both cord blood and the stem cell technologies share an inherently anti-feminist view of organisms as 'sets of replaceable parts'. As the feminist biologist Linda Birke argues,[13] life is no longer seen as given by women in childbirth, but by scientists, technologists and the equivalents of Smart Cells International, Cryo-Care (UK) and Kourion Therapeutics. It is no longer enough that women should give birth: now they must also give the prospect of extended life through ensuring that extracted cord blood enables their babies to enjoy the putative marvels of the stem cell technologies, whatever the risks to themselves in cord blood extraction.

Possibly those benevolent grandparents might want to think twice about the additional risk to which they are subjecting their daughter. In the next section I will be weighing up these risks to mother and baby in extraction of umbilical cord blood, as against the currently known benefits: it is by no means clear that the procedure is risk-free, as is commonly supposed, or that the benefits are clear, and so the 'wager' is not such a good one. Another incorrect common assumption is that the cord blood cells 'are normally discarded with the placenta after delivery', which I also evaluate critically, along with the equally dubious but equally widespread assumption that the umbilical cord blood belongs to the baby rather than the mother.

Risks and benefits

The collection immediately after the birth of your baby is totally painless for mother and baby and does not present any risk. It is completely non invasive. The collection of the blood is only done AFTER the baby has been delivered. A small prick in the umbilical cord enables the blood to be collected . . .[14]

The collection of these precious stem cells is totally safe and harmless to both mother and newborn.[15]

---

[13] Lynda Birke, *Feminism and the Biological Body* (Edinburgh, University of Edinburgh Press, 1999), p. 170.

[14] Cryo-Care (UK) Ltd advertising leaflet, 'Stem cell technology preserving the life of your child', p. 12.

[15] Cryogenesis International, www.cryo-gensis.biz, accessed 2 January 2006.

Contrary to the cheerful impression given by commercial cord blood banks and echoed by a surprising number of otherwise well-informed ethical and legal scholars,[16] the collection of umbilical cord blood takes place *during* childbirth (in the third stage of labour, after the delivery of the baby and up to the delivery of the placenta). As far as the mother is concerned, childbirth is not over after the baby has been delivered; indeed, the greatest risks to her lie in the third stage, since post-partum haemorrhage is the greatest cause of maternal death.[17] Once again, what women undergo in childbirth, and women's reproductive labour more generally, is not fully recognised – not just in the advertisements of commercial firms like this one, but also in the writings of bioethicists who have accepted the implicit claim that childbirth is over for the mother after the baby is delivered. They have effectively bought into the commercial cord blood banks' claims that nothing unnatural is going on – coincidentally similar to the little white lies told by the IVF clinics we met in chapter 3, the ones who tell potential egg donors that egg donation is not an invasive or risky procedure.

Contrary again to the advertising literature, the extraction of cord blood also presents sufficient risks to mother and baby for major professional bodies in obstetrics and gynaecology to have expressed substantial concerns.[18] These qualms can be subdivided into those involving the mother's health and those concerning the best interests of the baby. In addition, both mother and baby may be adversely affected if the attention of delivery room staff is distracted from the primary purpose of a safe delivery. The first breath, fetal adaptation and safe expulsion of the placenta are all complex and risky processes. In this crucial and chancy

---

[16] Waldby and Mitchell, *Tissue Economies*; Gunning, 'Umbilical cord blood banking'; Stephen R. Munzer, 'The special case of property rights in umbilical cord blood for transplantation' (1991) 51 *Rutgers Law Review* 493–568. Munzer, for example, writes that 'cord blood is harvested after a baby is born, and the procedure involves virtually no risk to the mother or the newborn' (at 495).

[17] C. Abouzahr, 'Antepartum and postpartum haemorrhage' in C. J. L. Murray and A. D. Lopez (eds.), *Health Dimensions of Sex and Reproduction* (Cambridge, MA, Harvard University Press, 1998), pp. 172–174.

[18] American College of Obstetricians and Gynecologists, *Opinion Number 183: Routine Storage of Umbilical Cord Blood for Potential Future Transplantation* (Washington, DC, ACOG, 1997); Royal College of Obstetricians and Gynaecologists Scientific Advisory Committee, *Cord Blood Banking*, opinion paper 2 (London, RCOG, 2001). In June 2006, the RCOG conducted a follow-up review, which confirmed the earlier view that there should be no interference in obstetric care for the speculative purpose of collecting cord blood stem cells. The latest RCOG guidance stipulates that if cord blood is to be taken, the procedure should only be done after the third stage of labour is complete, when the placenta is completely expelled, presumably even if that lessens the total amount of blood collected. Collection should also be done by a third party who has no duty of care to either mother or baby.

stage, doctors' and midwives' primary duty of care is to the mother and her baby, not to the priorities of a cord blood bank, whether commercial or public. Whereas the cord blood bank's interest lies in extracting the requisite amount of cord blood, the mother needs a speedy and safe third stage of delivery, minimising the risk of haemorrhage. There is some conflict between that requirement for the mother and the baby's need for maximal blood flow through the cord, although there the evidence is mixed. What seems quite clear, however, is that the greatest conflict lies between the interests of either the mother or the baby, and that of the cord blood bank.

To see how greatly a birth involving extraction of cord blood differs from the 'usual' birth, it is worth sketching in the contours of a normal third stage of delivery. In an 'undisturbed' or 'expectant management' third stage of labour, the baby would remain attached to the umbilical cord, while pulsation continued for several minutes. The placenta would usually be delivered within thirty minutes to one hour and would then be separated from the cord. This process mimics that of other mammalian deliveries, where mother and baby lie still while waiting for the placenta to appear. In 'active management', oxytoxic drugs are administered to hasten the separation of the placenta from the uterus, just as the baby's anterior shoulder appears. The baby takes a few breaths, the cord is clamped and cut within a few minutes, and controlled cord traction is used to deliver the placenta. Maximal quantities of cord blood, however, are only obtained when the placenta is still in the uterus and the cord has been clamped immediately, even before the baby's first breath. This process would contravene current standards of good practice in the third stage, both the 'undisturbed' or the more usual 'active' forms of management.[19]

Leaving the placenta attached to the uterine wall risks maternal haemorrhage. In terms of the mother's health during the delivery of the placenta, a systematic Cochrane review, the 'gold standard' of medical evidence, found in favour of routine administration of an oxytoxic drug to stimulate contractions of the uterine muscles and ensure quick and clean delivery of the placenta.[20] Together with early clamping of the

---

[19] Personal communication from Dr Susan Bewley, chair, Royal College of Obstetricians and Gynaecologists Ethics Committee and team leader, Women's Health Services, Guy's and St Thomas's Hospital, London, 2 January 2006.

[20] W. J. Prendiville, D. Elbourne and S. McDonald, 'Active versus expectant management in the third stage of labour', *Cochrane Database of Systematic Reviews*, issue 3, art. no. CD000007, 24 July 2000. See also W. Prendiville and D. Elbourne, 'Care during the third stage of labour' in I. Chalmers, M. Enkin and M. J. N. C. Keirse (eds.), *Effective Care in Pregnancy and Childbirth* (Oxford, Oxford University Press, 1989), pp. 1145–69. Another Cochrane review on management of the third stage of labour is expected to come out some time in 2006.

umbilical cord, while it is still pulsing, this measure was found to reduce the length of the third stage of labour and to lessen the risk of maternal haemorrhage, with no harm to the baby. Harvesting cord blood, however, might well be impaired by this procedure, since maximal extraction depends on the flow of blood from the pulsing cord. In a randomised clinical trial conducted by the private cord blood bank Eurocord comparing 100 *in utero* and 100 *ex utero* collections, significantly more blood was collected while the placenta was still attached to the uterine wall.[21] Cryo-Care does not specify a maximum sample, only a minimum of 60 ml., but it prides itself on obtaining two samples 'for added security'.[22] Whose security is served remains a moot point. As I wrote in an earlier article:

The final stage of labour often sees the mother exhausted by pain and effort, only eager to conclude the business at hand by expelling the placenta, and to have her baby with her. She may well also have to undergo painful stitching of the perineum, if an episiotomy has been performed. How can it possibly be part of the doctor's duty of care to impose an additional burden on her by performing cord blood collection *in utero*?[23]

It is also worth noting that if cord blood is taken from the pulsating cord during the third stage of labour and not harvested afterwards from the discarded placenta, it can hardly be seen as clinical waste, despite the image projected in the commercial cord blood bank literature. For example, Cryo-Care's literature says that 'stem cells are available in large numbers from umbilical cord blood immediately after birth, something which in the past was simply discarded with the placenta'.[24] I shall return to this point in the next section, on the property status of cord blood.

Clamping before the infant has drawn a first breath, or at an early stage, might well maximise collection of cord blood, but is likely to harm the infant. Most of the evidence concerning implications for the baby's wellbeing comes from comparative studies of early and late clamping of the umbilical cord, either while the cord is continuing to pulse or after it has ceased to do so. Intuitively we might expect that maximising blood flow to the infant through delayed clamping of the cord would be best for the baby, and thus that the interests of mother and baby would be in conflict. Delayed clamping can provide the infant with an additional

---

[21] Cited in Saskia Tromp, 'Seize the day, seize the cord', unpublished undergraduate medical dissertation (University of Maastricht, 2001). My thanks to Saskia Tromp for making this citation known to me when I was co-supervising her dissertation.

[22] Cryo-Care (UK) advertising leaflet, p. 13.

[23] Donna Dickenson and Paolo Vineis, 'Evidence-based medicine and quality of care' (2002) 10(3) *Health Care Analysis* 243–59, at 255.

[24] Cryo-Care (UK) advertising leaflet, p. 3.

30 per cent blood volume and up to 60 per cent more red blood cells, resulting in additional iron stores, less anaemia later in infancy, higher red blood cell flow to vital organs, better cardiopulmonary adaptation and increased duration of early breast-feeding. One review article concludes that delayed clamping increases haemoglobin concentration in infants at two to three months of age and reduces the risk of anaemia, without any associated increased risk of perinatal complications. The advantages of late clamping were especially pronounced for developing countries, where more mothers are anaemic, but also true in three out of four studies from industrialised countries.[25]

Other reviews have found a variety of adverse effects in early clamping, in addition to the concrete benefits from delayed clamping in terms of haemoglobin levels.[26] Immediate clamping has been reported to produce brain haemorrhage in premature infants.[27] In a systematic review of seven studies of a total of 297 infants, delayed cord clamping for premature babies was found to improve their overall health, resulting in fewer transfusions for anaemia or low blood pressure and less risk of intraventicular haemorrhage.[28] One might assume that for premature babies, in particular, any blood removed is taken at a cost to the infant's health. However, other studies indicate that there is no adverse effect from early clamping, particularly in full-term infants.[29] Indeed, it is

---

[25] Patrick van Rheenen and Bernard J. Brabin, 'Late umbilical cord-clamping as an intervention for reducing iron deficiency anaemia in term infants in developing and industrialised countries: a systematic review' (2004) 24 Annals of Tropical Paediatrics 3–16.

[26] Judith S. Mercer and Rebecca L. Skovgaard, 'Neonatal transitional physiology: a new paradigm' (2002) 15 Journal of Perinatal and Neonatal Nursing 56–75. See also G. M. Morley, 'Cord closure: can hasty clamping injure the newborn?' (1998) Obstetrics and Gynaecology Management (July); T. Peltonen, 'Placental transfusion: advantages and disadvantages' (1981) 137 European Journal of Pediatrics 141–6; and FIGO (International Federation of Gynaecology and Obstetrics), Ethical Guidelines regarding the Procedure of Collection of Cord Blood (1998), available at www.figo.org.

[27] G. K. Hofmeyr, P. J. M Bex, R. Skapinker and T. Delahunt, 'Hasty clamping of the umbilical cord may initiate neonatal intraventricular hemorrhage' (1989) 29 Medical Hypotheses 5. The validity of this study is disputed by Francesco Bartolini, Manuela Battaglia, Cinzia De Iulio and Girolano Sirchia, 'Response' (1995) 86(12) Blood 4900.

[28] H. Rabe, G. Reynolds and J. Diaz-Rossello, 'Early versus delayed umbilical cord clamping in preterm infants' Cochrane Database of Systematic Reviews, issue 4, art. no. CD003248pub2, first published 18 October 2004, with a more recent review in vol. 3, 17 May 2005. A review article by B. Lainez Villabona et al., 'Early or late umbilical cord clamping? A systematic review of the literature' (2005) 63(1) Anales Pediatria 14–21, agrees that late clamping could diminish the proportion of children with low iron reserves at three months by 50 per cent but notes that this study lost 40 per cent of patients during follow-up.

[29] G. R. Burgio and F. Locatelli, 'Transplant of bone marrow and cord blood hematopoietic stem cells in pediatric practice, revisited according to the fundamental principles of bioethics' (1997) 19 Bone Marrow Transplant 1163–8; F. Bertolini, M. Battagia, C. De Julio, G. Sirchia and L. Rosti, 'Placental blood collection: effects on newborns' (1995)

sometimes alleged that excessive flow of cord blood can result in abnormal red cell overload (polycythaemia), leading to later cardiovascular problems, although there is little evidence that polycythaemia is harmful in full-term babies.[30]

In addition to these clinical doubts about whether cord blood collection harms mother and baby, there is also a moral question: whether it is right to take any blood at all from the newborn, particularly because the long-term effects are unknown.[31] If there is a risk of harm to the infant here and now, it cannot be part of a clinician's duty to inflict present harm for the sake of speculative future gain and with the possibility of further future losses. The duty of non-maleficence, doing no harm, normally trumps that of beneficence in medical ethics,[32] especially when the beneficial effects to the infant are speculative future ones and when the more definite present harms to the mother are weighted into the equation. To comply with the maxim '*primum non nocere*', 'first do no harm', clinicians should not take cord blood against their better judgement. This is in fact the brunt of the advice given by the Royal College of Obstetricians and Gynaecologists – omitted, oddly enough, from the Cryo-Care advertising leaflet.

But what about the possibility of therapeutic gains from cord blood to the baby or others? Here, too, we need to separate out the moral question from the clinical evidence, which in any case is much less rosy than the commercial cord blood banks claim. The Cryo-Care leaflet, for instance, features a prominent caption on a picture of a mother helping a baby to walk: 'They gave Jesse a 0% chance of survival. But we had his cord blood and he's still alive.' Of course these statements may not be correlated, but the implication is clearly meant to be that *because* the parents had Jesse's cord blood, he is still alive. In addition to the better-documented blood diseases for which cord blood transplantation was first performed, the leaflet also lists as examples of 'diseases and disorders treatable with cord blood stem cells' several conditions for which there is little or no evidence of benefit, such as osteoporosis and immuno-deficiencies.

---

85 *Blood* 3361–2. For many years this was also the official opinion of the American College of Obstetricians and Gynecologists, at least as far as full-term pregnancies are concerned (Michael Greene, outlining a committee opinion statement of the ACOG, in Rebecca Haley, Liana Horvath and Jeremy Sugarman, 'Ethical issues in cord blood banking: summary of a workshop' (1997) 38 *Tranfusion* 367–73).

30 S. J. McDonald and J. M. Abbott, 'Effects of timing of umbilical cord clamping of term infants on maternal and neonatal outcomes (Protocol)' *Cochrane Database of Systematic Reviews*, issue 1, art. no. CD004074, first published online 20 January 2003.

31 Norman Ende, 'Letter' (1995) 86(12) *Blood* 4699.

32 Tom L. Beauchamp and James F. Childress, *Principles of Biomedical Ethics* (3rd edn, New York and Oxford, Oxford University Press, 1989), p. 122.

A private Rotterdam clinic, Advanced Cell Therapeutics, was recently reported to be offering umbilical cord blood transplants to adults suffering from multiple sclerosis. Its director, a general practitioner named Robert Trossel, claims to have found a method of adding messenger ribonucleic acid (mRNA) to stem cells derived from frozen cord blood. Trossel says that this procedure will 'instruct' cord blood cells to travel to the damaged myelin sheaths surrounding affected nerves in multiple sclerosis patients: 'a piece of research that would win a research scientist a Nobel prize,' as the newspaper report on Rossel's activities wryly noted. A stem cell scientist has remarked, 'I certainly cannot see how adding mRNA to frozen cells would instruct them to do anything, except die.'[33]

Cord blood transplantation was first performed in a case of Fanconi's anaemia in 1986[34] and continues to be most useful in blood disorders, particularly haematological cancers, where it can lessen patients' dependence on bone marrow transplants. Almost all the available evidence comes from allogeneic cord blood donation (from unrelated donors). Poor outcomes and low survival rates from allogeneic cord blood transplantation in adults with leukaemia were reported in two 2004 studies,[35] but other evidence is more optimistic, particularly in the treatment of childhood leukaemia.[36] There is almost no evidence concerning autologous (own-blood) transplantation, and indeed the probability of a need for autologous blood donation in families without a history of blood

---

[33] Robin Lovell-Badge, quoted in Sarah Bosely, 'Doctors' concern over MS clinic', *Guardian*, 20 March 2006, p. 3.

[34] E. Gluckman, H. A. Broxmeyer, A. D. Auerbach *et al.*, 'Hematopoietic reconstitution in a patient with Fanconi's anemia by means of umbilical-cord blood from an HLA-identical sibling' (1989) 321 *New England Journal of Medicine* 1174–8.

[35] M. J. Laughlin, M. Eapen, P. Rubinstein *et al.*, 'Outcomes after transplantation of cord blood or bone marrow from unrelated donors in adults with leukaemia' (2004) 351 *New England Journal of Medicine* 2265–75; V. Rocha, M. Labopin, G. Sans *et al.*, 'Transplants of umbilical cord blood or bone marrow from unrelated donors in adults with leukaemia' (2004) 351 *New England Journal of Medicine* 2276–85.

[36] Susan Wallace and Alison Stewart, *Cord Blood Banking: Guidelines and Prospects*, Cambridge Genetic Knowledge Park report (22 November 2004), available at www.cambridgenetwork.co.uk/pooled/articles, accessed 19 May 2005; J. N. Barker, D. J. Weisdorf, T. E. DeFor *et al.*, 'Rapid and complete donor chimerism in adult recipients of unrelated donor umbilical cord blood transplantation after reduced-intensity conditioning' (2003) 102 *Blood* 1915–19; M. N. Fernandez, C. Regidor and R. Cabrera, 'Letter: umbilical cord blood transplantation in adults' (2005) 352 *New England Journal of Medicine* 935, reporting a four-year survival rate of 65–82 per cent. Gesine Koegler *et al.*, 'A new human somatic stem cell from placental cord blood with intrinsic pluripotent differentiation potential' (2004) 200(2) *Journal of Experimental. Medicine* 123, report a new intrinsically pluripotent type of human somatic stem cell from cord blood, but this procedure had not yet been clinically tested at the time of writing.

disorders is rated at about 1 in 20,000 for the first twenty years of life[37] – again making the 'punt' offered by commercial blood banks considerably less attractive.

In addition, there is consistent evidence that autologous transplantation is less advantageous than tissue-matched allogeneic donation. Contrary to intuition, the blood of others may be clinically better for the patient than her own.[38] An increased immune response from allogeneic transplant actually diminishes the patient's chances of relapse in cases involving bone marrow transplantation.[39] As yet there are no studies comparing patients who received an autologous cord blood cell transplant with those receiving an allogeneic one, but it seems likely, particularly for genetically related disorders, that autologous blood would also be less effective than allogeneic. If the source of the disorder is 'in the blood' – genetically based – one's own blood might do more harm than good.[40]

So babies who receive a gift of cord blood stem cells in their Christmas stocking would probably be better off with a transplant from someone else, if they ever need treatment. This is a nice moral, I think, worthy of Titmuss's depiction of blood as the great metaphor of social solidarity.[41] Indeed, cord blood is the ultimate selfless gift, more so than peripheral blood, since the mother has no expectation of reciprocity for herself and does not derive any clinical benefit from donation, as do, say, haemochromatosis patients. The Hegelian emphasis on mutual recognition is much better exemplified in allogeneic banking than in the idea of setting up a private cord blood account, like a bank account, for one's own baby. By contrast, the model of the private cord blood account does not embody any ongoing recognition of the mother as donor by the recipient, her child,

---

[37] George J. Annas, 'Waste and longing: the legal status of placental blood banking' (1999) 340 *New England Journal of Medicine* 1521–4.

[38] Vanderson Rocha *et al.*, 'Graft-versus-host disease in children who have received a cord-blood or bone marrow transplant from an HLA-identical sibling' (2000) 342(25) *New England Journal of Medicine* 1846–54, found that as an alternative to bone marrow for haematopoietic stem-cell transplantation, umbilical cord blood from a tissue-matched sibling may lower risk of graft-versus-host disease (GHVD), in a study of 113 recipients of cord blood compared with 2,052 recipients of bone marrow.

[39] Juliet N. Barker and John E. Wagner, 'Umbilical-cord blood transplantation for the treatment of cancer' (2003) 3 *Nature Reviews Cancer* 526–32, report results for blood cancers treated with umbilical cord blood-derived haematopoietic stem cells in several studies involving both child and adult patients, confirming the lower incidence of graft-versus-host disease.

[40] J. L. Wiemels, G. Cazzaniga, M. Daniotti, O. B. Eden, G. M. Addison, G. Masera *et al.*, 'Prenatal origin of acute lymphoblastic leukaemia in children' (1999) 352 *Lancet* 1499–1503.

[41] Richard Titmuss, *The Gift Relationship: From Human Blood to Social Policy* (Ann Oakley and J. Ashton (eds.), 2nd edn, London, LSE Books, 1997).

or by society as a whole. Instead it merely reduces altruistic donation to a bet: 'it's a good punt'.

To summarise this section, it is simply not true that umbilical cord blood collection is risk-free for both mother and infant: a careful study of the clinical evidence base does not bear out this casual assumption. Whether or not those risks are major is not the point: the proponents of routine cord blood collection typically claim they do not exist at all, which is easily proved wrong. If there is a certain level of immediate risk to the baby or mother from the collection of cord blood, genuinely benevolent grandparents and parents will want to think again about the speculative long-term benefits of extracting cord blood. They, and the clinicians involved, are opening themselves up for remorse and regret if things turn out wrong.[42] Possible harm to the baby through cord blood extraction also changes the equation in cases involving deliberate conception of a tissue-matched 'saviour sibling', whose cord blood can be used to treat an existing child.[43] Even though the possible harms to the new baby may seem minor compared to saving the older child, they should at the very least be taken into account. I do not intend to pursue that side issue here, however: I merely want to note that once we abandon what appears to be an *a priori* rather than an evidential belief that cord blood extraction is risk free, all sorts of other consequences ensue.

If cord blood is property, whose is it?

We saw in chapter 1 that both civil and common law systems are loath to recognise tissue taken from the body as property. In the past, excised tissue would often have been diseased, so that the only value to the person from whom it was removed lay precisely in having it removed. Cord blood presents the opposite phenomenon: a form of tissue removed because it is *valuable*. Hypothetical though the clinical value of cord blood may be, particularly autologous blood, there is clearly money in it: Cryo-Care charges nearly £1,000 for collection and twenty years' storage, and the potential market is every pregnant woman in the United Kingdom, plus partners and grandparents. That there is money in cord blood, however,

---

[42] See Donna Dickenson, *Risk and Luck in Medical Ethics* (Cambridge, Polity Press, 2003), pp. 59–64, for a more extended discussion of the proper boundaries of remorse and regret in probabilistic medical decision-making.

[43] Robert J. Boyle and Julian Savulescu, 'Ethics of using preimplantation genetic diagnosis to select a stem cell donor for an existing person' (2001) 323 *British Medical Journal* 1240–43; K. Devalder, 'Preimplantation HLA typing: having children to save our loved ones' (2005) 31 *Journal of Medical Ethics* 582–6.

is not enough to make cord blood rightfully property, let alone to resolve the question of whose property it should be.

Under traditional common law doctrine, cord blood could either be construed as waste, something once owned but later abandoned, or as *res nullius*, never having been anyone's thing. If cord blood is seen as abandoned material, then it may be open to the first comer to claim it, in Lockean fashion, by mixing her labour with it: for example, by extracting and storing stem cells. This is the implication, at least, of the *Moore* and *Kelly* decisions.[44] If cord blood is *res nullius*, then it is inherently incapable of being claimed by anyone. As we have seen, commercial cord blood literature, echoed by many scholars, naturally leans towards the first construction: that cord blood is property which would otherwise have been abandoned. This emphasis in private cord blood bank advertising is frequently teamed with a moralistic emphasis on the evils of wasting a potentially life-saving resource. As the Cryo-Care leaflet puts it:

stem cells are available in large number from umbilical cord blood immediately after birth, something which in the past was simply discarded with the placenta. This makes the collection of your baby's stem cells a once in a lifetime opportunity. Cryo-Care offers a service to collect, process and preserve these precious restorative cells.[45]

We have also seen, however, that this impression is medically inaccurate and misleading: for maximal extraction, cord blood is not simply squeezed out of the discarded placenta after childbirth, but is taken deliberately during the third stage of labour, while the placenta is still attached to the uterine wall. Besides, the infant *needs* the blood, as we have seen from the dominant consensus in the evidence. So the waste analogy seems doubly inappropriate, prevalent though it has been in the literature from the time of George Annas's article 'Waste and longing: the legal status of placental blood banking'. In my view, cord blood should not be regarded as abandoned, but neither should it be seen as *res nullius*, as incapable of belonging to anyone. Consistently with my approach in previous chapters, I want to argue that it should be construed as the mother's property because she has put her labour into it, but that her rights in it should not be all-encompassing: they should be limited to certain sticks in the property bundle.

On the incorrect abandonment analogy, however, cord blood becomes the property of the cord blood bank because the mother is deemed to have

---

[44] *Moore* v. *Regents of the University of California*, 51 Cal. 3rd 120, 793 p. 2d, 271 Cal. Rptr. 146 (1990); *R* v. *Kelly* [1998] 3 All ER 741.

[45] Cryo-Care (UK) advertising leaflet, p. 3.

abandoned it, whereas the bank has put effort and skill into harvesting and storing it. Yet the mother has by no means jettisoned the cord blood as valueless: on the contrary, it is so precious to her that she has endured an additional procedure to harvest it. She has also commissioned the cord blood bank to act as her agent, for a fee, in storing the blood. This contradiction is heightened by the uncertain position of the cord blood bank's claim to have put effort and skill into taking the blood. In fact it is delivery room staff who 'harvest' the blood. (One can imagine that a legal case might arise in which an obstetrician or midwife launches a joint claim to a clinical sample of blood which turns out to have particularly therapeutic value, much as Dr Golde, who extracted the T-cells and other tissue from Moore, became a joint owner of the cell line together with the regents of the university hospital.) Once again, the abandonment analogy simply fails, as does the labour-desert claim of the cord blood bank to own the cord blood once it has supposedly been abandoned.

To reinforce their rights under the false abandonment analogy, US commercial blood banks often negotiate contracts with the parents which explicitly stipulate that if the annual storage fee is not paid, the blood becomes the property of the bank. In effect such firms are charging the mother for storing what is rightfully hers, and illicitly seizing it if she fails to pay them for the privilege. Annas likens their tactics to a pawn-broker's,[46] but at least a pawnbroker pays the client while the valuable object is kept in store; here, the client pays the pawnbroker. Perhaps a better analogy is a lock-up storage depot, although most people would blench at a contract stipulating that the depot could claim all their valuables if they missed a payment. These contracts are also much more open to challenge through an action in conversion than was the behaviour of Dr Golde in the *Moore* case; Golde had the minimal good grace not to charge Moore for storing his own tissue.

These commercial US umbilical cord blood banks, then, effectively charge the mother for the privilege of giving her blood to the baby. Cryo-Care, in apparent contrast, emphasises that the stored blood remains the property of the parent (half marks only, since 'parent' implies 'father' or 'mother' equally). No charge is imposed for the retrieval of the blood, although because the firm demands full payment up-front, the question of what happens if payments lapse does not arise. In effect, then, Cryo-Care personnel are also treating the stored blood as their property, but attempting to make a virtue of the fact that they do not charge the mother if she wants to take back what I think is hers all along.

[46] Annas, 'Waste and longing', 1524.

Yet at the same time commercial cord banks play on the sentiment that this substance is the baby's own precious blood.[47]

[T]he collection of *your baby's stem cells* [is] a once in a lifetime opportunity . . . you are ensuring the safe storage of *your baby's stem cells* . . . the cells being used are *one's own* . . . *The owner or parent/guardian* . . . can retrieve the preserved cells at any time.[48]

This confusion is echoed in the academic literature. Just as otherwise well-informed scholars typically deny that collecting cord blood poses any risks to mother or baby, in the same uncritical way these same authorities simply assert that the blood belongs to the baby.[49] Why do so many authors think that the cord blood is the baby's property? The reasoning is often skimpy, but most commonly rooted in biological, genetic[50] or immunological identity.[51] Sometimes the reasoning is deductively Scholastic, as in Munzer's *a priori* argument – real 'angels on the head of a pin' stuff:

The term 'cord blood', used loosely, applies both to blood in the umbilical cord and to blood within the embryonic part of the placenta. This loose usage creates an ambiguity as to whether, after birth, blood is harvested from the placenta, the umbilical cord, or both. The ambiguity hinders a precise description of the harvesting procedure, but otherwise is of no consequence, for it is always the blood of the newborn that is at issue.[52]

---

[47] One might well speculate on the salience of redemption through precious blood in a Christian culture, no matter how attenuated that culture may be in some modern Western societies.

[48] Cryo-Care (UK) advertising leaflet, pp. 3, 5 and 13.

[49] Munzer, 'The special case', p. 510; Annas, 'Waste and longing', 1522; and Gunning, 'Umbilical cord blood banking', all claim that cord blood belongs to the baby because of genetic or immunological identity. None of these sources rehearses possible arguments in favour of the blood being the mother's property. Waldby and Mitchell, in *Tissue Economies*, simply treat it uncritically as the infant's, without offering even the minimal justification of biological identity. Sugarman *et al.* also take it for granted that in principle the blood is the infant's own, although in practice competitors may arise in the shape of commercial banks (Jeremy Sugarman, Emily G. Reisner and Joanne Kurtzberg, 'Ethical issues of banking placental blood for transplantation' (1995) 274 *Journal of the American Medical Association* 1763–85). In passing, the decline of the term 'placental blood' in favour of 'cord blood' may either reflect or contribute to this general view: the placenta, attached to the uterine wall, seems more obviously part of the mother's body than the cord stretching between mother and infant. Each of us bears a constant bodily reminder of 'his' or 'her' own umbilical cord in the shape of one's navel, which seems so obviously 'ours' that the cord once attached to it might seem so too.

[50] Annas, 'Waste and longing', 1522.

[51] Munzer, 'The special case', 499.

[52] *Ibid.* p. 500.

Munzer simply defines away the little biological difficulties by saying that 'it is always the blood of the newborn'. Unyielding commitment to the *idée fixe* that the blood belongs to the baby forces Munzer into some very tortured contortions indeed:

Perhaps the closest analogy of cord blood is blood lining the uterus, which either can serve to nourish an implanted fertilized ovum or leaves the body during menstruation. Yet, the analogy is imperfect. Blood lining the uterus is the blood of a menstruating woman whose body surrounds it. Cord blood is different because, though it is fetal/neonatal rather than maternal blood, it is often circulating outside the normal contours of the body of the fetus or newborn, and further is, prior to birth, surrounded by the body of the pregnant woman.[53]

We seem to be back in the days of the phlogiston explanation of combustion. Just as the mythical negative substance phlogiston was supposedly added to produce combustion, resulting in a lowered weight for the substance burned, so this complicated explanation tenaciously insists that cord blood belongs to the infant even when it circulates outside the infant's body. In fact, however, there is constant exchange of gases, glucose and antibodies between mother and fetus during fetal development. Maternal and fetal circulations are entirely intertwined, separated only by a layer of endothelium one cell thick.[54] In genetic and immunological terms, placenta and cord blood combine traits of both the mother and the fetus. So there is little basis in biology for any doctrinaire distinction between fetal and maternal blood, if that is the basis for arguing that cord blood belongs to the baby. A short sharp dose of Occam's razor is in order to cut through this tangle, as well as to prune away the image of the woman as a container, also notable in the quotation from Munzer.

In fact, one might logically expect Munzer to take the view that cord blood belongs to the mother, since he subscribes in part to a 'labour-desert' model of property under which investing work in an object confers rights in it.[55] Indeed, Munzer does consider whether a labour-desert model of property might apply to umbilical cord blood, but rejects it because the fetus in the womb does not invest labour in producing tissue.[56] 'Just as the lilies of the field do not have to work or spin, neither do fetuses in the womb have to do any work – in the rudimentary sense of exerting effort to make or physically appropriate something – to produce cord blood.' It never seems to occur to Munzer that women do 'toil and spin' in pregnancy and childbirth: to trade one proverb for another, 'Adam delved and Eve span'. The supposedly rudimentary requirement

---

[53] *Ibid.* p. 511.   [54] My thanks to Susan Bewley for these physiological points.
[55] Munzer, 'The special case', p. 497.   [56] *Ibid.* p. 512.

of exerting effort to make a baby is certainly fulfilled by what women do in childbirth: as one childbirth manual puts it, 'You've never worked so hard in your life.'[57]

If, as Marx thought, productive labour is distinguished by intentionality and control, the decision to allow cord blood to be extracted requires both those qualities. Women must decide in advance that they intend this additional procedure to be performed, and that they will be doing so, at a time when they will simply want childbirth to be over as quickly as possible, because they view the extra effort as vitally important for their baby. That seems to me, as someone who has gone through childbirth twice, to require considerable powers of intentionality and control.

In the previous chapter I argued that although women produced value for the stem cell technologies through undergoing the laborious practices of superovulation and egg extraction, they were alienated from their productive and reproductive labour because their contribution was not recognised. A similar denial of women's agency and labour takes place when their property in cord blood, derived from their labour in childbirth, is also ignored. In the case of cord blood a product of value is also created, but in this case the value of the product is recognised, whereas that of ova for the stem cell technologies is not. In another way, however, the cord blood case is more insidious: a property in cord blood is indeed recognised, but not attributed to the woman who produces it through her labour in pregnancy and childbirth.

As I argued in chapter 3, this lack of recognition is a form of exploitation, but in the case of cord blood, it is even clearer that the source of the exploitation does not lie in women's exclusion from the profits to be made in the biotechnologies that take their labours for granted. Instead, as I wrote in chapter 3, the sources of the injustice are threefold: 'the commodification of what should not be commodified, the performance of procedures which contravene the duty of "first do no harm", and the co-opting of women's altruism into the process'. True, part of the first injustice, commodification, is the seizure of surplus value by the private cord blood bank – all the more so because that value is seized from the mother when she is charged for the privilege of having the bank store what is rightfully hers. But the issue is not whether women should receive part of the proceeds made by the private cord blood bank, and the injustice would not disappear if banks were to charge lower fees. What is at issue here is who has a property in the tissue, and the answer to that cannot be the cord blood bank, not even acting as the child's agent, because the blood does not inherently belong to the child either.

---

[57] Sheila Kitzinger, *The New Experience of Childbirth* (London, Orion, 2004).

In my analysis, the mother is not consenting to harvesting and storage of the baby's cord blood, on the baby's behalf, as most commentators presume; cord blood is simply the mother's own property. This is also the position taken in a recent legal advice note to the Royal College of Obstetricians and Gynaecologists.[58] Reviewing the possibilities that the blood is either the mother's property, the property of the child, the property of the hospital or no one's property, this report concludes that the UK Human Tissue Act 2004, following on from the report of the Retained Organs Committee, clearly vests ownership of the placenta and cord blood in the mother.[59] In terms of both law and physiology, this analysis seems to me to be correct. If the placenta is part of the mother's body throughout the third stage of labour, and if the cord blood produced by the placenta is extracted during that stage, then clearly that blood also belongs to the mother. If blood is taken after the placenta has been expelled from the mother's body, and if the mother has not expressed a desire to retain the afterbirth, then conceivably the blood extracted from the placenta might be viewed as abandoned – but that is not the procedure most cord blood banks want to see, because it does not produce maximal quantities of blood.

The infant would normally receive all the blood supplied through the conduit of the cord from the mother, until clamping occurs (under 'active management') or until the placenta is expelled naturally (in 'expectant management'). The mother is the donor of the blood and the infant the recipient, in the usual case. When cord blood is taken, a portion of that blood is donated by the mother to the public or private cord blood bank rather than to the infant. It is donated for the infant's benefit, in private banking, but it only 'belongs' to the infant because the mother has given it to the baby. For these physiological reasons, I think it is better to view cord blood as either a conditional gift or possibly even a sort of settlement in trust[60] from the mother.

Whereas most commentators assume that the cord blood belongs to the baby on the basis of genetic identity, I argue that it is the mother's on labour-desert grounds. In chapter 2 I denied that Locke intended to set up a property right in our bodily tissues that we have not laboured

---

[58] Bertie Leigh, *Umbilical Cord Stem Cell Banking: Legal Review*, report to the Royal College of Obstetricians and Gynaecologists Umbilical Cell Cord Banking Committee (September 2005).

[59] Leigh, *Umbilical Cord Stem Cell Banking*, p. 5.

[60] For more detailed analysis of the trust model in the slightly different context of public biobanks, see J. Winickoff and R. Winickoff, 'The charitable trust as a model for genomic biobanks' (2003) 349 *New England Journal of Medicine* 1180–4. Biotrusts will be discussed at greater length in chapter 6.

to create. Genetic or biological identity is insufficient to create such a right. Cord blood, however, is a tissue which the mother labours in child-birth to create – at increased risk to herself, if she chooses to donate part of the blood for stem cell banking. I do not necessarily advocate that she should be encouraged to do so, even to allogeneic banks, not least because of the possible risks to the baby, any more than I advocate that women should 'donate' ova through the risky and painful processes of ovarian stimulation and egg extraction. In the next section, this issue will be explored in greater depth. For now, I merely assert that some women will want to do so in each case, and that in each case they should be protected from exploitation. The first step in protecting women is recognising what they do, and what entitlements it brings. In the case of cord blood, as with ova for the stem cell technologies, there can be no objections against my argument on the grounds that I am trying to give women a property right in the baby born through the labours of preg-nancy and childbirth. Cord blood, like enucleated ova, is a thing rather than a person, and to that extent something in which property rights could be held.

Why is it so widely assumed, instead, that cord blood belongs to the baby? It seems to me that the fetus's share in the genetic or immuno-logical identity of the blood is being privileged over the mother's and, further, that genetic identity is privileged over gestational. Again, there is a parallel with the arguments advanced in chapter 3, and particularly with the assumption that paternal genetic identity confers rights in cases involving 'surrogate' motherhood. In the *Baby M* 'surrogacy' case, the court effectively held that the father's genetic parenthood was privileged over both genetic and gestational motherhood, by finding that the genetic father already had sole rights over the child, and that his contract with the genetic and gestational mother merely covered her willingness to be impregnated and carry 'his' baby to term.[61] A similar case, *Anna J* v. *Mark C*, held that the matter was even clearer where the gestational mother was not the genetic mother: the legal parents were the genetic progenitors, the husband and wife in the commissioning couple.[62] I believe that genetic identity is likewise privileged in the common discourse about cord blood – but not the mother's genetic identity.

As I have argued elsewhere, it is no mere coincidence that what fathers contribute is never more than genetic identity, whereas mothers con-tribute both genetic and gestational identity. Paternal genetic parenthood and 'father-right' were supreme over maternal genetic and gestational

---

[61] *In the matter of Baby M*, 217 N.J. Supr. 313 (1987), 109 N.J. 396 (1988).
[62] *Anna J* v. *Mark C*, 286 Cal. Rptr. 369 (1991).

parenthood in the law of coverture, which persisted in concrete statutory form in many common law jurisdictions until the very end of the twentieth century.[63] When the baby is viewed unquestioningly as the owner of cord blood, father-right is not at issue, but we still see exactly the same prejudice in favour of genetic over gestational rights.

We also witness a widespread misreading of Locke as implying that we have a generalised property right in our own bodies, whereas I have insisted all along that we only have such a right in tissue which we have laboured to create, but which does not constitute a separate person. In this sense I agree with Munzer: the infant does not have a property right in his cord blood, because he has not laboured to create it. The infant's mother, however, has laboured, and does have rights. The next question is which rights.

Respecting altruism, recreating the commons

In this final section I will argue that although the mother does possess property rights in cord blood, those rights fall short of what James Harris calls 'full-blooded ownership'.[64] Harris posits an ownership spectrum, at whose upper end lies the sort of property with which the owner is entirely free to do as she pleases – use, abuse or transfer. That is the meaning of 'full-blooded ownership'. Further down the spectrum lies what Harris (somewhat confusingly) terms '*mere* property': something which belongs to a person within strict limits, which include non-commodification.[65]

I want to claim that the mother's property rights in cord blood are of this second type. She does not have the right to commodify her cord blood (even at a cost rather than a gain to herself) by paying a commercial blood bank. She does, however, have the right to donate it to a public allogeneic bank. (In so doing, she effectively settles the property as the object or *res* of a trust, which she is likewise empowered to do.) Nor does she have a *duty* to donate to a public cord blood bank, despite the demonstrable benefits of allogeneic cord blood banking and the possibility that painful bone marrow donations could be ended if sufficient cord blood were available for transplantation.[66] Such a duty is rejected even in French policy – which, as we shall see in chapter 7, heavily emphasises public benefit and duty to the *patrie*. According to the French national ethics committee's opinion on cord blood banks, public allogeneic banking symbolises the

---

[63] *Property, Women and Politics*, p. 160.

[64] James W. Harris, *Property and Justice* (Oxford, Oxford University Press, 1996), p. 29.

[65] *Ibid.* p. 28.

[66] Jeffrey L. Ecker and Michael F. Greene, 'The case against private umbilical cord blood banking' (2005) 105(6) *Obstetrics and Gynecology* 1282–84.

desirable values of solidarity and *fraternité*, but mothers should not be made to feel guilty because they cannot or do not wish to donate.[67]

Elsewhere in this book I have laid emphasis on the notion of property as a bundle of rights, using Honoré's typology. I have already said that I do not regard the mother's property in cord blood as 'full-blooded', to use Harris's terminology. The precise 'sticks' in the bundle of rights can now be further delineated. In the case of cord blood, the mother does not normally require right (1), immediate physical possession, or current use (right (2)). She does need to protect herself against unauthorised taking, for example in fraudulent contracts such as those imposed by some private cord blood banks (right (6)). I suggest that she should possess right (7), to transmit it to others by gift, but not right (8), to sell the blood. In fact neither private nor public cord blood banks buy cord blood, so this is largely a moot question; public banks rely on donations, whereas private banks charge the mother a fee to store the blood, rather than paying for it. Rights to income that can be derived from the object's use by others, right (4), and to the cord blood's capital value, right (5), are largely irrelevant for the same reasons. Even in a system of private banking, the blood's value lies in the provision of the banking service to parents, not in selling the blood to other buyers. However, if clinics like the Rotterdam one become more widespread, that picture may change: cord blood is being 'sourced' from some unknown location and being used at a profit to treat MS sufferers. As a precaution, I would prefer to deny the rights to income and capital value to all parties, the mother included.

What about right (3), determining the ways which others can use the cord blood? This is perhaps the most contentious question. I will shortly go on to depict systems in which the mother retains some such control, where her own placental blood carries a marker even when stored in a public bank, so that it can be used at her request for her own child. She may also need downstream rights to give or withhold consent to future uses, consistent with the position I have taken about the appropriateness of donors retaining some such rights in biobanks more generally. But she should not have a unilateral right to withhold her blood from use by a recipient in urgent clinical need on any such basis as ethnic, religious or national identity. Obviously, the day-to-day control over how cord blood donation is used should be vested in an appropriate management body, not in the donors. But that body should be bound by constraints to protect freely donated cord blood from commodification. Otherwise, as Waldby and Mitchell note of the creeping privatisation and commercialisation of

[67] CCNE (Comité Consultatif National d'Ethique), *Umbilical Cord Blood Banks*, opinion number 74.

the UK blood service, gift simply renders the body 'an open source of free biological material for commercial use'.[68] Given the tremendous interest in stem cell lines derived from umbilical cord blood, commercial pressure will inevitably be brought to bear. A public cord blood bank needs something like a board with 'lay' representatives from donors to police those pressures. Perhaps individual mothers should retain rights to determine how their cord blood will be used through these representatives.

Why do I think these are the rights the mother requires? Only these entitlements genuinely respect the motives behind the mother's altruism and recognise the extent of her sacrifice, in setting risk to herself aside. A system of private banking, by contrast, belittles what women do in donating cord blood by reducing their selflessness to the level of 'a good punt'. Banking blood should not be seen as a smart calculation or a good investment, because neither image does justice to what women do in producing that blood in the first place. In an even more blatant manner than in the unrecognised dependence of the stem cell technologies on enucleated ova, private cord blood banking also exploits women not only by misleading them about the medical risks they run, but in its entire premiss: that it is private cord blood banks which add value to a 'product' which would otherwise be mere 'waste'.

In the *Moore* case, Broussard J likewise favoured a policy permitting rights (3), (6) and (7) (to determine how others use the property, to be protected against unauthorised taking, and to transmit the property by gift) but not rights (4), (5) or (8) (income, capital value and sale rights). As Broussard put it:

It is certainly arguable that as a matter of policy or morality it would be wiser to prohibit any private individual or entity from profiting from the fortuitous value that adheres in a part of a human body and instead to require all valuable excised body parts to be deposited in a public repository which would make such materials freely available to all scientists for the betterment of society as a whole.[69]

Allogeneic public cord blood banks are exactly that type of repository, benefiting not only research but also therapy. If anything, they recognise and respect altruism to a greater extent than Broussard could have foreseen. Moore at least benefited from the splenectomy which yielded the tissue to be banked, whereas the mother who donates cord blood derives no such benefit for herself – indeed, she is voluntarily subjecting herself to greater risk. Furthermore, she can rightly be said to be donating that which is hers, because she has put her labour into it, which cannot be said of Moore.

[68] Waldby and Mitchell, *Tissue Economies*, p. 24.   [69] Broussard in *Moore*, at 172.

Public cord blood banks possess one more great attraction: they set up a new form of commons. In the era of the new genetic enclosures, that is an appealing counter-tactic to the privatisation of tissue and the commodification of the body. Few commentators have recognised this possibility, perhaps because too many have naively accepted that the blood belongs to the infant. If that premiss is taken for granted, it is all too easy to slip into the notion that the private cord blood 'account-holder', the adult who that infant has become, is a sort of venture capitalist in his own body.[70] There seems no sphere immune from commodification and 'the new enclosures' on that account. A commons in cord blood, on the other hand, recreates many of the desirable features of the old agricultural commons, without any risk of the 'tragedy of the commons': there is no incentive for overuse. A commons in cord blood, like the old agricultural commons, is open to all, regardless of wealth. Whereas ethnic minority parents can rarely afford private banks, a public bank can also offer suitable tissue matches for ethnic minorities through geographically targeted collection efforts.[71] By contrast, implementing equality in access to private cord blood banks poses complicated problems for government intervention[72] and merely subsidises yet another private healthcare industry at the taxpayer's expense. At the end of the day, it also results in an inferior service to all: autologous blood transplantation, as we have seen, is less effective therapeutically than allogeneic.

Nor is the notion of public allogeneic banks merely a utopian vision; indeed, their pedigree is better established than that of the private 'Johnny come latelies'. (Their future is also less legally precarious, at least in Europe, where the European Tissue Directive 2004/23/EC limiting commodification of tissue must be incorporated into national law by April 2006.)[73] Worldwide, by 2003, there were already over 70,000 units of placental blood stored in public banks, with an international search facility available to match blood samples with recipients.[74] Even in the USA, public banking has been established in twenty-two individual repositories

---

[70] Waldby and Mitchell, *Tissue Economies*, p. 130.

[71] National Academies, 'Report proposes structure for national network of cord blood stem cell banks', available at www.sciencedaily.com/releases/2005/04/050418095036.htm.

[72] Moshe Zilberstein, Michael Feingold and Michelle M. Selbel, 'Umbilical cord-blood banking: lessons learned from gamete donation' (1997) 349 *Lancet* 642–5.

[73] Wallace and Stewart, *Cord Blood Banking*. It might be argued that the directive's wording only covers payment for tissue, whereas the opposite takes place in private cord blood banking: mothers pay the bank to store their own tissue. However, the legislative intent is clearly to cut short the activities of profit-making firms dealing in tissue, which would include private cord blood banks.

[74] Royal College of Obstetricians and Gynaecologists Scientific Advisory Committee, opinion paper 2.

such as the New York Blood Center[75] and is to be extended into a more cohesive national system, with an appropriation of US$10 million for a national system in the 2004 federal budget.[76] In France, public placental blood banks date back to the early 1990s, comprising traceable units which can be claimed back for a particular child's treatment.[77]

Since 1996, the UK National Blood Service has operated a public cord blood bank at four specialised centres in maternity units, augmented in 2004 by a separate national bank for Scotland, operated by the Scottish Blood Transfusion Service.[78] Most of the donations are used to treat unrelated patients, but there is also some provision for 'directed' collection and banking in at-risk families. Compared to the general pressure on all expectant mothers which the private cord blood bank literature promotes, this sort of public service provision will probably appeal most to those from families affected by the sorts of diseases which cord blood transplantation can treat. At the same time, the UK and French public model of cord blood banking allows for and encourages altruism. By contrast, as the French national ethics committee notes, 'Preserving placental blood for the child itself strikes a solitary and restrictive note in contrast with the implicit solidarity of donation.'[79]

Of course, it may be argued that women will not donate cord blood altruistically in sufficient numbers, that they will only give to their own babies. If that were the case, then private banks would indeed have the edge. I think this assessment is unduly pessimistic. Although cord blood donation does pose additional risks to the mother, it is less onerous than bone marrow donation; yet there are approximately 8 million bone marrow donors throughout the world.[80] If the mother believes that she is depriving her own baby of sufficient blood in order to donate to a public bank, however, she will not want to donate. That problem can be

---

[75] Sugarman *et al.*, 'Ethical issues of banking placental blood'; P. Rubinstein, R. E. Rosenfeld, J. W. Adamson and C. E. Stevens, 'Stored placental blood for unrelated bone marrow reconstitution' (1993) 81 *Blood* 1679–90; Giuseppe Roberto Burgio, Eliane Gluckman and Franco Locatelli, 'Ethical reappraisal of 15 years of cord-blood transplantation' (2003) 361 *Lancet* 250–2.

[76] National Academies, 'Report proposes structure'; Ecker and Greene, 'The case against', 1283.

[77] CCNE, opinion number 74, p. 3. The French banks are supervised by the French Authority for Transplantation, the Authority for Blood and the Safety of Health Products Agency; they operate in a limited number of sites, like the UK bank.

[78] S. Armitage, R. Warwick, D. Fehily, C. Navarrete and M. Contreras, 'Cord blood banking in London: the first 1000 collections' (1999) 24 *Bone Marrow Transplant* 139–45; S. J. Proctor, A. M. Dickinson, T. Parekh and C. Chapman, 'Umbilical cord blood banks in the UK have proved their worth and now deserve a firmer foundation' (2001) 323 *British Medical Journal* 60–1.

[79] CCNE, opinion number 74, p. 7.   [80] *Ibid.* p. 2.

minimised if cord blood is only taken after the placenta is delivered. In public banks there is less pressure to maximise the donation, since cord blood is immunologically 'naïve', lacking in a strong response against tissue from another body, making pooled donations effective and allowing less perfect tissue matching for a transplant to succeed.[81] A private bank, by contrast, will want to take as large a sample as possible, for 'security', and so the parents feel that they are getting value for money.

The notion that women will not donate cord blood altruistically, but only for their own babies, smacks of one of Hegel's less attractive precepts: that women do not understand public duty, but only the narrower moral life of the private realm. On this account, Antigone is the perpetual thorn in the side of the state: she places duty to her dead brother above the rule of law. Women remain immured in the ahistorical preoccupations of the family, as Antigone did in the defence of her brother's body, a dead thing.[82] Womankind 'changes by intrigue the universal end of government into a private end, transforms its universal activity into a work of some particular individual, and perverts the universal property of the state into a possession and ornament for the Family'.[83] Ironically, however, it is private banks which encourage the view of a potential public good, cord blood, as 'a possession and ornament for the Family.' But cord blood is not 'the universal property of the state', nor is it the baby's possession: it belongs to the mother, and it is ultimately hers to give, if she so chooses.

I have argued throughout this chapter that recognition of cord blood as the mother's property is essential to avoid exploitation, consistently with a different and more attractive Hegelian emphasis on mutual recognition. Just as the view of woman as receptacle in the stem cell technologies fell short of that requirement, so does the common depiction of labouring mothers as mere conduits for transference of precious cord blood to their babies. If we are to view women as genuine subjects rather than either receptacles or conduits, we will have to leave the moral choice of whether to donate their placental blood to public banks up to them. Even if this policy risks lower rates of donation, that seems to me infinitely preferable to the deception, moral pressure and exploitation commonly practised in private cord blood banking. And compulsory altruism for women only is not an attractive policy.

---

[81] Waldby and Mitchell, *Tissue Economies*, p. 113; Ecker and Greene, 'The case against', p. 1262; Rogers and Casper, 'Lifeline in an ethical quagmire'.

[82] *Property, Women and Politics*, p. 107.

[83] G. W. F. Hegel, *Phenomenology of Spirit* (A. V. Miller (tr.), Oxford, Oxford University Press, 1977), p. 475.

5   The Gender Politics of Genetic Patenting

In 1997, the US biotechnology company Biocyte was granted a European patent for isolating and storing umbilical cord blood cells. Although later revoked by the European Patent Office, the Biocyte patent exemplified the way in which surplus value is generated from women's bodies in another manner to that discussed in the previous chapter, where the commercial value of cord blood lay primarily in the 'service' offered by private blood banks to expectant parents. But not all patents depend on female bodies, useful though the Biocyte example is in the context of this book – to mark the transition from female bodies to all bodies. *All* bodies are potentially feminised in the politics of patenting. The 'sex' of the DNA involved is irrelevant to the process of patenting, even though some of the most prominent patenting cases have concerned female tissue. The 1994 *Relaxin* case, for example, involved a patent on a DNA sequence generated from a polypeptide hormone secreted by the *corpus luteum* in pregnant women. Objections to the patent, however, such as the challenge unsuccessfully mounted by the German Green Party, had nothing to do with protecting women as a group, but rather with the general 'human right to self-determination'.[1]

By 2005, the number of patented human genes had increased to 4,270, representing 18 per cent of the entire human genome.[2] Despite the gargantuan scale of genetic patenting, however, a cynic might note that there is an inverse proportion between the real physical or legal threat commonly evoked and the emotional heat generated.[3] As one small example,

---

[1] *Howard Florey/Relaxin* [1995] *European Patent Office Reports* 541. For a more complete discussion of the *Relaxin* case, see Derek Beyleveld and Roger Brownsword, 'Patenting human genes: legality, morality and human rights' in J. W. Harris (ed.), *Property Problems: From Genes to Pension Funds* (London, Kluwer Law International, 1997), pp. 9–24.

[2] K. Jensen and F. Murray, 'International patenting: the landscape of the human genome' (2005) 310 *Science* 239–40. Of these 4,270 patents, 63 per cent were held by private firms.

[3] One need not be a cynic to hold this view; it is fairly common in the patenting literature. See e.g., S. J. R. Bostyn, 'One patent a day keeps the doctor away? Patenting human genetic information and health care' (2000) 7 *European Journal of Health Law* 229–64;

a report from the human rights organisation The Corner House notes rather wryly, 'In rural Dorset, the ethics of patenting genes has even made it on to the front page of a local free paper, *The Blackmore Vale Magazine*, an organ more usually preoccupied with local farm sales and village events.'[4] With all due respect to the *Blackmore Vale Magazine*, I want to suggest that the real affront is the symbolic reduction of everyone's genetic patrimony – and I use the gendered term 'patrimony' advisedly – to the status of the objectified female body.

The 'new enclosures' of the genetic commons by biopatents have occasioned fervent campaigns by non-governmental organisations and have bled the academic inkpots dry.[5] After what we have seen of the risks imposed on women 'donors' in cord blood and ova 'harvesting', however, it may seem surprising that anyone should find genetic patenting so threatening. How is anyone actually harmed? DNA sampling for patentable material involves few of the risks imposed on women from whom cord blood or ova are taken, and very much less effort. Yet while those risks and that effort are routinely ignored by the promoters of private cord blood accounts and stem cell research, patenting the human genome appears to evoke great fear.

David B. Resnik, 'The morality of human gene patents' (1997) 7 *Kennedy Institute of Ethics Journal* 43–61; and Glenn McGee, 'Gene patents can be ethical' (1999) 7 *Cambridge Quarterly of Healthcare Ethics* 417–30.

4 Alan Simpson, Nicholas Hildyard and Sarah Sexton, 'No patents on life: a briefing on the proposed EU directive on the legal protection of biotechnological inventions', available at www.thecornerhouse.org.uk, first published September 1997, accessed 24 August 2004, p. 1.

5 In a huge literature, see e.g., Lori B. Andrews, 'Genes and patent policy: rethinking intellectual property rights' (2002) 3 *Nature Reviews Genetics* 803–8; Nuffield Council on Bioethics, *The Ethics of Patenting DNA* (London, Nuffield Council on Bioethics, 2002); Maurice Cassier, 'Brevets et éthique: les controversies sur la brevetabilité des gênes humains' (2002) 56 *Revue française des affaires sociales* 235–59; Donna Dickenson, 'Patently paradoxical? Public order and genetic patents' (2004) 5 *Nature Reviews Genetics* 86; Rebecca S. Eisenberg, 'How can you patent genes?' (2002) 2 *American Journal of Bioethics* 3–11; Mark M. Hanson, 'Religious voices in biotechnology: the case of gene patenting' (1997) 27 *Hastings Center Report* 1–30; Bartha M. Knoppers, 'Status, sale and patenting of human genetic material: an international survey' (1999) 1 *Nature Reviews Genetics* 23; Stephen Munzer, 'Property, patents and genetic material' in J. Burley and J. Harris (eds.), *A Companion to Genethics* (Oxford, Basil Blackwell, 2002), pp. 438–54; Pilar Ossorio, 'Common heritage arguments against patenting DNA' in A. Chapman (ed.), *Perspectives on Gene Patenting: Religion, Science and Industry in Dialogue* (Washington, DC, American Association for the Advancement of Science, 1999), pp. 89–108; Alain Pottage, 'The inscription of life in law: genes, patents and biopolitics' (1998) 61 *Modern Law Review* 740–65; Sigrid Sterckx, *Biotechnology, Patents and Morality* (2nd edn, Aldershot, Ashgate, 2000); Sivaramjani Thambisetty, *Human Genome Patents and Developing Countries* (London, Department for International Development, Commission on Intellectual Property Rights, 2002).

The holder of a patent over a human DNA sequence or stem cell line has no direct control over any particular human body containing that sequence or cell line.[6] The US Patent Office has declared that a patent claim on the entire genome of any individual would violate the Thirteenth Amendment, prohibiting slavery.[7] The wording of article 5.1 of European Directive 98/44/EC states that:

> The human body and the simple discovery of one of its elements, including the sequence of partial sequence of a gene, cannot constitute patentable inventions. However, an element isolated from the human body or otherwise produced by means of a technical process, including the sequence or partial sequence of a gene, may constitute a patentable invention.

No one individual's body is reduced to a condition of slavery by the patenting of an element isolated from the human body. In the *Relaxin* case the European Patent Office rejected the objection that granting a patent would amount to a form of modern slavery over the pregnant women who had provided the genetic material to be patented. There is no risk of any one person being forced to undergo any procedure or endure any form of bodily invasion by the patent-holder without their consent, still less of becoming the patent-holder's slave. It is important to avoid this confusion, since all too often the debate on the rights and wrongs of patenting the human genome slides into the unrelated non-question of whether it is right or wrong to own a human being.[8]

What else might differentiate patenting of the human genome from the cord blood or ova examples? Is there some good reason why the former should be much more worrying than the latter? The answer cannot lie in informed consent. It is simply not tenable to claim that women from whom cord blood or ova are taken have given free and informed consent, but that patients whose gene sequences are patented suffer some sort of battery, assault or involuntary servitude. Even if the consent procedures for ova and cord blood collection were transparent and fully voluntary – and we have already seen that they are typically not – the difference cannot lie in bodily trespass without consent, because in the case of genetic patenting there is frequently no bodily trespass. This is particularly true if genetic samples are taken from samples collected for some other

---

[6] This position is generally agreed, although it is fair to say that it has never been tested in a legal case: see Canadian Biotechnology Advisory Committee, *Patenting of Higher Life Forms and Related Issues: Report to the Government of Canada Biotechnology Ministerial Coordinating Committee* (Ottawa, Canadian Biotechnology Advisory Committee, 2002), p. 8.

[7] Bostyn, 'One patent a day', 236.

[8] Pilar Ossorio, 'Legal and ethical issues in biotechnology patenting' in J. Burley and J. Harris, *A Companion to Genethics* (Oxford, Blackwell, 2002), pp. 408–19.

legitimate purpose, or if the patented sequence is 'invented' through large-scale scanning of existing genetic databases. Nor does taking a DNA swab run such obvious risks of exploiting the vulnerable donor as collection of cord blood or ova does.

Certainly there are concrete harms in neo-liberal patenting politics: licence fees for genetic screening, for example, such as Myriad Genetics attempted to impose in taking out patents on human BRCA01 and 02 genes and charging substantial fees for diagnostic tests involving those genes.[9] Developments in both the USA and Europe threaten to reinforce similar neo-liberal policies, such as patents on essential drugs, which have already produced widespread misery in Third World countries.[10] Those threats, however, do not fully explain the widespread outrage that has greeted recent developments in the politics of patenting. The 1998 European Patent Directive aroused and continues to arouse great European public anxiety about eugenics and dignity, not simply about the costs to national health systems.[11] France and other countries are still resisting implementation of the Directive on ideological rather than practical grounds.[12] In chapters 7 and 8, I will show that in the examples of France and Tonga, the new enclosures of biopatenting also pose an affront to a nation's or people's entire world view, and that in the Tongan case, they represent a new form of colonialism. While the 'new enclosures' is a metaphor drawn from European history, in the Tongan instance the same process is seen in the context of Western imperialism.

I hasten to say that I am no advocate of a neo-liberal approach to genetic patenting. The reader who has persevered thus far would be unlikely to think me a free marketeer, I hope. Nor do I feel that public

---

[9] For further detail on the *Myriad Genetics* case, see Andrews, 'Genes and patent policy'; Australian Law Reform Commission, *Genes and Ingenuity: Gene Patenting and Human Health*, report number 99, available at www.austlii.edu.au/other/alrc/publications/reports/99/01.html, accessed 8 September 2004; and Bryn Williams-Jones, 'History of a gene patent: tracing the development and application of commercial BRCA testing' (2002) 10 *Health Law Journal* 121–44.

[10] Sigrid Stercx, 'Lack of access to essential drugs: a story of continuing global failure, with particular attention to the role of patents' in Christian Lenk, Nils Hoppe and Roberto Andorno (eds.), *Ethics and Law of Intellectual Property: Current Problems in Politics, Science and Technology* (Aldershot, Ashgate, 2006), ch. 9. David Coles has identified a vicious circle in European biotechnology policy, whereby lack of investment by biotechnology companies produces ever more liberal policies to placate them ('The European Union strategy on biotechnology, after the 2005 EC report', paper presented at the seventh workshop of the EC PropEur project, Paris, 6 May 2006).

[11] E. Richard Gold and Alain Gallochat, 'The European Biotech Directive: past as prologue' (2001) 7 *European Law Journal* 331–66.

[12] Jean-Jacques Gomez, 'Intellectual property in human genetics: the French legal approach', paper presented at the first workshop of the EC PropEur project, Cardiff, July 2004; Cassier, 'Brevets et éthique'.

opposition to neo-liberal patenting policies is necessarily misguided. On feminist grounds alone, there is good reason to distrust a free-for-all in biopatenting, because it would harm women in the developing world particularly badly.[13] There are also concrete benefits from stricter patent regimes, which could conceivably prevent a commercial market in ova from developing, for example. In the wake of the Hwang controversy, US politicians, feminists and bioethicists have recently debated using patent law as a means of preventing future abuses, barring patents on stem cell lines and other 'products' in which women's ova had been used illicitly. And as I said in chapter 1, I emphatically do not think that just because women's bodies have been commodified, men have no reason to object when theirs are too.

Rather, I simply want to know why public and academic opposition has been so much less obvious in the cases where solely female tissue is involved, and whether the fear of all bodies' feminisation has something to do with the much higher level of antagonism in the politics of patenting. Where both men's and women's tissue or DNA is taken or used indiscriminately, it seems, there is a great deal of public anxiety, even when the other harms or risks are much less than in the cases involving only women's tissue. The political direction of my argument, let me reiterate, is *not* to claim that we should be no more worried about genetic patenting than we are about extraction of cord blood and ova. As I made clear in chapter 1, I am emphatically not taking an *a priori* position in favour of maximal commodification of both sexes.

Let us proceed step by step, avoiding any such foregone conclusions or any moral panics. Arguably, it is not the actual feminisation of all bodies that we face in biopatenting, but an ungrounded fear that all bodies are being feminised. This moral panic, it might be argued, impedes our awareness of the real but underrated new ways in which surplus value is being extracted from women's bodies, and of genuine abuses of the patenting system involving both sexes. In chapter 1 I introduced the fear of the body's feminisation without evaluating how well-grounded that fear might be. Here in chapter 5, where in genetic patenting we first encounter a form of tissue take-over that affects both sexes, I intend to be more critical: are we right to fear a general feminisation of all bodies, or is that fear exaggerated? Although I cannot evaluate that premise in sociological or psycho-analytical terms, I can and do make connections

---

[13] Maria Julia Bertomeu and Susanna E. Sommer, 'Patents on genetic material: a new originary accumulation' in Rosemarie Tong, Anne Donchin and Susan Dodds (eds.), *Linking Visions: Feminist Bioethics, Human Rights and the Developing World* (Lanham, MD, Rowman and Littlefield, 2004), pp. 183–202.

with the wellsprings of our political culture, already examined in chapter 2. That culture, dating back at least to Athens, informs the notions
of human dignity, public morality and recognition of labour in particularly gendered ways, as I demonstrated there, and it also conditions the
gendered politics of genetic patenting.

I do not claim that fear of feminisation is the only 'real' source of
opposition to widespread genetic patenting. Other entirely genuine factors might include the way in which patents impede rather than assist
research (quite contrary to their purpose and to the utility requirement
in patent law)[14] or the high cost of diagnostic genetic testing when a
monopoly patent-holder gets greedy.[15] These are excellent reasons for
opposing patenting of the human genome on a large scale, but I do not
propose to concentrate on these pragmatic arguments, even though I
agree with them. My concern is rather to analyse the way in which more
theoretical objections such as human dignity or public morality typically
incorporate an element of fear of feminisation.

When all bodies are treated by a new biotechnology such as patenting
in ways that were previously reserved for women, a fear of loss of human
dignity might well arise. In legal discourse the terms 'human dignity'
and 'public morality' do possess a concrete reality. The concept of *ordre
public*, usually translated as 'public morality', is enshrined in Article 27
of the Trade-Related Intellectual Property (TRIPS) Agreement and in
Article 53 of the European Patent Convention, which excludes as offensive to public morality the practices of human cloning, germline genetic
modification, use of the human embryo for industrial or commercial purposes and processes for modifying animal genetic identity where harm
outweighs benefit.[16] In relation to patenting, the notion of *ordre public* is
not defined in relation to positive law, with few case law precedents.[17]

---

[14] Andrews, 'Genes and patent policy'; Timothy Caulfield, E. Richard Gold and Mildred
K. Cho, 'Patenting human genetic material: refocusing the debate' (2000) 1 *Nature
Reviews Genetics* 227–31.

[15] Gert Matthijs, 'Editorial: patenting genes' (2004) 329 *British Medical Journal* 1358–60.
The fee for an individual diagnostic test purchased directly from the BRCA patent-holder
Myriad Genetics was roughly US$2,500 at the time the article appeared.

[16] Article 6 of the 1998 EC Directive further limits the *ordre public* exclusion by invoking
an extreme utilitarian argument: provided some public benefit is likely to result from
exploitation of the patent, the exclusion is unlikely to be enforced. See W. R. Cornish,
M. Llewelyn and M. Adcock, *Intellectual Property Rights (IPRs) and Genetics: A Study
into the Impact and Management of Intellectual Property Rights within the Healthcare Sector*
(Cambridge, Cambridge Genetic Knowledge Park, July 2003), s. 2.C.3(b), 'Morality'.
Although the notion of *ordre public* is confined to European patent law, the US Patent
Law 2000 excludes inventions whose use is inherently immoral, such as a letter bomb.

[17] Sigrid Stercx, 'Embryo stem cell patenting', paper presented at the fifth workshop of the
EC PropEur project, Bilbao, December 2005.

More explicitly, a patent will not necessarily be found contrary to public morality because it infringes the law in some or all of the contracting European states. Rather, *ordre public* has developed in what meagre case law applies to it as 'the culture inherent in European society and civilisation'.[18]

Just as that culture is highly gendered, so is *ordre public* and the associated notion of human dignity. We have seen that the processes involved in collecting ova and cord blood pose a concrete risk to the women involved, and that the very manner in which these risks are downplayed can itself be argued to be antithetical to women's agency and dignity. Yet the language of human dignity is rarely, if ever, used in that context. Dignity, according to Article 2 of the UNESCO Universal Declaration on the Human Genome and Human Rights, 'makes it imperative not to reduce individuals to their genetic characteristics' – a formulation which must in turn reduce to hollow laughter any sufferer from what has playfully been called 'genetic double-X syndrome', otherwise known as being a woman.

Human DNA: object or person?

Why should it matter if 18 per cent, or 80 per cent, or even the entirety of the human genome is made subject to private patents? There may well be pragmatic objections, but what exactly is the objection in and on principle? After all, human DNA in the form used in a patent application is much more like a thing than a person, and is therefore a potential object of property-holding. Since in a non-slave-owning society there are no rights of ownership over persons, the widespread concern over whatever ownership rights patenting actually implies would be understandable if human DNA were more 'person' than 'thing' – but it is not.

It is fallacious, I would argue, to say that human DNA is 'special' because it is uniquely human. Firefly DNA is uniquely firefly-ish, but that does not in itself make it any more special than any other organism's genetic material, that of *homo sapiens* included. But what about the larger claim that *all* DNA is inherently unsuitable as an object of property? If there can be rights of ownership over animals and plants, which our legal system clearly allows, then that claim is obviously untenable; I can grow an aspidistra and keep a cat without falling foul of the law. There is a distinction, however, between owning an individual aspidistra and owning the entire aspidistra genome. I do not wish to condone spectacular patent claims on entire genomes, such as the attempt by Syngenta and Myriad Genetics in 2003 to patent not only the rice genome, but also flowering

18 Nuffield Council on Bioethics, *The Ethics of Patenting DNA*, p. 34.

in plants more generally, including banana, wheat, maize and forty other species. This claim would even have extended to unknown species, if they existed.[19] As embodied in individual plants and animals, DNA is 'ownable', however.[20] Yet if anything there seems to be more outrage about the idea that 'I' as an individual could be patented than that the human genome or its components might be.

There are three good reasons for thinking that human DNA in its isolated, patentable forms is more thing than person. The first is the very wide range of forms in which that DNA appears: not only complete genes, but also partial genes, expressed sequence tags, individual mutations known to cause disease, polymorphisms not associated with disease, cloning vectors formed from bacterial DNA and used to replicate DNA sequences, expression factors used to express proteins in replicated DNA sequences, amino acid sequences and fragments of DNA used to locate particular parts of DNA sequences.[21] The one form in which DNA never appears in a successful patenting application, in fact, is for an entire human being. True, the artist Donna Rawlinson MacLean has recently filed a patent application for an entity called 'Myself', consisting of her entire genome,[22] but it is hard to imagine her claim succeeding.

Secondly, human DNA can only be patented where isolated from the human body, e.g. through the use of cloning techniques and identification of the series of bases of which it is composed, rather than in its naturally occurring form.[23] Not even the most fervent advocate of the human being as an embodied entity, rather than as some sort of Cartesian ghost in the bodily machine, would presumably want to include a *dis*embodied genetic sequence as part of the *embodied* human being.

Finally, the genome is as much information as matter.[24] It has been said that 'The DNA molecule itself may be thought of as a tangible storage

[19] Paul Oldham, 'The patenting of plant and animal genomes', paper presented at the seventh workshop of the EC PropEur project, Paris, May 2006.

[20] My thanks to Prof. Ross Harrison, Quain Professor of Jurisprudence at University College London, for helping me to draw this distinction in his commentary on an earlier version of this chapter, presented at the London Legal and Philosophy Seminar series at UCL in February 2006.

[21] Nuffield Council on Bioethics, *The Ethics of Patenting DNA*, p. 25.

[22] Lori Andrews, 'Shared patenting experiences: the role of patients', paper presented at the fifth workshop of the EC PropEur project, Bilbao, December 2005. Patent claim available at http://blather.newdream.net/p/patent.html.

[23] Article 5 of the EC Directive 98/44/EC states that 'The human body at the various stages of formation and development, and the simple discovery of one of its elements, including the sequence or partial sequence of a gene, cannot constitute patentable inventions.' However, it goes on to say that 'An element isolated from the human body or otherwise produced by means of a technical process, including the sequence or partial sequence of a gene, may constitute a patentable invention, even if the structure of that element is identical to that of a natural element.'

[24] Nuffield Council on Bioethics, *The Ethics of Patenting DNA*, p. 27.

mechanism for information about the structure of proteins',[25] although a genetic patent is more frequently regarded as a form of intangible property, like copyright. Either way, in its status as both information and molecular substance, a genetic sequence differs from any other chemical compound, but it does not differ in such a way as to remove it from the world of objects. Conceived of as information, a blueprint for how to build a particular human, it might be confidential, or emblematic of that person, but it is not the person herself and therefore in principle it can be owned.

If these three arguments are correct, then patenting the human genome does not literally involve objectification, because it does not reduce something that is *not already* a thing to the status of a thing. DNA is already a thing, on my account. However, if we use objectification in the Marxist sense, then the argument might possibly be more plausible. As defined in chapter 2, following Marxist concepts, objectification is the process by which use value is attributed to something external to ourselves, which is made to satisfy our needs and wants. Commodification also entails the attribution of exchange value, in addition to the use value involved in objectification. In genetic patenting it is clear that human DNA has become both something to which use value is attributed and something which itself generates exchange value. Only objects separate from the self can be objectified and commodified, but that is not actually a problem. We have just seen that isolated DNA sequences are indeed external to the embodied self, although their status also exemplifies the way in which new biotechnologies disaggregate the body. In principle, they might be viewed as things that can be objectified and commodified, although the ethical issues around commodification are additional to and separate from those involved in objectification. Because human DNA has the qualities of an object does not necessarily mean it should be likened to a commodity. Merely because something has been objectified and commodified, however, does not mean it has been *wrongly* objectified and commodified. The question is whether patenting of the human genome constitutes wrongful objectification, first, and wrongful commodification, second. Certainly it is widely perceived as doing both, but why?

In a general mêlée, where the boundaries between the lived body and the external world become progressively shakier, perhaps it seems all the more important to defend every bit of the body, even an isolated DNA gene sequence, from being reduced to something which can be used and commodified at will. When patenting of the human genome is described as an affront to public morality, *ordre public* or human dignity, that sort

---

[25] Eisenberg, 'How can you patent genes?', 6.

of defensive reaction is evident.[26] Fearing a slippery slope in which all human bodies are reduced indiscriminately to things, opponents of commodification may be tempted to reject the possibility of discriminating between those sorts of human tissue that are more like things, and others genuinely central to our personalities as moral agents. Female reproductive tissues such as cord blood or ova extracted for the stem cell technologies, both of which are much nearer the 'person' end of the spectrum than an isolated DNA sequence, seem to have been left out of this defensive strategy. There is little point reinforcing every chink in the walls of Troy if the Greeks (in this case, the forces of biotechnological commodification) are allowed to bring in gigantic wooden horses.

It might well be thought that those who protest against genetic patenting are confusing property in the person with property in the body. That is, because they wrongly think that moral agents do own their bodies, or should own their bodies, they become fearful when somebody else owns even the smallest segment of anyone's bodily tissue. It does seem to me that such a misunderstanding is widespread and that fear of genetic patenting is also common; possibly the two are correlated, and the first may possibly cause the second. An uncommon number of fallacies are at work here, of which the most prominent is the wrongful notion that if I am to own myself and not be a slave, I must own my body. Other common confusions include taking my DNA swab or blood sample to be essentially 'me'; assuming that what is patented is that particular DNA swab or blood sample, rather than a cloned version of a gene or genetic sequence; and failing to differentiate the limited rights granted under patent law from 'full-blooded' ownership.[27]

As well as these fallacies, however, there is a more symbolically plausible interpretation of why patenting is so widely feared as undermining public morality. If we understand our bodies as belonging to us in Ricœur's sense,[28] as expressive of our agency, genetic patenting apparently threatens our identity for quite profound reasons. The question in

---

[26] A prominent example is the report by the French Deputy Alain Claeys on why France should continue to resist ratification and implementation of the 1998 European Directive on patenting (*Rapport sur les conséquences des modes d'appropriation du vivant sur les plans économique, juridique et éthique, Troisième partie*, report number 1487, Office Parlementaire d'Evaluation des Choix Scientifiques et Technologiques, Assemblée Nationale, available at www.assemblee-nationale.fre/12/oecst/il1487.asp, accessed 23 September 2004).

[27] Ossorio, 'Legal and ethical issues in biotechnology patenting'.

[28] Paul Ricœur, *Oneself as Another* (Kathleen Blamey (tr.), University of Chicago Press, 1992), especially Fifth Study, 'Personal identity and narrative identity', cited in Catriona MacKenzie, 'Conceptions of the body and conceptions of autonomy in bioethics', paper delivered at the Seventh World International Association of Bioethics conference, Sydney, November 2004.

this interpretation is not whether the stuff of our bodies is physically separated from us. True, our bodies primarily belong to us because we are embodied in them and perceive the world through them; but they also express our agency in a more symbolic than physical sense. What belongs to me in this sense is whatever is constitutive of who I am. Genes, in particular, might be thought to sum up who we are, what we inherit from our ancestors, and what we will pass on in turn to our descendants. These aspects combine to give DNA a 'sacred quality', which 'shares many characteristics with the immortal soul of Christianity'.[29] The human genome has been described variously as the Bible, the Book of Man and the Holy Grail. Even the smallest piece of DNA – the most minuscule relic, no matter how long separated from the individual body or how infinitesimal a proportion of its total genetic component – takes on the aura of sainthood.

Fear of a slippery slope is further exaggerated if patenting is wrongly construed as 'full-blooded ownership', as allowing the patent-holder all the rights in the property bundle, rather than as a time-limited monopoly over some aspects of management of the patented material, in exchange for free disclosure of information to the public at the outset of the patent term. (For example, in the European Patent Office decision about the Harvard 'oncomouse', developed for cancer research, only the negative right to prevent others from using the 'invention' was awarded, not the positive right for Harvard researchers to use the mouse themselves.) Patent rights do not equate to complete ownership, but some critics of patenting use the language of ownership as an ontological trump claim.[30] If human genetic material partakes of the sacred, or is essential to human dignity, in a more secular formulation, then it makes no difference how small a segment is patented or how few powers the patent process actually conveys. In this Pascal's Wager variant, the infinite loss represented by any incursion on human dignity makes any further calculations inappropriate.

But why has the human genome taken on this iconic quality? Cord blood and ova might be expected to carry equal or greater emotional and symbolic freight: after all, they are crucially involved in the supposedly sacred process of human reproduction. Whereas ova can only be separated from their 'owner' through risky and painful processes, a DNA swab or a blood sample can be 'alienated' from its 'source' without physiological harm. Human genetic material used for patenting thus meets Penner's criterion of 'separability', which defines a rightful object of property as

---

[29] Dorothy Nelkin and Susan Lindee, *The DNA Mystique: The Gene as a Cultural Icon* (New York, W. H. Freeman and Co., 1995), p. 39.
[30] Hanson, 'Religious voices in biotechnology', 8.

something which is only contingently associated with its possessor.[31] By contrast, ova fail this criterion to the extent that their removal might cause death: we have already encountered the potentially fatal risk of ovarian hyperstimulation syndrome.

As Penner writes, 'What distinguishes a property right is not just that they [sic] are only contingently ours, *but that they might just as well be someone else's*'.[32] If we take the metaphor of genetic solidarity *au pied de la léttre*, a property in any part of my genome might just as well be someone else's. Any of my genes could easily be seen as belonging to anyone whose genome contains the same allele. The entire human genome might just as well belong to the director of MegaBioBucks as to me, since he is as much human (although fictional) as I am. However, if it might just as well belong to this fortunate fellow, he can only own it in his capacity as a human being who shares in the human genome, not in his role as CEO of MegaBioBucks. This distinction is borne out by the second aspect of contingency, according to Penner: that there is nothing special about my ownership of the object, so that 'the relationship the next owner will have to it is essentially identical'.[33]

Somehow, however, the argument that no individual genome is being patented fails to reassure many opponents of genetic patenting. Rather, the reverse is true: there is widespread dismay at the fact that the patent system dissociates the human source of the genetic material from the invention itself. Perhaps this phenomenon has something to do with alienation, in either the Hegelian or the Marxist senses. In the Hegelian view, the issue might be property as a form of social recognition rather than as mere physical possession.[34] What is at issue, on a Hegelian account, is the manner in which the contribution of the human 'source' is not recognised in a patent system that seems increasingly dissociated from the human element, particularly in an era of large-scale sequencing of entire genomes. Human dignity is not respected, in this view, when the patent is on something other than the actual cells removed from any one person's body; rather, it is affronted, because the human being is reduced to something increasingly thing-like.

In a Marxist formulation, what is wrong is the 'unnaturalness' of genetic patenting. Just as the conditions under which women perform the task of reproducing the species become progresssively more external and less 'natural' in the new reproductive technologies, so a Marxist analysis of genetic patenting might stress the way in which 'reproducing' the entire

---

[31] James Penner, *The Idea of Property in Law* (Oxford, Clarendon Press, 1997), p. 111.
[32] *Ibid.* p. 112, original emphasis.   [33] *Ibid.* p. 112.
[34] William E. Connolly, *Political Theory and Modernity* (Oxford, Blackwell, 1988), p. 117.

human genome shifts from a natural process to the artificial techniques involved in producing patentable material. However, we saw in chapter 2 that the Marxist account is too ready to accept the category of the 'natural' as, in fact, natural. What is natural, particularly what women do in pregnancy and childbirth, cannot confer added value, on a conventional Marxist account. If an objection to genetic patenting is to be built up on Marxist foundations, it will have to deal with the counter-objection that the processes by which patentable material is created are avowedly unnatural. Precisely because they are artificial, they can confer value. This point leads 'naturally' into my next discussion, of the patenting requirement for an 'inventive' step and its relation to brute matter.

The inventive step and 'dumb' matter

The criteria for patenting include the crucial requirements of an 'inventive' or 'non-obvious' step. A related distinction is that the object of a patent should not represent the *discovery* of something pre-existing, but rather an *invention*. European patent law explicitly excludes mere discoveries from patentability, while US law admits both discoveries and inventions but jibs at 'laws of nature and natural phenomena'.[35]

How can a patent on a gene or genetic sequence possibly be said to represent an invention rather than a discovery? As Rebecca Eisenberg puts it, 'How can you patent genes?' Her answer is this:

One cannot get a patent on a DNA sequence that would be infringed by someone who lives in a state of nature on Walden Pond, whose DNA continues to do the same thing it has done for generations in nature. But one can get a patent on DNA sequences in forms that only exist through the intervention of modern biotechnology.[36]

The argument widely accepted by patent offices, and enshrined in both the TRIPS Agreement and European Commission Directive 98/44/EC,[37] maintains that patents do not cover genes as discovered in their naturally occurring form. Instead a genetic patent involves the *inventive step* of creating genes artificially, by cloning and isolating them from the human body. While the material basis of the invention was originally a form of human tissue, that tissue has been reduced to the status of mere matter, no different from any other naturally occurring substance. The distinctively human element now lies not in the tissue itself, but rather in the inventive step by which recombinant DNA technology transforms 'dumb' matter.

---

[35] *Diamond* v. *Diehr*, 450 U.S. 175, 185 (1981).
[36] Eisenberg, 'How can you patent genes?', 4.
[37] Article 27 of TRIPS Agreement and Article 3.1 of European Directive 98/44/EC.

The further the object of a patent claim is from the natural state – the more *manmade* – the more likely it is to fulfil the inventive step criterion.[38] According to the influential holding in *Diamond* v. *Chakrabarty*, 'anything under the sun made by man' is patentable.[39]

A feminist analysis, however, alerts us to the arbitrariness and partiality of the distinction between the controlling mind and 'mere' matter. Generally mistrustful of a simplistic body-mind distinction, feminist theorists can provide analytical allies for those who wish to resist the increasingly untenable split between the inventive step and the material on which it is practised.[40] A view of the body as something separate from one's agency is widely seen as antithetical to feminism.[41] The logic of mind-body dualism, which I questioned at the very beginning of chapter 1, is reflected in the linked notions of the inventive step and dumb matter, and so comes to underpin patent law. That much seems obvious; what a feminist perspective can add is a new insight into the way in which the inventive step requirement is also gendered.

The trend in genetic patenting is increasingly towards the information model, as opposed to the chemical molecule model. Large-scale sequencing of entire genomes is less about identifying new chemical entities than about analysing patterns among genes. Most patents these days merely describe an association between a gene and a particular disease or condition, which looks much more like the discovery of a pre-existing correlation than a true invention.[42] Yet patent courts continue to regard DNA sequences primarily as chemical substances isolated and 'invented' by patent applicants.[43] At the same time, patent law judgments contradict themselves by upholding restrictions on diagnostic testing for genes in individual human bodies, not in their isolated state as produced by the inventive step. Genes predisposing to cystic fibrosis, breast cancer, Huntington's Disease and many other conditions have been successfully patented, drawing on the argument that they are not present in the human body in their patented form.[44] But diagnostic tests assay the presence of

---

[38] Nuffield Council on Bioethics, *The Ethics of Patenting DNA*, p. 29.

[39] *Diamond* v. *Chakrabarty*, 447 U.S. 303 (1980).

[40] See e.g., Moira Gatens, *Imaginary Bodies: Ethics, Power and Corporeality* (London, Routledge, 1996).

[41] Laura Brace, *The Politics of Property: Labour, Freedom and Belonging* (Edinburgh, Edinburgh University Press, 2004), p. 188. For a more extended discussion of feminist theory and subjectivity, see my ch. 6, 'Another sort of subject?', in *Property, Women and Politics*, pp. 139–52.

[42] Nuffield Council on Bioethics, *The Ethics of Patenting DNA*, p. 49.

[43] Bostyn, 'One patent a day', 233.

[44] Lori Andrews and Dorothy Nelkin, *Body Bazaar: The Market for Human Tissue in the Biotechnology Age* (New York, Crown, 2001), p. 50.

those genes in actual human bodies; how can patent rights logically be upheld on diagnostic tests for those genes *in situ*?

The inventive step analogy looks more and more threadbare. Why is it still accepted by the patent courts? One possible answer might be that it chimes with a powerful, highly gendered, cultural world view in which an implicitly male guiding force fertilises a passive, feminised 'nature'. We have already observed a new form of this long-dominant conception in the example of stem cells, where the enucleated ovum represents 'dumb' matter, waiting to be transformed by the energising force of inserted genetic content. In a much older antecedent, the Athenian woman's labours in spinning, weaving, food processing and animal husbandry all created a product and added value to what was by nature mere substance, but this contribution was not recognised. Women themselves were regarded as somewhere between person and thing in Athens. Aristotle considers wives to be 'bought' – although more indirectly than slaves – through sharing in the husband's supposedly greater economic contribution to the household, and in the children, who in his view are created predominantly by the male's active, energising, soul-creating power. In physical reproduction, too, Aristotle only recognises the male contribution as active, and children therefore 'belong' to the father. A similar view lived on until very recently in the Anglo-American law of coverture.[45]

In both the classical and the Christian sources of Western culture, that which engenders is privileged over the mere matter on which it operates. At the heart of the *Credo* in the Catholic Mass lies the believer's affirmation in Christ as '*genitum, non factum*'. This ancient primacy of the genetic is reinforced in such modern legal decisions as the 'surrogacy' cases *Baby M* or *Anna J*, which illustrate not only genetic essentialism but also deep-rooted patriarchal values. The sexual contract now transcends physical sex, extending into the new reproductive technologies, where it continues to assure what Pateman terms 'male sex-right' over women's reproductive capacities.[46] Men can, of course, only contribute genetic identity, not gestational parenthood, but in these decisions and elsewhere in our culture genetic identity is sacrosanct.

Because genetic essentialism in this masculinised form is central to our religious, social and legal culture, the human genome occupies a central place in our hagiography and demonology. Many commentators have remarked on the widespread assumption that 'genes are us'.[47] What they have not usually noticed is that genetic essentialism serves a patriarchal

[45] *Property, Women and Politics*, ch. 3.

[46] Carole Pateman, *The Sexual Contract* (Cambridge, Polity Press, 1988), p. 1.

[47] For example, Hanson, 'Religious voices in biotechnology'; Ruth Chadwick, 'Are genes us? Gene therapy and personal identity?' in G. K. Becker, *The Moral Status of Persons*

purpose and reflects profoundly patriarchal values. If the genetic is the true source of human identity, and if the genetic is reduced to the level of a commodified object through patenting, then human identity is reduced to the same level. That is why genetic patenting evokes greater fears than commodification of human ova or cord blood, which are seen as instances of 'mere' matter, feminised flesh, even waste. If this argument is correct, then the fear of widespread genetic patenting is actually a fear of being reduced to 'mere' matter, and also to female status. Biopatenting does not actually reduce all bodies to female status, but it is feared because it appears to. We do all have 'feminised' bodies now, however, to the extent that all bodies are the site of these insidious fears about objectification and commodification.

No one's entire genome can be patented, but that possibility is not the real source of anxiety. Rather, fear about patenting is the prime instance of the general concern I identified in chapter 1: that somehow commodification in biotechnology transforms us all into passive subjects rather than active agents. What generally distresses us about what is widely, if wrongly, seen as a loss of pre-existing property in our own bodies is the idea that we have thereby lost our agency, our selfhood: that we have become mere objects of property-owning. Although none of us has become an object of property-holding through patenting of the human genome, genetic patenting both magnifies and reflects that fear, which in my analysis is also a fear of feminisation.

As Waldby and Mitchell write, 'Intellectual property in biological entities is organized through a mind-body split that makes the contribution of the body . . . primarily the woman's body – understood as dumb matter that must be animated by the contribution of mind.'[48] Religious commentators have complained that patenting reduces all existence to mere accidents of matter, and so eliminates the transcendent or holy.[49] I think this is only half right, at the very most. The gendered politics of patenting does reduce the material substratum of genetics to mere feminised

(Amsterdam, Rodopi, 2000), pp. 183–94; Guido de Wert, Ruud ter Meulen, Roberto Mordacci and Mariachiara Tallachini, *Ethics and Genetics: A Workbook for Practitioners and Students* (Oxford, Berghahn Books, 2003), pp. 118–20; Heather Widdows, 'The impact of new reproductive technologies on concepts of genetic relatedness and non-relatedness' in Heather Widdows, Itziar Alkorta Idiakez and Aitziber Emaldi Cirion (eds.), *Women's Reproductive Rights* (Basingstoke, Palgrave Macmillan, 2006), pp. 151–64; Neil C. Manson, 'How not to think about genetic information' (2005) 35 *Hastings Center Report* 3; Nelkin and Lindee, *The DNA Mystique*.

[48] Catherine Waldby and Robert Mitchell, *Tissue Economies: Blood, Organs and Cell Lines in Late Capitalism* (Durham, NC, Duke University Press, 2006) p. 74.

[49] For examples, see Hanson, 'Religious voices in biotechnology', particularly the commentary by Leon Kass at 13.

'dumb' matter, but it actually exaggerates the importance of the implicitly masculine inventive step and of the genome itself, construed as the 'blueprint' that shapes mere DNA into something looking like a human being.

The fear of genetic patenting as reducing all bodies to 'dumb matter' is not a good basis for resisting commodification. There are better arguments against widespread biopatenting, whose opponents do their cause no favours if they succumb to genetic essentialism and fear of feminisation. More convincing, perhaps, is the notion that the genetic 'commons' is being 'enclosed'. That argument can also be profitably analysed from a feminist perspective, relying as it does on the notion that all bodies are open and accessible once the protections afforded by traditional rules of commons are undermined. The notion of mere matter as a sort of wilderness waiting to be tamed by inventive steps also parallels the notion of *terra nullius*, which will be examined in chapter 8 in relation to the Tongan case study. Now, however, I want to consider the second of the two instances in which all bodies appear to be reduced to female status by biotechnology: biobanks.

6   Biobanks: Consent, Commercialisation and Charitable Trusts

If genetic patenting evokes widespread fear that all bodies are being reduced to objectified female status, biobanks provoke an even more elemental fear of feminisation. When DNA or tissue is taken without consent, it might be thought that a sort of rape is taking place. What makes the parallel plausible is that this kind of taking is widely perceived not merely as a form of theft or assault, but also as a case in which *consent* to the assault is presumed. All bodies are frequently assumed to be open and accessible in biobanking, just as women's bodies are, in a society where the rape conviction rate has now dropped well below 10 per cent. More than nine times out of ten, police, prosecutors and juries don't believe the woman said no; they presume she really did consent. Similarly, the offence of marital rape was non-existent in the English common law until 1991; a wife's consent was simply presumed, with her body open and accessible. The original common law doctrine, enunciated by Chief Justice Matthew Hale in the seventeenth century, was that by accepting the so-called marriage 'contract', the woman 'hath given up her body to her husband' 'which she cannot retract'.[1] A similar phenomenon applies in biobanking, when citizens' consent is presumed by virtue of their having accepted the social rather than the sexual contract.

The prime example of presumed consent in biobanking was the original version of the Icelandic genomic database. In the 1998 law creating an electronic repository of the country's medical records, participation in the project was presumed unless individuals explicitly 'opted out'. The exclusive licence granted to the private company building the database included access to diagnoses, test results, information about treatments, genetic and epidemiological data. Every Icelander's medical and genetic data were thus assumed to be objects in the public domain. This

---

[1] See *Property, Women and Politics*, ch. 3 for a more extended discussion of the 'marriage contract'.

objectification was matched by the commodification of assigning the database to the monopoly control of the US-based firm deCODE Genetics.[2] The legislation allowed Icelanders six months to opt out, but anyone who decided afterwards that they wished to have their data withdrawn was assumed to have 'really' consented. The insertion of fresh data could be blocked after that date, but data already entered could not be withdrawn.[3] Icelanders had given up their biodata to deCODE in a form of 'consent' which, like the wife under coverture, they could not retract.

Six years later that statute was overturned as unconstitutional, and subsequent national biobanks such as those in Australia, Estonia and the United Kingdom have required explicit consent at the time of donation.[4] UK Biobank now offers participants a choice of three options for withdrawal: 'no further contact' (cutting off future communication with the donor but allowing UK Biobank to use previously stored samples and data, as well as to seek further information from health records in future; 'no further access' (permitting use of samples and data but barring use of future information); and 'no further use' (destroying all stored samples and information, in addition to cutting off future contact).

However, biobanks created with the consent of donors, from scratch, are vastly outnumbered by biobanks of existing material, created without explicit consent in many cases. In 1999, a 'conservative estimate' put the number of stored tissue samples in the USA at over 307 million, from more than 178 million people.[5] At that time the quantity of samples was thought to be increasing at a rate of over 20 million a year. In the United Kingdom, the Retained Organs Commission, appointed in the wake of the Alder Hey hospital scandal concerning tissue stored from dead children without their parents' consent, uncovered large tissue

---

[2] For further discussion of the Icelandic database, see, among others, Gisli Palsson and Paul Rabinow, 'Iceland: the case of a national Human Genome Project' (1999) 15(3) *Anthropology Today* 14–18; Ruth Chadwick, 'The Icelandic data base: do modern times need modern sagas?' (1999) 319 *British Medical Journal* 441–4; Skuli Sigurdsson, 'Yin-yang genetics, or the HSD deCODE controversy' (2001) 20(2) *New Genetics and Society* 103–17.

[3] Hilary Rose, 'Gendered genetics in Iceland' (2001) 20(2) *New Genetics and Society* 119–38.

[4] For Australia, see Mark Stranger, Donald Chalmers and Dianne Nicol, 'Capital, trust and consultation: databanks and regulation in Australia' (2005) 15(4) *Critical Public Health* 349–58; for Estonia, see Rainer Kattel and Riivo Anton, 'The Estonian genome project and economic development' (2004) 8(1–2) *Trames: Journal of the Humanities and Social Sciences* 106–28.

[5] RAND corporation report, summarised in Rebecca Skloot, 'Taking the least of you: the tissue-industrial complex', *New York Times*, 16 April 2006, available at www.nytimes.com/2006/04/16/magazine/16tissuehtml, accessed 24 April 2006.

banks at many other hospitals and academic institutions.[6] Although the retention without parental consent of dead children's tissue was widely felt to be unacceptable, tissue removed from tumours and in other procedures involving adults was rarely seen to be problematic: rather, as necessary for research, audit and education. The UK Human Tissue Act 2004, which took effect in 2006, aims to prevent such 'accidental' accumulations of tissue in future, but there remain a set of important issues about existing collections. Furthermore, once a stem cell line has been created, it falls outside the remit of the Human Tissue Act 2004, as do gametes and embryos.[7]

I hasten to say that I do not think biobanks actually constitute a form of rape, or in fact that the supposed assaults they involve are more serious than those discussed in chapters 3 and 4, on the taking of ova and cord blood. Genomic databases, in fact, typically involve no physical interventions on patients at all: at most an attack on their privacy or confidentiality.[8] Many of the samples held in tissue biobanks are no more than blocks or slides containing tiny amounts of tissue, and often the sampling involves no additional procedure or risk to the patient. The particular concern that genomic databases arouse may be nothing more than 'gene angst', a negative form of genetic exceptionalism – the belief, already encountered in the previous chapter, that there is something mystically sacrosanct about genes.[9] (One might also speculate that because men are on the whole more likely to be affected by genetic diseases than women, particularly x-linked conditions, they may be more heavily represented on disease-specific genetic databases.) The point is that much media coverage treats biobanks, whether tissue banks or genetic databases, as if they *were* almost a form of rape, or indeed something much more serious. My sarcasm is intentional. As in chapter 5, what I am really asking is why, like genetic patenting, biobanks seem to evoke such widespread fear and trembling, when the physical harm done by biobanking is much less than that involved in ova and cord blood 'harvesting'. (We saw in chapter 4 that

---

[6] For a summary of the ethical issues in the Alder Hey and Bristol scandals, see Veronica English, Rebecca Mussell, Julian Sheather and Ann Sommerville, 'Ethics briefings: retention and use of human tissue' (2004) 30 *Journal of Medical Ethics* 235–6.

[7] Kathleen Liddell and Susan Wallace, 'Emerging regulatory issues for human stem cell medicine' (2005) 1(1) *Genomics, Society and Policy* 54–73.

[8] John-Arne Skolbekken, Lars Oystein Ursin, Berge Solberg, *et al.*, 'Not worth the paper it's written on? Informed consent and biobank research in a Norwegian context' (2005) 15(4) *Critical Public Health* 335–47.

[9] For the concept of 'gene angst', see Jasper A. Bovenberg, 'Towards an international system of ethics and governance for biobanks: a "special status" for genetic data?' (2005) 15(4) *Critical Public Health* 369–83, at 370. For a sceptical view of genetic exceptionalism, see Mary Anne Warren, 'The moral significance of the gene' in J. Burley and J. Harris (eds.), *A Companion to Genethics* (Oxford, Blackwell, 2002), pp. 147–57.

in contrast to widespread public scrutiny of tissue banks affecting both sexes, regulation of private cord blood banking has been minimal.) Fear of feminisation of all bodies, disproportionate to the actual harm done, is one possible answer, and that answer is linked to absence of consent. As Dorothy Nelkin and Lori Andrews note, the scale and spread of biobanks imply to many people that we may all become research subjects without our consent.[10]

The Icelandic database also represents another theme with which this book has dealt: the enclosure of the commons, genetic and otherwise. (The Icelandic government also granted deCODE property rights to the bacteria living in hot springs throughout the country: another form of privatising the commons.) Although in fact Icelanders' genetic homogeneity has been shown to be no greater than that of most other peoples, despite their geographical and historical isolation, much was made during the genome 'saga' of the Icelandic national genome as an antique and unique heritage. What Hilary Rose terms a prevailing masculinist discourse urged Icelanders to exploit this communal resource, this national genetic commons, in an epic rivalry with Norway, which had successfully exploited its own communal resource of oil.[11] This notion was widely accepted, with the great majority of the Icelandic population supporting the database and its policy of presumed consent. In an ironic twist, a masculinist discourse of competition and conquest of nature opened the way for the Icelandic population to be both feminised and privatised.

This chapter begins by examining the issue of consent in biobanking, which has come to be widely regarded in public policy and the bioethics literature as the primary ethical issue. I do not share this general opinion: commodification is the more important issue, to my mind, and consent something of a fig-leaf. In this view I am not alone: a recent focus group study revealed that many members of the British public feel that the 'expert agenda' of policy-makers and medical ethicists is too fixated on consent and too naïve about commercialisation.[12] Another article likewise revealed that British respondents distrust commercial involvement and want genetic databases to be publicly owned.[13] A consistent consent regime, however, would also imply property rights for patients far

---

[10] Lori Andrews and Dorothy Nelkin, *Body Bazaar: The Market for Human Tissue in the Biotechnology Age* (New York, Crown, 2001), p. 11.

[11] Rose, 'Gendered genetics in Iceland', 130.

[12] Mairi Levitt and Sue Weldon, 'A well placed trust? Public perceptions of the governance of DNA databases' (2005) 15(4) *Critical Public Health* 311–21.

[13] Kuliki Korts, Sue Weldon and Margaret Lilja Gudmansdottir, 'Genetic databases and public attitudes: a comparison of Iceland, Estonia and the UK' (2004) 8(1–2) *Trames: Journal of the Humanities and Social Sciences* 131–49.

beyond those minimal entitlements given by many biobanks, particularly the recently established UK Biobank.[14] Personal rights such as consent are not actually opposed to or separate from a property rights approach; in my view, and that of other commentators in bioethics and biolaw,[15] limited property rights for donors and patients will in fact give teeth to personal rights.

I then go on in the second section of this chapter to ask what those rights should be, given that the risk, labour and intentionality involved in donating biobank samples are minimal compared to those in ova and cord blood donation. In chapters 3 and 4 I established that women who give ova for the stem cell technologies or cord blood for banking do indeed possess property rights in those tissues, but that those rights must be subdivided into a limited number of 'sticks' in the property 'bundle'. Here in chapter 6, I want to ask whether donors to other tissue banks can be said to demonstrate sufficient labour, risk-taking and purposiveness to ground any property rights on a labour-desert basis. I conclude that their entitlements are considerably less, but that they do have some rights. We need to think in terms of a spectrum of those who are entitled to property rights in tissue, as well as a disaggregated concept of what those rights might be.

Thus, the biobank example enables us to develop a more nuanced concept of property in the body, something like a phenomenological account, more sensitive to the range of situations encountered in the new biotechnologies. I still uphold my original assertion in chapter 3 that the most legitimate form of property in the body is women's property in their reproductive tissue. Yet if the 'bundle' notion is to be seriously meaningful in legal and political terms, it seems ill-advised to restrict its use to cases involving women's reproductive tissue, such as ova and cord blood. Those instances are the 'gold standard' against which other forms of property in the body can be judged. Might there be other examples – such as biobanks – in which some more limited form of property entitlement could also be granted?

It is not only women who need to be protected from unauthorised taking, for example: who need right (6) in the bundle, security. Might that element of the property bundle rightfully be extended to biobank

---

[14] Roger Brownsword, 'Biobank governance – business as usual?', paper presented at the fourth workshop of the EC PropEur project, Tuebingen, 20 January 2005.
[15] Brownsword, 'Biobank governance: business as usual?'; Graeme Laurie, *(Intellectual) Property: Let's Think about Staking a Claim to our Own Genetic Samples* (Edinburgh, Arts and Humanities Board Research Centre, 2004); Ken Mason and Graeme Laurie, 'Consent or property? Dealing with the body and its parts in the shadow of Bristol and Alder Hey' (2001) 9 *Medical Law Review* 710–29.

participants? There are certainly *pragmatic* advantages in granting that right, and perhaps others, such as the right to downstream management of the tissue (right (3)). Establishing such a right would protect patient groups who have donated tissue from exploitation. In the *Greenberg* case, for example, parents of children with Canavan's disease succeeded in a claim of 'unjust enrichment' against a researcher who had taken out patents on a genetic sequence identified through their contributions and who had then attempted to charge a fee for diagnostic use.[16] But there is a *conceptual* hurdle to leap first.

Do other claimants than ova and cord blood donors have sufficient grounds to be regarded as having some form of property right in the first place, so that the bundle notion can then be brought into play? We might, for example, grant biobank donors proportionally fewer rights, since they contribute proportionally less labour, but still allow them some of the rights in the bundle. The same might apply to people who donate DNA swabs used in patenting, the concern of chapter 5. This suggestion would mean extending the notion of a spectrum of property rights to the prior question of a spectrum of those who are entitled to claim rights in the first place. I want to examine that question critically in the rest of this chapter. To my mind, it is at least as crucial as the much more frequently discussed issues of consent and confidentiality.

Consent, empowerment and gift

The reason why informed consent has been presented as the foremost issue concerning biobanks is not simply to do with the Alder Hey scandal in the United Kingdom, nor with the outcry (primarily elsewhere than in Iceland itself) against the presumed consent regime operated by deCODE's genomic database. A focus on consent also fits the framing assumptions of bioethics in the liberal Anglo-Saxon context,[17] as being all about individual autonomy and patient choice – but it fits that paradigm in a particular gendered way. As I argued when introducing the notion of the sexual contract developed by Carole Pateman, whereas men are presumed to be 'the lords and owners of their faces', or bodies, women's bodies are assumed to be available when public benefit so requires. That, I would argue, explains why 'the lady vanishes' in ova extraction for stem

---

[16] *Greenberg and others v. Miami Children's Hospital Research Institute*, District Court Northern District of Illinois, 00 C 6779 (2002) and Southern District Court of Florida, 02-22244 (2003), discussed in Lori Andrews, 'Harnessing the benefits of biobanks' (2005) 33 *Journal of Law, Medicine and Ethics* 1.

[17] Garrath Williams, 'Bioethics and large-scale biobanking: individualistic ethics and collective projects' (2005) 1(2) *Genomics, Society and Policy* 50–66.

cell research; why umbilical cord blood is not widely regarded as belonging to the mother; and why, by contrast, consent is sacrosanct when tissue is taken from men as well. Only where male subjects lose the right to autonomy by transgressing societal norms, for example, through criminal actions, does consent cease to matter for them. That, it has been said, explains why the issues of confidentiality, privacy and consent to be included in the UK forensic database have attracted so little attention, although the forensic database is far larger than UK Biobank, where those issues have dominated the debate.[18]

Of course, an argument in favour of bypassing consent in biobanking can be framed on utilitarian grounds,[19] but the debate in that case quickly shakes down into the familiar individual rights versus progress of science mode. The terms of the debate, in other words, assume that consent is an issue, but that it may not be the major issue when public welfare trumps it. As we saw in chapters 3 and 4, in the extraction of female tissue for the stem cell technologies and for cord blood banking, it would actually be progress for the debate in those areas to be framed in terms of women's rights versus scientific benefit. In the extreme case of the vanishing lady in stem cell research, few commentators originally noticed that women's rights were involved at all, because few noticed that women's tissue was involved at all. A feminist analysis helps us to see that individual informed consent is a culturally specific and gendered interpretation of the ethical issues in biobanking. That analysis offers one set of limitations in the consent model. A second and equally important analysis, in terms of empowerment, should also alert us to the reasons why a limited property rights model is needed to supplement and strengthen informed consent.

In an incisive analysis of the ethical premises behind UK Biobank, a £61 million public project established in April 2006 and intended to recruit 500,000 participants in an attempt to understand the interactions between environment and genetic predisposition to disease, Roger Brownsword typifies the biobank's ethical stance as strong on consent but weak on property.[20] That combination, he believes, is untenable, and the weakness of the property rights afforded to participants makes a mockery of the much-trumpeted consent mechanisms. As Brownsword points out, control for UK Biobank donors ends at the point when the sample is taken: the original donor has no property rights in the sample

[18] Williams, 'Bioethics and large-scale biobanking'.
[19] Paul van Dienst and Julian Savulescu, 'For and against: no consent should be needed for using leftover body material for scientific purposes' (2002) 325 *British Medical Journal* 648–51.
[20] Brownsword, 'Biobank governance: property, privacy and consent', later version of 'Biobank governance – business as usual?'.

and therefore no way of preventing the sample from being used for purposes to which he or she objects: for example, usage by profit-making firms. Given the indications that UK populations are more concerned about use of biobanked material by corporations for private profits than about consent mechanisms in themselves,[21] this provision is likely to lead to widespread distrust in UK Biobank, once it becomes widely known. If donors had a property right to manage downstream uses of their samples, not just to withdraw them, that distrust could be avoided.

Nor will UK Biobank recruit participants who express a wish to have their samples withdrawn when they die or if they become mentally incapacitated. Just as the wife in the marriage 'contract' could not vary the terms of the contract even if her husband agreed,[22] so participants in UK Biobank cannot choose a model of participation that would give them these meaningful rights. Their only choice is between participation on UK Biobank's terms or no participation at all. Far from being driven by individual choice and free consent, UK Biobank actually restricts both the available choice and the terms of consent. Donors are not empowered by consent of this sort but rather disempowered by it.[23]

As Brownsword notes, UK Biobank maintains an untenable distinction between participants' rights in the information derived from their samples and their comparative lack of rights in the samples themselves. Participants can at most insist that their samples be withdrawn, although we have already seen that gift rightfully implies ongoing interests by the donor in how the gift is used.[24] That same altruism which impelled donors to give in the first place, I would argue, naturally and rightfully implies that they will prefer altruistic rather than narrowly profit-making uses to be made of their gift. After all, the satisfaction of having demonstrated concern for public welfare is the only consideration received in return for their gift. Donors to UK Biobank, however, have no right to insist that any products or services developed through their gift should be used to benefit the National Health Service rather than commercial biotechnology companies.

---

[21] Levitt and Weldon, 'A well placed trust?'.

[22] In the common-law doctrine of coverture, the wife's legal personality was subsumed in that of her husband: she was effectively dead at law. As Blackstone's *Commentaries* put it, 'The very being or legal existence of the woman is suspended during the marriage, or at least is incorporated and consolidated into that of her husband.' (Cited in *Property, Women and Politics*, p. 83)

[23] A similar point is made by Laurie in *(Intellectual) Property*.

[24] See also James Penner, *The Idea of Property in Law* (Oxford, Clarendon Press, 1997), p. 90: 'Giving is not mere abandonment, involving no further interests of the donor.'

It is hard to avoid the conclusion that informed consent is a hollow reed, a fig-leaf, or whatever botanical metaphor the reader prefers. Originally intended to refer to a single intervention by a single physician, informed consent cannot plausibly be stretched to fit biobanks' requirement for blanket permission approving multiple uses by multiple users.[25] Where there is no right to withhold consent to specific uses viewed as unethical, short of withdrawing from UK Biobank altogether, the participant is not empowered but rather disempowered by informed consent. Underneath the rhetoric of rights, a utilitarian strategy favouring biotechnology firms and researchers actually takes priority, Brownsword thinks. Whereas the US Genetic Privacy Act of 1985, giving tissue bank donors property rights in their own tissue, was repealed six years later under pressure from corporate biotechnology, UK Biobank has chosen to avoid giving donors property rights in their tissue from the outset. The question is whether that position is internally contradictory, and even counter-productive, in terms of its potential for disempowerment and distrust. As Brownsword remarks, 'whereas the voices of those who have property rights simply cannot be ignored, the voices of those who have an interest, but without the backing of property, are just so much "noise"'.[26]

Do biobank participants deserve property rights?
If so, which ones?

Politically speaking, property rights for biobank participants are a desirable adjunct to personal rights such as privacy and consent. Philosophically speaking, however, can they be justified? Participants in UK Biobank donate samples of blood and urine, involving little or no risk, minimal time and not a great deal of effort, although it does require a modicum of intentionality. If we do not believe that genetic identity confers a property right – and I have been at pains throughout this book to deny that it does – is the labour that UK Biobank participants put into their donation sufficient to ground a property right? More generally, do biobank donors in general deserve proprietary rights? If so, which rights in the bundle?

On a Hegelian justification, in which property instantiates the will of the donor imposing itself upon the world, biobank donors would certainly

[25] Mark A. Rothstein, 'Expanding the ethical analysis of biobanks' (2005) 33(1) *Journal of Law, Medicine and Ethics* 89–101; Roberto Andorno, 'Population genetic databases: a new challenge to human rights' in Christian Lenk, Nils Hoppe and Roberto Andorno (eds.), *Ethics and Law of Intellectual Property: Current Problems in Politics, Science and Technology* (Aldershot, Ashgate, 2006), pp. 45–73.

[26] Brownsword, 'Biobank governance – business as usual?', 38.

merit property rights. By making the gift of their tissue samples, voluntary biobank participants have publicly stated their will to benefit research, the health service, science, progress or whatever other public good motivates their personal gift. A Lockean justification is harder to argue. Certainly, compared to mothers in childbirth who allow umbilical cord blood to be taken, or even more clearly, women who undergo the heightened risks and long-term effort involved in ova extraction, the donation of blood and urine seems a very minimal sort of labour. Given that Locke does not believe we own our bodies straightforwardly, there is no automatic right in our tissue. Such a right must be established through mixing one's labour and biobank donors, quite simply, have not done a great deal of work.

But the same can be said, in many instances, of biobank owners and managers. In a recent US case, a federal court awarded ownership of 10,000 patients' tissue samples to Washington University, rather than to the researcher who collected them over two decades.[27] Dr William Catalona, a urologist and originator of an antigen test for prostate cancer, decided to leave Washington University in part because he felt that his employer was denying him reasonable access to the biobank that he had created. When he took up a post at another institution, he wrote to the donors and asked for their permission to transfer the samples to his new place of employment. Although Catalona did obtain consent for the transfer from most of his donors, Washington University successfully sued to retain possession of the collection, even though the donors' consent forms allowed participants to withdraw their samples at any time.

What the *Catalona* case demonstrates is that the institutional proprietor of a biobank need not actually have put any effort into processing the samples in order to be recognised as the rightful owner. Washington University never claimed to have done any more than to store the tissues; Catalona and his team did the skilled work of extracting and processing the material provided by his patients. On a Lockean basis, and in conformity with other cases in which skill and labour have been recognised as grounding a property right in tissue,[28] the decision should have gone the other way. The judge, however, ruled that possession, sometimes known as nine-tenths of the law, effectively established ownership rights for the university, even though it is generally accepted in jurisprudence

---

[27] Jocelyn Kaiser, 'Court decides tissue samples belong to university, not patients' (2006) 312 *Science* 436. See also Skloot, 'Taking the least of you', for the background to the case.

[28] *Doodeward* v. *Spence* (1908) 6 CLR 406; *R* v. *Kelly* [1998] 3 All ER 741.

that possession is merely a descriptive concept, whereas ownership is a normative one.[29]

A tissue economy, in Waldby and Mitchell's formulation, is a mechanism for adding value to the raw material of human tissue.[30] At first it might appear that Washington University is the Tommy Hilfiger of the biotechnology sector, adding little to the value of a product except its own 'brand'. (The Hilfiger firm outsources production abroad and does nothing except add its own labels, which can double the sale price of the product.)[31] If we admit that Washington University did pay for specialised equipment and storage facilities, however, it can be seen that some added value was actually imparted by the university. Compared to the effort undergone by the prostate cancer patients, whose samples were taken in the course of treatment rather than as a separate voluntary donation, it is not so clear that the university's contribution fails altogether to meet the labour-desert criteria. There is a three-way balancing act going on here, between the patient's, Catalona's and the university's contribution.

Whereas in the case of private cord blood banking it seemed quite clear that the woman's contribution entailed extra effort, but that of the private cord blood bank added little value and in fact cost the donor money, the balance is not quite so clear in the case of Catalona's patients. They have not undergone any risk over and above that entailed in their operations for prostate cancer; nor have they exhibited any active intention to benefit another, as does the woman who willingly prolongs her labour in order to donate cord blood. In either Hegelian or Lockean terms, their claim to ownership is undeniably less. If property represents the will of the agent imposing itself upon the world, on a Hegelian model, they have exhibited far less in the way of active will. If property results rightfully from the mixing of labour with resources, in the Lockean manner, they have undertaken little or no labour. Contributors to UK Biobank have a somewhat better claim: perhaps they have had to make special journeys to donate, or taken time off work, or overcome needle phobia in order to donate blood. It seems that their efforts should count for more than those of Catalona's patients, and probably more than the actions of someone who contributes a cheek swab for DNA analysis, but not as much as those of women who undergo the extraction of cord blood. Those women, in turn, seem to exhibit less intentionality, agency and

---

[29] Penner, *The Idea of Property in Law*, p. 145.
[30] Catherine Waldby and Robert Mitchell, *Tissue Economies: Blood, Organs and Cell Lines in Late Capitalism* (Durham, NC, Duke University Press, 2006), p. 31.
[31] Naomi Klein, *No Logo* (London, Picador, 2000).

risk-taking than women who undergo the long-term, threefold processes involved in donating ova.

What this analysis suggests is that 'the appropriate choice of a bundle of rights may differ for different types of biological material'.[32] We can envision a spectrum, or possibly several spectra, based on the criteria of agency, intentionality, labour and risk-taking. Alternatively, and perhaps more neatly, we could collapse all those criteria within the single concept of labour as a form of 'desert', conferring property rights.[33] Some forms of tissue donation, such as voluntarily offering one's ova for research, will fall near the higher end of the spectrum, and will in turn either merit more of the rights in the bundle or stronger forms of those rights. For example, right (3) (controlling management of the resource) is probably the most important 'stick' in the bundle for all groups of patients and tissue donors. That was the issue in the *Catalona* case: whether Catalona's patients should have the right to determine 'downstream' uses of their tissue. Although the case was framed in terms of right (1) (to physical possession of the tissue), and of the patients' right to withdraw their tissue from the biobank, right (1) was only sought because right (3) was the motivation. The form of right (3) which Catalona's patients sought to establish was fairly minimal: approval of their tissue accompanying Catalona to his new position. Although they have a minimal labour-desert claim to have a property right in their tissue in the first place, they can safely be afforded this single 'thin' stick in the property bundle.

That does not mean that *all* the rights in the property bundle should go to Catalona's patients, still less to his former employer or even to Catalona himself. If none of the parties to biobanks – the patient, the researcher or the researcher's institution – can rightfully possess all the sticks in the bundle, who can? Much as the law, like nature, abhors a vacuum, perhaps the answer is 'no one'. Even the much-maligned Icelandic databank operator, deCODE Genetics, is not the legal owner of the database; no one is made expressly the owner by the legislation, although the biobank operator has limited rights of usage, though not of sale.[34] This position is similar to that taken by the French and German national ethics committees in saying biobanks cannot be the legal owner of the material

---

[32] B. Bjorkmann and B. O. Hansson, 'Bodily rights and property rights' (2006) 32 *Journal of Medical Ethics* 209–14, at 214.

[33] Here I am using the terminology adopted by Stephen R. Munzer in *A Theory of Property* (Cambridge, Cambridge University Press, 1990).

[34] Jane Kaye, Hordur Helgi Helgason, Ants Nomper, *et al.*, 'Population genetic databases: a comparative analysis of the law in Iceland, Sweden, Estonia and the UK' (2004) 8(1–2) *Trames: Journal of the Humanities and Social Sciences* 15–33, at 18.

they house,[35] or more generally, in denying that the human body can be an object of property. In contrast to UK Biobank's bold assertion that it and it alone is the legal owner of the material stored, the joint French and German model lays more stress on the duties of the bank than on its rights, and on return of the benefits of research to the contributors. It is forbidden to engage in commercial transactions, since 'the contents of the bank are the fruit of voluntary donation by those concerned. They cannot from one moment to the next become the property of the researcher or the curator.'[36]

The notion of a trust may go some way towards plugging the legal vacuum. Even if contributors to biobanks do not possess full proprietary rights, as do the beneficiaries of a trust, the trust model stresses the duties of administrators of the biobank, while severely restricting their own property rights. Trusts are an appropriate mechanism for governing biobanks on three principal grounds:

(1) Biobanks are typically large-scale entities, accumulated over a period of many years. The contribution of each individual tissue donor is hard to distinguish, particularly because over the long time frames typically involved, donors may die, lose mental capacity or simply forget that they ever made a contribution. Some form of joint rather than individual control is appropriate for such pragmatic reasons.

(2) Communal benefit was presumably the donor's motivation in donating tissue in the first place. Although the 'gift relationship' has been used and abused to deny donors any ongoing right in the management of many tissue collections, including UK Biobank, altruism is still a good thing. The trust provides a mechanism for honouring donors' altruism while protecting them from exploitation – the consequence of one-way altruism. In place of the 'open' or 'blanket' consent that biobank donors are normally asked to assign, the trust mechanism affords ongoing scrutiny.

(3) In a charitable trust the beneficiary's rights are exercised at a distance; there is an absence of direct control and thus weaker rights overall. Actually, that is perfectly appropriate for biobank donors because they have done less to merit a property in their tissue. Their weaker rights of ownership can be acknowledged through the creation of a charitable trust to govern the biobank, enabling them to exercise those rights *at a distance*. I would still want to give women who donate ova

---

[35] CCNE (Comité Consultatif National d'Ethique) and Nationaler Ethikrat, *Opinion Number 77, Ethical Problems Raised by the Collected Biological Material and Associated Information Data: 'Biobanks', 'Biolibraries'* (Paris, CCNE, 20 March 2003).
[36] *Ibid.* p. 6.

to stem cell lines *direct* access to their rights, however, because they
have done much more to merit them. In both cases, we will be mainly
concerned with sticks (1) (physical possession), (3) (management),
(4) (income) and (6) (security against taking) of the bundle, but in
the case of biobank donors, those rights will be exercised vicariously
through trustees.

The notion of the trust as a model for biological repositories was
mooted by Karen Gottlieb in 1998.[37] As set out in an influential 2003
article by David and Richard Winickoff,[38] the charitable biotrust sets
out a far more precise programme of duties and entitlements that the
rather vague notions of 'stewardship' and 'custodianship', used by many
biobanks that are actually more like brokers to the private sector.[39] Other
legal mechanisms for compensating donors of human tissue have also
been suggested, such as Harrison's hybrid notion of a government agency
to compensate donors.[40] That proposal, however, mainly concerns financial compensation and lacks the concerns with ongoing control in the trust
model.

Under a trust agreement, the donor or settlor formally transfers her
property interest in tissue to the trust, appointing trustees who have legal
fiduciary duties to use the property for the benefit of a third party, the
beneficiary. In charitable trusts, the beneficiary must be a class of persons (neither an individual nor the community at large). Such a collective grouping might be as broad as national health service patients, or as
narrow as sufferers from a particular disease. Each donor sets up an individual trust instrument, assigning certain property interests to the same
trustee, a non-profit organisation that holds and manages the biobank
in accordance with the agreed charitable purpose. Full disclosure of all
pending commercial arrangements must be made to the settlor at the time

---

[37] Karen Gottlieb, 'Human biological samples and the law of property: the trust as a model
for biological repositories' in R. F. Weir (ed.), *Stored Tissue Samples: Ethical, Legal and
Public Policy Implications* (Iowa City, Iowa University Press, 1998), pp. 183–97.

[38] David E. and Richard N. Winickoff, 'The charitable trust as a model for genomic
biobanks' (2003) 349(12) *New England Journal of Medicine* 1180–4. For a commentary on the original paper by the Winickoffs, see J. Otten, H. Wyle and G. Phelps,
'The charitable trust as a model for genomic banks' (2004) 350 *New England Journal of
Medicine* 85–6. David Winickoff is now working with the US Veterans' Administration,
the largest provider of publicly funded medical care in the USA, to apply aspects of
the charitable trust model in genomic databanking. See David E. Winickoff and Larissa
B. Neumann, 'Towards a social contract for genomics: property and the public in the
"biotrust" model' (2005) 1(3) *Genomics, Society and Policy* 8–21, note 4.

[39] Waldby and Mitchell, *Tissue Economies*, p. 79. For example, UK Biobank's literature
often describes the bank as the 'steward' of the samples it contains.

[40] Charlotte H. Harrison, 'Neither Moore nor the market' (2002) 28 *American Journal of
Law and Medicine* 77–104.

she gives her agreement. If the biobank fails or goes bankrupt – a real risk in the 'easy come easy go' world of modern biotechnology[41] – its assets cannot simply be transferred to the highest bidder or a creditor. Unlike corporate executives' legal obligations to their shareholders to maximise profits, the fiduciary duties of trustees are not primarily profit-orientated. Thus, donors can be protected from unwanted commercialisation of their donations or transfer without any secondary consent to an unknown third party. They may also appoint representatives from their number to the board of trustees, which mitigates the paternalistic nature of the trust. Accountability is also enhanced by setting up an ethical review committee and a donor advisory committee, in a further elaboration of the biotrust model.[42] These bodies may even help to create a 'Habermasian space' for vigorous public debate on biomedical research more generally.[43] Overall, the charitable biotrust can also be viewed as a beneficial Hegelian form of public property, demonstrating that property mechanisms can be used to enhance agency and subjectivity, to encourage a Hegelian interaction with the world and to transcend selfish individualism.

Like the 'bundle of sticks' notion of property, the trust demonstrates how flexible and productive traditional legal concepts can be when applied to modern biomedicine. Recognising the power imbalance between donors and the repository, as highlighted in the *Catalona* case, also enables the trust mechanism to ask many of the same questions to which the bundle concept likewise alerted us. In both instances, the principal issue to many donors is not the right to capital from a resource, or the right to sell a resource: rather, there are wider concerns about rights to manage and rights to be protected against unauthorised taking. When tissue donors file legal actions for the right to capital or income, as in the *Moore* case, it is often because they have no other option. What Moore really wanted was acknowledgement that his tissue had been taken fraudulently; his action in conversion was merely the most plausible legal means to that end.[44]

Applying these traditional concepts of the bundle of rights, from the common law, and the charitable trust, from the law of equity, can provide valuable protection against widespread objectification and commodification of tissue. In the biobank example, I have sought to

[41] See e.g., Hilary Rose, 'An ethical dilemma: the rise and fall of UmanGenomics – the model biotech company?' (2004) 425 *Nature* 123–4.

[42] Winickoff and Neumann, 'Towards a social contract', 11.

[43] Juergen Habermas, *Between Facts and Norms: A Discourse Theory of Law and Democracy* (William Rehg (tr.), Cambridge, MA, MIT Press, 1996), p. 298, cited in Winickoff and Neumann, 'Towards a social contract', 18.

[44] Waldby and Mitchell, *Tissue Economies*, p. 89.

show how the two traditional concepts work in tandem to unpack a very modern problem. By allowing biobank donors a limited number of sticks in the bundle, but restricting them to collective remedies at a remove through trustees, I have suggested how we can solve the prior question of whether trust participants have any property to settle in the first place.[45] The mechanism of a charitable trust is increasingly recognised as a good pragmatic solution. I have also tried to give it a robust philosophical grounding.

[45] Andrea Boggio, 'Charitable trusts and human research genetic databases: the way forward?' (2005) 1(2) *Genomics, Society and Policy* 41–9. In their reply to Boggio, Winickoff and Neumann ('Towards a social contract', at p. 13) likewise remark that the trust model only presupposes parts of the spectrum of property rights.

7   The New French Resistance: Commodification Rejected?

> French doctrine exemplifies simultaneously the simplicity of an axiom and the ambition of a mission: *the body is the person*, and this is one of the modern aspects of France's eternal civilising mission: to defeat the mercantilism of industrial society with the force of this idea.[1]

Having ended the last chapter on the pragmatic note of biotrusts, I now begin the section of the book which presents two extensive applied examples. In this chapter I evaluate the first of two cases exemplifying resistance to biotechnological commodification: France. The next chapter will explore the example of Tonga, thus balancing case studies from the developed and developing world. In neither chapter, however, am I concerned only to tell the narrative of the case. Both France and Tonga offer alternative conceptualisations of what it means to be a subject and of the relationship between the human subject and the body. The official French view that 'the body is the person' has been dismissed as a 'taboo' by the French political scientist Dominique Memmi.[2] If we lift the pejorative neo-colonial connotation of 'taboo', however, merely defining 'taboo' or 'tapu' as a boundary of inviolability, the possible parallel between the French attitude and the Tongan begins to become obvious, and should become clearer in the next chapter.

These two chapters are intended, then, not merely as case-specific analyses in applied ethics, but also as explorations in political theory, comparative cultural attitudes and jurisprudence. Specifically, France and Tonga will allow me to scrutinise further two central concepts in this book: enclosure of common property in the body and fear of feminisation. In the case of France, I conclude that a gendered discourse around commodification does lay central stress on preserving the *patrimoine*, the masculinised

---

[1] Jean-Pierre Baud, *L'affaire de la main volée: une histoire juridique du corps* (Paris, Editions du Seuil, 1993), p. 15.

[2] Dominique Memmi, *Les gardiens du corps: dix ans de magistère bioéthique* (Paris, Editions de l'Ecole des Hautes Etudes en Sciences Sociales, 1996), p. 20, contrasting the 'corps-tabou' and the 'corps-outil' (the body as taboo and the body as tool).

141

common property of the nation, but that this discourse diverts attention from the ways in which commodification is actually taking place.

France has publicly resisted the models of globalised commodification adopted in US and UK biotechnology, as, for example, when the government blocked a research collaboration between the US firm Millennium Pharmaceuticals and a leading genomics laboratory, le Centre d'Etude du Polymorphisme Humain, on the grounds that 'French DNA' should not be given away. This example, however, itself suggests why the 'new French Resistance' is not altogether liberating. The absolutist conception of all bodies as belonging to the French state – indeed, as constituting the body politic[3] – is so potentially invasive that a counter-ideology of inviolability of the body is maintained assiduously. This inviolability is defended particularly strongly against commercialisation, but only at the moment when tissue is taken from the individual subject, who is not to be paid or compensated, although commercial enterprises who subsequently use the tissue are not similarly constrained.

In fact, the French insistence on the gift relationship actually leaves the individual patient or research subject powerless, while affording copious opportunities for commercial interests to commodify and use the biological material given freely by the patient. French law generally lacks the notion of property as a bundle, which affords English and US jurisprudence potential opportunities for protecting the subject against unauthorised taking, for example.[4] Rather, property is conceived of in terms of the multiple and absolute powers conveyed by *dominium* in Roman law: article 544 of the civil code gives each property-holder the rights of use (*usus*), profit (*fructus*) and even abuse (*abusus*) over the objects of the holding. Combined with formulations of political power retained from the absolutist monarchies, this equally absolutist approach to property in the body lacks the sorts of 'checks and balances' for individual patients that I have tried to develop in elaborating the notion of the bundle of rights.

None the less, France has overtly rejected a policy of commodification, sometimes bringing its policies into dispute with other nations and the European Commission in the process. In relation to intangible property, France is probably the most prominent bulwark against the tide

---

[3] As Baud puts it, 'un "corps mystique de la République" appelé aussi "corps politique"' (*L'affaire de la main volée*, p. 74). Baud claims that originally the members of the body politic were the subject of the monarch, the secular counterpart to the mystic body of the Church, but that the notion has persisted under the Republics in a jurisprudence which created and maintains it.

[4] Andrew Grubb, '"I, me, mine": bodies, parts and property' (1998) 3 *Medical Law International* 299–313.

of precedents and policies favouring wholesale genetic patenting, as, for example, when the French Justice Minister Elizabeth Guigou declared in 2000 that human genetic patents violate French ethical principles.[5] France continues to refuse to ratify the 1998 European Biotechnology Directive 98/44/EC sanctioning most forms of patenting of the human genome, with an official governmental report maintaining stoutly that the Directive would have to be renegotiated before France would sign up.[6] The politics of non-commercialisation of the body have been played out in the bioethics legislation of 1994 and 2004,[7] as well as in the opinions of the first European bioethics national commission, the Comité Consultatif National d'Ethique (CCNE). Thus, article 511–4 of the Loi of 29 July 1994 stipulates a term of five years' imprisonment for purchasing tissue, cells or body parts from any person, with the penalty rising to seven years for whole organs (article 511–2). French national documents and commissions frequently present their views as firmly principled, as against those of the laxly 'pragmatic' or 'utilitarian' Anglo-Saxon countries.

Commercialisation and its discontents: the CCNE as exemplar of French principles

I begin this chapter in good French fashion, by means of an *exposé de texte*: analysis of the background assumptions, modes of reasoning and linguistic overtones of some key documents from the CCNE, particularly those on non-commodification of the human genome and human tissue, and of the opinion on the European Biotechnology Directive in which the CCNE rejected government attempts to compromise with the pro-commodification position of the European Commission. The CCNE has consistently taken the strongest possible stand against non-commodification, which it calls 'an intolerable disrespect for the person, a radical violation of our law, a decay which would threaten our entire civilisation'.[8] How can we best understand the rationale of these principles, and of the CCNE as their defender?

---

[5] Timothy Caulfield, E. Richard Gold and Mildred K. Cho, 'Patenting human genetic material: refocusing the debate' (2000) 1 *Nature Reviews Genetics* 227–31.

[6] Alain Claeys, *Rapport sur les conséquences des modes d'appropriation du vivant sur les plans économique, juridique et éthique, Troisième partie*, report no. 1487 (Paris, Office Parlementaire d'Evaluation des Choix Scientifiques et Technologiques, Assemblée Nationale) available at www.assemblee-nationaleofre/12/oecst/il1487.asp, accessed 23 September 2004.

[7] The relevant 2004 law is Loi no. 2004–800 du 6 aout 2004 relative à la bioéthique. For the full titles of the 1994 laws, see n. 9 below.

[8] Comité Consultatif National d'Ethique, *Recherche biomédicale et respect de la personne humaine* (Paris, Documents Français), para. 2.3.2 ('Un irrespect intolérable de la personne, une violation radicale de notre droit, une menace de pourrissement pour toute notre civilisation').

Established in 1983 by the decree of 23 February and given a formal statutory basis by the 'lois bioéthiques' of 1994[9] and 2004,[10] the CCNE has a total membership of thirty-nine persons, plus a president appointed by the President of the Republic. Within the full group, there are three separate methods of appointment. The first 'college' consists of five members likewise appointed by the President, 'belonging to the principal philosophical and spiritual families';[11] the second of nineteen persons, with particular competence in the domain of ethics, appointed by the National Assembly, the Senate, the Conseil d'Etat, the Cour de Cassation, and the ministries of Justice, Health, Research and Communication.

The final 'college' of fifteen members is selected from nominations by the major professional and research bodies, such as the national academies of medicine and science, the Institut Pasteur, the Collège de France and the nationally funded research bodies INSERM and CNRS. Although the third group is meant to possess particular competence in the domain of research, it is not necessarily limited to scientists and physicians; nor is the second group heavily weighted toward philosophers. Jurists carry considerable authority and are well represented in most working groups, with a tendency to conflate ethical and legal thinking by referring to existing law in order to derive ethical principles.[12]

From within the full group of thirty-nine, plus selected 'outsiders', working parties are set up to examine particular issues, which the Committee itself has had the right to select since 1997 under the power of *autosaisine*.[13] Despite the stereotype of French ethics methods as deductive, the subjects discussed by the Committee arise empirically, either from official requests made mostly by institutional sources or through suggestions under *autosaisine* by individual members of timely topics from the world of practice.

---

[9] (1) Loi no. 94–548 du 1 juillet 1994 relative au traîtement de données nominatives ayant pour fin la récherche dans le domaine de la santé; (2) Loi no. 94–654 du 29 juillet 1994 relative au don et à l'utilisation des éléments et produits du corps humain, à l'assistance médicale à la procréation et au diagnostique prénatal; (3) Loi no 94–653 du 29 juillet 1994 relative au respect du corps humain.

[10] Articles L.1412-1, -2, -3, -4, -5, -6.   [11] Article L.1412-2.

[12] I am grateful to Simone Bateman, member of the committee from 1992–1996, for this insight.

[13] This description of the Committee's structure is taken from the thousand-page tome produced on the CCNE's twentieth anniversary and edited by its current president: Didier Sicard (ed.), *Travaux du Comité Consultatif National d'Ethique* (Paris, Quadrige/Presses Universitaires de France, 2003), and from the very detailed list of appointee qualifications in article L.1412-2 of the 2004 legislation. I am also grateful to several past and current members of the CCNE whom I interviewed: Anne Fagot-Largeault, Simone Bateman and Nicole Questiaux.

Since January 2005, the CCNE has been supplemented, or perhaps outranked, by a new agency, L'Agence de la Biomédicine, created by the 2004 legislation (article L.1418–1). The Committee's function is and will remain advisory, but in fact it has sometimes had considerable influence over legislation: it was consulted during the drafting of both the original bioethics laws (1994) and their long-awaited revisions in the summer of 2004. Individual members of the CCNE also played a role in drafting the bill, although not necessarily in their official capacity.

In some cases, such as its Opinion number 64 on the European Bioethics Patenting Directive of 1998,[14] the CCNE has openly rejected government policy. Nominally decisions are meant to be unanimous, but in fact in that opinion there were three dissenters. Each of the three presidents to date has laid a different level of stress on attaining unanimity and on presenting a definite opinion to the government, rather than elucidating the pros and cons of the argument so that ministers and legislators can then make up their own minds. Thus, for example, the second president, Jean-Pierre Changeux, explicitly rejected the view that the task of the committee was merely to state possible arguments. That agreement was possible in the twenty-nine opinions over which he presided was due, he believes, to concentration on practical regulation rather than foundational debate on concepts such as the status of the embryo.[15]

Whereas there has been tacit agreement to bury the subject of the embryo's status, however, the Committee has continued to blazon its public unity around the concept of non-commodification. Indeed, non-commodification has such a totemic status in the opinions of the CCNE, the bioethics laws and the civil code that it appears to be the equivalent of le drapeau tricolore: all parties rally behind its symbolic imagery, whatever their disagreement on other issues. In this symbolic role, the principle of non-commodification also functions to proclaim French exceptionalism: to distinguish France from supposedly less ethical nations, particularly the Anglo-Saxon countries, who, in turn, are rarely differentiated from each other. For example, in its 1990 Opinion number 21, *That the Human Body should not be Used for Commercial Purposes*, the CCNE wrongly but proudly states that 'The view of French law on this problem is clear. It does not accept that the human body should be used for commercial purposes. The body is not an object and cannot be used as such; for instance, blood and organs are not for sale, a position which is rarely

---

[14] Comité Consultatif National d'Ethique, *Avis no. 64: L'avant-projet de loi portant transposition, dans le code de la propriété intellectuelle de la directive 98/44/CR du parlement Européen et du Conseil en date du 6 juillet 1998, relative à la protection juridique des inventions biotechnologiques* (Paris, CCNE, 2000).
[15] Introduction by Jean-Pierre Changeux, in Sicard, *Travaux du CCNE*.

encountered elsewhere.' The UK blood collection system, an obvious exception based on free donation, is not mentioned.

In 1984, the year after its establishment by ministerial decree, the CCNE's very first opinion had already denounced the commercial use of fetal tissue.[16] However, it is in two opinions specifically concerning the human body and the human genome that the committee's position is most clearly seen, shorn of the polarising debate around the status of the embryo.[17] The first of these two reports, *That the Human Body should not be Used for Commercial Purposes*, begins by reiterating the consistent stand taken against commercial use of human tissue throughout the Committee's opinions to date. In the French civil code,[18] as restated in the CCNE opinion, 'the human body or one of its components cannot be the object of a contract'. No distinction is made here between sale and donation:

> For instance, an organ such as the kidney, cannot be sold by the person to whom it belongs and, even if it is donated free of charge, cannot be sold by a third party, however much the would-be recipient or his entourage insist on it. Such insistence may be tantamount to blackmailing dependent individuals, for example prison inmates or misused minorities. Human dignity is at stake if financial gain becomes the result of physical weakness, however temporary.[19]

This rapid move to questions of social justice and power relations typifies the French style: individual consent from the kidney seller is not sufficient to outweigh questions about protecting the vulnerable.[20] However, despite the obvious contrast with the discourse of rights and autonomy more prevalent in Anglo-Saxon bioethics, there is also a surprisingly Lockean proviso in the CCNE opinion: 'The body or its organs are neither paid [*sic*] nor sold, but that is no reason to refuse payment to those whose work is involved. In that case, what is expressed in monetary terms is not the value of a body or a component of the body, but that of the work of observation, sampling, analysis and processing which they make possible.'[21] That is, once labour has been mixed with the tissue, those

---

[16] Comité Consultatif National d'Ethique, *Opinion Number 1: On Sampling of Dead Human Embryonic and Foetal Tissue for Therapeutic, Diagnostic and Scientific Purposes* (22 May 1984), available at www.ccne-ethique.fr/english/avis/a_001.htm.

[17] Comité Consultatif National d'Ethique, *Opinion Number 21: That the Human Body should not be Used for Commercial Purposes* (13 December 1990) and *Opinion Number 27: That the Human Genome should not be Used for Commercial Purposes* (2 December 1991).

[18] Article 1128 of the civil code: 'Only things in commerce can be the object of contracts.' Although this argument is the basis of French jurisprudence on property in the body, it is obviously circular: tissue is not in commerce precisely because commerce in tissue is widely taken to be forbidden by this very article.

[19] CCNE *Opinion Number 21*, p. 2.

[20] For the effect of this emphasis in research ethics, see Giovanni Maio, 'The cultural specificity of research ethics – or why ethical debate in France is different' (2002) 28 *Journal of Medical Ethics* 147–50.

[21] CCNE, *Opinion Number 21*, p. 2.

performing the labour may rightfully lay claim to it: the logic of the majority opinion in *Moore*. In fact this aspect of the CCNE's reasoning is conventionally liberal. As we have already seen, the effect of this argument is not to empower the individual patient but to give free rein to commercial interests.

If the CCNE position on tangible property in human tissue is actually quite conventionally liberal, despite French exceptionalism, its opinions on intangible property in the genome are rather more unique. In its 1991 Opinion number 27, *That the Human Genome should not be Used for Commercial Purposes*, the committee sets out two relevant principles 'to which the Committee attaches the most fundamental importance'. One of these is our old friend, 'the inviolable principle that the human body cannot be put to commercial use'.[22] The other is the argument that the human genome is the common property of humanity as a whole, translated in French as *patrimoine de l'humanité*. Although this principle may seem familiar to non-French readers from its appearance in the United Nations Declaration on the Human Genome and Human Rights,[23] for example, and in the related concept of the genetic commons in the Anglophone bioethics literature,[24] it takes a rather different form in French thought.

Patrimoine, patriarchy and protection

The narrow meaning of *patrimoine* is essentially heritable private property: those things of monetary value which come under the control of an individual. Even in this narrow construction, *patrimoine* conveys a social meaning, as 'the social extension of the person'.[25] Historically, under

---

[22] CCNE *Opinion Number 27*, p. 2.

[23] Proposed by the general conference of UNESCO in 1997 and adopted by the General Assembly in 1998.

[24] For arguments about the biomedical or genetic commons, see in addition to James Boyle, 'The second enclosure movement and the construction of the public domain' (2003) 66 *Law and Contemporary Problems* 33–74: Robert Mitchell, 'Registered genes, patents and bio-circulation', paper presented at the BIOS Vital Politics conference, London School of Economics, September 2003; Stephen R. Munzer, 'Property, patents and genetic material' in J. Burley and J. Harris (eds.), *A Companion to Genethics* (Oxford, Basil Blackwell, 2002), pp. 438–54); Seana Shiffrin, 'Lockean arguments for private intellectual property' in Stephen R. Munzer (ed.), *New Essays in the Legal and Political Theory of Property* (Cambridge, Cambridge University Press, 2002), pp. 138–67; Pilar Ossorio, 'Common heritage arguments against patenting DNA' in A. Chapman (ed.), *Perspectives on Gene Patenting: Religion, Science and Industry in Dialogue* (Washington, DC, American Association for the Advancement of Science, 1999), pp. 89–108; Carol M. Rose, 'The comedy of the commons: customs, commerce and inherently public property' (1986) 53 *University of Chicago Law Review* 742; and the foundational article by Garrett Hardin, 'The tragedy of the commons' (1968) 162 *Science* 1243.

[25] Claire Crignon-de Oliveira and Marie Gaille-Nikodimov, *A qui appartient le corps humain? Médecine, politique et droit* (Paris, Les Belles Lettres, 2004), p. 106.

the strongly patriarchal system of Roman law, this was of course a male person, and we should remain alert throughout this discussion to the connection between *patrimoine* and patriarchy. In the French context, this link is particularly suspect because of another connection, that between solidarity and fraternity. French bioethics opinion, at least as expressed in the CCNE's opinions, reiterates the importance of solidarity. As the US sociologist Paul Rabinow has written, 'After all we have learned about the historical restrictions on the public sphere from feminist historians, especially of France, it is hard to see how the passing of all forms of *fraternity* is to be regretted.'[26] Rabinow might have added feminist political theorists, such as Carole Pateman, who have drawn attention to the explicitly fraternal nature of the social contract and its exclusion of women.[27] It is certainly true that the leading concepts and debates in France concerning medical ethics lack a consciously feminist voice and that the offices charged with women's affairs have little input into bioethics policy.[28]

What I want to do here, however, is primarily to examine how French public policy and jurisprudence concerning property in the body, particularly property in the genome, also rely on an implicit broader meaning of *patrimoine*. The wider connotations of *patrimoine* concern this social meaning, and by linguistic inference the links with *patrie*. These two meanings, narrow and broad, are linked by the notion of heredity.[29] As elaborated by the nineteenth-century jurists Aubry and Rau, *patrimoine* even in its narrow sense already carries a notion of indivisibility and thus of communality, at least within its original community of ownership – a family whose common goods would have constituted a *patrimoine*. Furthermore, even in its narrow sense, *patrimoine* concerns rights of disposition between testators and inheritors, not to be alienated to others outside the circle of inheritors.[30] 'Thus the *patrimoine* is always that of a continuous

---

[26] Paul Rabinow, *French DNA: Trouble in Purgatory* (Chicago, University of Chicago Press, 1999), p. 22, original emphasis.

[27] Carole Pateman, 'The fraternal social contract' in *The Disorder of Women* (Stanford, CA, Stanford University Press, 1989), pp. 33–57.

[28] Jennifer Merchant, 'Confronting the consequences of medical technology: policy frontiers in the United States and France' in Marianne Givvens and Dorothy McBride Stetson (eds.), *Abortion Politics: Public Policy in Cross-Cultural Perspective* (New York and London, Routledge, 1996), pp. 189–210, at p. 206. Even Simone Veil, the Minister for Health who was the guiding spirit behind the 1974 abortion law, never analysed the questions raised by women's *rights*; the statute was justified rather by minimising maternal *distress*, in a paternalistic manner.

[29] Crignon-de Oliveira and Gaille-Nikodimov, *A qui appartient le corps humain?*, p. 184.

[30] C. M. Aubry and F. F. Rau, *Cours de droit civil français* (Brussels, Méline, Cans, 1850), summarised in Crignon-de Oliveira and Gaille-Nikodimov, *A qui appartient le corps humain?*, pp. 184–5.

succession of individual proprietors.' ('De ce fait, le patrimoine est tou-
jours celui d'une succession continue d'individus propriétaires.')[31]

There are restrictions on how something belonging to the *patrimoine*
can be alienated, of which 'no commercial usage' is one of the most
important in biomedicine, particularly in relation to the national genetic
heritage. That prohibition, in my interpretation, applies solely to the original alienation from the *patrimoine*, which can only be justified if it is a
gift from one member of the community to another. Rabinow traces this
nationalistic emphasis back to the French Revolution, when the wealth of
the nation was no longer to be identified with the detested monarchy and
Church, but rather with the sovereign people itself. By as early as 1794,
the sale or destruction of this wealth had already come to be prohibited:
it was to be preserved for the newly sovereign people alone.[32] Rabinow
goes on to note: 'Previously the task of patrimony had been dutiful transmission of goods; today it is protection.' In its frequently invoked role as
guardian of national identity, *patrimoine* now functions to protect French
cultural and biological identity against the threats posed by globalised
biotechnologies. Thus, as Rabinow puts it, 'the invocation of "genetic
patrimony" fits snugly with the main symbols of French bioethics: menace, integrity, identity'.[33]

One way of viewing the limitations imposed by *patrimoine*, in modern
terms, is the parallel with provisions of a will which constrain the uses to
which an heir can put his or her inheritance. A better analogy, I would
say, is the manner in which ancient systems of property transmission typically emphasise keeping the wealth of the household intact more heavily
than the individual rights of any member of the household, even the head.
Thus, in archaic mainland Greece wealth was seen as belonging to the
household, not to individual heads except as temporary stewards of the
property of the *oikos*.[34] Although the purpose of the property system was
to preserve the wealth of the household, a principal effect of the classical system was the subordination of women. Filtered through a Roman
rather than a Greek lens, the communal model also continues to influence
French law through the concept of *patrimoine*, and retains its gendered
connotations. In its modern form, consciously revived by many French
jurists and philosophers,[35] this wealth includes not only fungible property

---

[31] Mikhail Xitaras, *La Propriété* (Paris, Fondements de la politique, Presses Universitaires
de France, 2004), p. 396.
[32] Rabinow, *French DNA*, p. 125.   [33] Rabinow, *French DNA*, p. 126.
[34] For a further discussion of the effect on women of this model, see *Property, Women and
Politics*, p. 52 *et seq.*
[35] Martin Remond-Gouilloud, 'L'avenir du patrimoine', *Esprit*, November 1995, p. 216.

but also the genetic 'endowment' of the nation, along with some forms of tissue.[36]

It might be thought that contributing to the patrimony by donating blood or tissue is neither altrustic nor egoistic, because those contributing are themselves members of the nation which enjoys the wealth of the *patrimoine*. However, this mutual gift relationship fails to take into account the way in which 'the new enclosures' transfer what was previously communal wealth into the hands of a new, globalised set of proprietors. While the individual French tissue donor is limited to altruistic donation, *en aval*, downstream, commercial interests are not constrained by such norms of gratuitous donation. Elements belonging to the modern market system inevitably and increasingly creep in unless stringently guarded against. The civil code, with its emphasis on the inviolability of *patrimoine*, is a product of a non-market society and of a period in which tissue and organs were not detachable from the living body.

What we see here is in fact a pre-market model, similar to that which obtained in the Athenian *oikos*, but more closely related to that of the absolutist French state. In France the effect of democracy, in its direct Rousseauesque variant, was to transfer the personality of the monarch wholesale to the entire people.[37] It is the sovereign people which exercises power and enjoys rights in this formulation of democracy; individuals are also accorded rights by virtue of their membership in the collectivity, but not as individuals *per se*. The collectivity, or body public, is primary. Liberal democracy, by contrast, conceives of the individual in the state of nature as the basic building block, and of the state as secondary, formed through the social contract and limited by the rights of individuals. Just as liberal democracy's building block is frequently said to be the autonomous property-holding individual,[38] so in the French model of direct democracy the unit of power is the collectivity of individuals, and the locus of wealth the collective *patrimoine*.

---

[36] Baud, *L'affaire de la main volée*, p. 206, cited in Rabinow, *French DNA*, p. 206, alleges that placental tissue is routinely assumed to be made available by the mother for albumin extraction. However, I can find no evidence of this practice in the CCNE Opinion (number 74) on umbilical cord blood, which emphasises that cord blood extraction should be voluntary.

[37] David Held, *Models of Democracy* (1st edn, Cambridge, Polity Press, 1987), ch. 3. See also Gilbert Hottois, *Essais philosophie bioéthique et biopolitique* (Paris, Librairie Philosophique J. Vrin, 1999). Rousseau explicitly connects the democratic citizen's status as political subject with the social body, so that, as Hottois puts it, 'It is the State (public law) which institutes and creates the individual subject, and it creates him insofar as he is a citizen' (at p. 61).

[38] C. B. MacPherson, *The Political Theory of Possessive Individualism: Hobbes to Locke* (Oxford and New York, Oxford University Press, 1962).

Just as the physical and moral person of the absolutist monarch embodied the state, so now do the persons of all French citizens collectively
comprise the French republic. French law does not accord the individual a property right in his or her own body; in important respects it
still conceives of the citizen's body, particularly but not exclusively the
human genome, as belonging to the state. This incarnation of the state
in the collective bodies of its citizens can also be seen as the outcome of
two merging traditions, according to the French bioethicist Anne Fagot-
Largeault:

> In the Roman Catholic tradition, the church is viewed as the (mystical) body of
> Christ (in the protestant tradition there is no such mediation of an institutional
> body between man and God). In the French (and English) tradition of monarchy,
> the King incarnated the nation, i.e. there was a kind of mutual incorporation of
> the King in his subjects, and of the subjects in their King. Both traditions merged
> in France: the Gallican church and the Catholic King embodied the 'patria'
> (or 'crown'), that is, the spiritually and politically structured community, the
> 'domain' of which could not be 'alienated' . . . This notion of an organic com-
> munity transcending individuals seems to have been secularized, and resumed
> rather than reversed, by the French Republic. What the 1789 revolution brought
> about was the guarantee that no member of the community may freely dispose
> of the body of any member (not even his/her own).[39]

Reading French bioethics and jurisprudence in light of this double
meaning reveals unexpected meanings behind the official doctrine. Both
the civil code and the bioethics laws firmly declare that 'The human body,
its elements and its products cannot be the object of a patrimonial right'
('Le corps humain, ses éléments et ses produits ne peuvent faire l'objet
d'un droit patrimonial') and that the human body is therefore inviolable
('Le corps humain est inviolable.')[40] This is strange: it looks as if the
human body is explicitly excluded from the *patrimoine*, whereas I have
been arguing that the reverse is the case. Exactly what does this pair of
statements mean?

The patrimonial right of which the human body cannot be a subject
refers to the narrower sort of *patrimoine*, an individual's worldly goods.
The broader meaning of *patrimoine*, that which belongs to the body
politic or the state, takes precedence over the narrow meaning of individual worldly goods in the French context. It is this very dominance of
patrimoine as equivalent to the French nation itself which necessitates

---

[39] Anne Fagot-Largeault, 'Ownership of the human body: judicial and legislative responses
in France' in Henk ten Have and Jos Welie (eds.), *Ownership of the Human Body: Philosophical Considerations on the Use of the Human Body and its Parts in Healthcare* (Dordrecht,
Kluwer, 1998), pp. 115–40, at p. 133.
[40] Civil code, art. 16–1; loi nationale 94–653, 29 juillet 1994, art. 3.

strongly reiterated assurances in law and jurisprudence that this dominance is no longer absolute. Thus, in an ironic sense, it is precisely because the human body is identified with *patrimoine* in its broader sense, that the narrower sense of *patrimoine* must be invoked in the assertion that the human body cannot be the object of a patrimonial right. Because the state's rightful potential control over the body of its citizens is unbounded, it becomes particularly crucial to restate the doctrine of human dignity and inviolability of the body. What at first appears an attractive and consistent insistence – that the human body is in no way a thing and cannot become property – actually flows from the diminished nature as subjects of French citizens. They are subjects insofar as they are members of the *patrie* and share in its *patrimoine*, but they lack full control over their bodies insofar as those bodies are part of the *patrimoine*. They are in fact both subjects and objects.

Because the individual body is the object of the nation's *patrimoine*, the inviolability of the body extended under the Napoleonic code to a state prohibition on self-mutilation, including vasectomy and sterilisation. The underpinning principle was that the body was inviolable except in cases of therapeutic necessity. Doctors performing either procedure were subject to criminal charges, although in fact sterilisations (particularly on mentally handicapped individuals) were performed far more frequently than vasectomies,[41] indicating that the notion of the body's inviolability is strongly gendered. Current legislation (Loi no. 2001–588 du 4 juillet 2001) now allows both sterilisation and vasectomy, but under strict terms, including a required period of four months between the first consultation and performance of the procedure. Similarly, IVF is restricted in France to married couples or to heterosexual partners of at least two years' standing.[42] Such narrow boundaries on eligibility are most easily understood in terms of the notion of reproduction as a patrimonial state interest, even though it is presented in terms of the natural order[43] and of the child's

---

[41] Fagot-Largeault, 'Ownership of the human body,' 118. For further discussion of how French bioethics legislation retains concepts from the absolutist and Enlightenment periods, see Nan T. Ball, 'The reemergence of Enlightenment ideas in the 1994 French bioethics debates' (2000) 50 *Duke Law Journal* 545–87.

[42] Code de la santé publique, art. L.152-2: 'l'homme et la femme formant le couple doivent être vivants, en âge de procréer, mariés ou en mésure d'apporter la preuve d'une vie commune d'au moins deux ans' ('the man and woman forming the couple must be alive, of the age to procreate, married or able to prove that they have lived together for at least two years').

[43] For a critical view of the 'natural' state, see Simone Bateman, 'La nature fait-elle (encore) bien les choses?' ('Does nature (still) know best?') in Patrick Pharo (ed.), *L'homme et le vivant: sciences de l'homme et sciences de la vie* (Paris, Presses Universitaires de France, 2004), pp. 391–404.

best interests.[44] (They are, needless to say, detrimental to lesbian parents, although a recent case allowing a lesbian partner to formally co-adopt her partner's children may be a straw in a differently prevailing wind.)[45]

A very telling example of the difference between Anglo-Saxon and French perspectives in this regard can be found in the CCNE's Opinion number 74 (2002), *Umbilical Cord Blood Banks for Autologous Use or for Research*. Rather than posing the question in terms of benefits to individual babies or the choice of individual couples, the CCNE opinion condemns the private banking of cord blood for autologous use as a breach of social solidarity:

> Preserving placental blood for the child itself strikes a solitary and restrictive note in contrast with the implicit solidarity of donation. It amounts to putting away in a bank as a precaution, as a biological preventive investment, as biological insurance . . . There is major divergence between the concept of preservation for the child decided by parents and that of solidarity with the rest of society.[46]

A coherent and consistent role is played in France by the notions of social solidarity and *ordre public*, likewise derived from the absolutist state but consciously reinforced in the nineteenth century as a deliberately constructed counter-weight to the instability of the Republic and the power of the Church.[47] Solidarity is not necessarily seen as pre-existing: the CCNE opinion on biobanks, for example, speaks of 'constructing' it consciously through benefit-sharing.[48] Nor is it unproblematic: the CCNE opinion on *Consent in favour of a Third Person*[49] clearly sets out the conflict between solidarity and autonomy, neither of which necessarily trumps the other. What is noteworthy is simply the prevalence of solidarity-centred arguments in the French context, linked to the notion of the body politic and to *patrimoine* in its broader sense.

Gift and altruistic donation

Solidarity is linked to gift, whose centrality in French bioethics is generally dated back to the two World Wars. Before the First World War,

---

[44] For further discussion of the justification, see Jean-François Thery, Frédéric Salat-Baroux and Christine Le Bihan-Graf, *Les lois de la bioéthique: cinq ans après*, étude adoptée par l'Assemblée générale du Conseil d'Etat (Paris, La Documentation française, 25 November 1999), p. 19.

[45] 'La justice reconnaît pour la première fois une famille homoparentale', *Le Monde*, 23 September 2004.

[46] CCNE Opinion Number 74, *Umbilical Cord Blood Banks for Autologous Use or Research*.

[47] Paul Rabinow, *French Modern: Norms and Forms of the Social Environment* (Chicago and London, University of Chicago Press, 1989), p. 184.

[48] CCNE and Nationaler Ethikrat, Opinion Number 77.

[49] CCNE Opinion Number 70, *Consentement en faveur d'un tiers* (Paris, CCNE, 2001).

blood was paid for in France, and some commentators fear that the effect of European Community membership will be to reinstate a market system.[50] During the 1980s, an intense national debate over altruistic donation was provoked by 'le drame du sang contaminé', when over 2,000 lawsuits were filed by patients who had received transfusions infected with HIV. Was the débâcle due to bad medicine or bad ethics? Could more intensive scrutiny of donors prevent future crises, or was it offensive to screen those who were coming forward purely out of the goodness of their hearts? Although such scruples might seem oversensitive, it was argued by some that a policy of screening would encourage homophobia, given the higher prevalence of the HIV virus in the gay population. Others feared that the position of the donor at the centre of a system founded on trust and solidarity would be threatened, so that 'calling him into question, even if only partially, would risk undermining the entire structure'.[51]

Two major statutes and a Constitutional revision later, however, the position of altruism in blood donation remains dominant in public policy, as does the concept of solidarity on which it rests. It has in fact been said that the debate over HIV-infected blood secured that principle on an even firmer footing in law, establishing that society owed a debt to the victims of technological 'progress', particularly techniques such as blood pooling, on the one hand, and on the other, separation of blood products into albumins, immunoglobulins and factor VIII.[52] Contract law was the unexpected means through which these cases were settled in favour of the patients, even though there is no contract between patient and doctor in the French public medicine system. Rather, the majority of tribunals involved held that the *contrat de fourniture* between the transfusion centres and the hospitals could be invoked by the patients not as third parties, but by a 'tacit stipulation' in favour of the patient.[53] Whilst in the short term this interpretation benefited patients, in the long term it undermined the strict separation between things and persons: contract law is a strange thing to invoke in the ostensible case of *une chose hors commerce*.[54] Here, however, we have something akin to the flexible use of separate sticks in the property 'bundle' in the common law: judicious judicial

---

[50] Marie-Angèle Hermitte, *Le sang et le droit: essai sur la transfusion sanguine* (Paris, Editions du Seuil, 1996), p. 15.

[51] Philippe Steiner, 'Don du sang et don d'organes: le marché et les marchandises "fictives"' (2001) 42(2) *Revue française de sociologie* 357–73, at 361: 'le donneur était au centre de l'affaire, le pivot de toute la chaine de la transfusion sanguine . . . le remettre en cause, fût-ce partiellement, risquait de mettre à bas tout l'édifice'.

[52] Hermitte, *Le sang et le droit*, p. 17.   [53] *Ibid.* p. 276.   [54] *Ibid.* p. 280.

interpretation of property in the body precisely *as* property in order to afford protections that a system based entirely on personal rights may lack.[55]

Although one CCNE opinion after another reiterates the centrality of gift in French bioethics, the position of gratuitous donation is in fact problematic, and the importance of non-commodification merely secondary. What is illicit is not commodification in itself, but commodification of that which belongs to the *patrimoine*.[56] (Gametes also belong to the *patrimoine* in a particularly significant way, so that semen is regarded as a gift from one couple to the other. This model imposes strict demands on both the receiving couple (who must be either married or cohabiting for three years) and the donor, who is also required to be in a stable relationship and already the father of at least one healthy child.) Once genetic material or tissue has been removed from the realm of the national *patrimoine* into the private market under procedures laid down and controlled by the state, the state has willingly abnegated its powers over the tissue of individuals and market rules can then apply. For example, in the CCNE Opinion number 9 on *Products Derived from Human Cells* (1987), a tissue sample is to be considered as freely donated by the patient to the medical or hospital, allowing the clinicians to develop a product which can be commercialised. Limitations on the price of the product are suggested – so that the price, in good Lockean fashion, should only reflect the added value of the labour to the material, which has no price – but these suggestions have never been enforced. The patient, however, retains no further rights in the tissue or to benefits from its commercialisation once it enters the market domain: exactly the same result as *Moore*.

But how can tissue belonging to the *patrimoine* be alienated in the first place? Why is it permissible to diminish the national heritage by gift, any more than by sale? The answer must lie in social solidarity. Gift of blood or tissue to another citizen of the *patrie* is permissible because it does not diminish the total holding of the French nation. Indeed, 'donation' is well-nigh compulsory after death: France operates an 'opt-out' system according to which it is presumed that the deceased person would have consented to organ donation, unless she explicitly withdrew

---

[55] For a more developed argument in favour of this strategy for French law, see Baud, *L'affaire de la main volée*.

[56] For an excellent discussion of the intricacies into which these requirements lead, see Simone Bateman (as Simone Bateman Novaes), *Les passeurs de gamètes* (Nancy, Presses Universitaires de Nancy, 1994).

consent, while alive, to posthumous organ retrieval.[57] Because the interests of the *patrie* take precedence over individual rights, and because the most vulnerable may be more tempted than the rich to sell their blood or tissue in a commercial system, the state has an obligation to protect citizens from themselves by forbidding anyone who might be tempted to sell their blood, rather than give it away. Happily, this paternalistic interest coincides with the logic of gift: the more vulnerable will be no more tempted than the wealthiest to give their tissue away, and the total *patrimoine* will be enhanced, to everyone's benefit.

Thus, human tissue may well be *une chose hors commerce*, a thing outside the realm of commerce,[58] but that does not mean that it cannot be alienated by gift. Provided that gift is mediated through procedures laid down by the state, as Fagot-Largeault argues, 'Human body parts may be said to be common property of that community. Exchanges are made possible by the community acting as the actual owner of all body parts, with the consent of individual persons.'[59] Does this presumption that the state already owns one's body parts actually *dis*courage altruism? France has the worst record in Europe of gratuitous organ donation from living donors: for example, only 2.7 per cent of French adult end-stage renal patients receive a donated kidney from a relative, as against 49 per cent in Norway.[60] (However, the two countries are not strictly comparable, since most transplants in France are cadaveric.)

The French jurist Dominique Thouvénin, in her sceptical dismissal of both gift and gratuity,[61] argues that the principal function of gift is to establish an irrevocable transfer from donor to recipient.[62] The notion of conditional gift, mooted by some Anglophone scholars as a mechanism for enhancing donor control,[63] is entirely absent in French jurisprudence.

---

[57] Loi no. 76–1181 du 22 decembre 1976 relative aux prélèvements d'organes ('loi Caillavet'), art. 2.

[58] For a fuller discussion of the French law on *choses hors commerce*, see Isabelle Moine, *Les choses hors commerce: une approche de la personne humaine juridique* (Paris, LGDJ-Monchrestien, Bibliothèque de droit privé, 1997).

[59] Fagot-Largeault, 'Ownership of the human body,' 137.

[60] Steiner, 'Don du sang et don d'organes', pp. 367–8, quoting figures for 1990 produced by H. Lorentzen and F. Paterson ('Le don des vivants: l'altruisme des Norvégiens et des Français?' in J. Elster and N. Herpin (eds.), *Ethique des choix médicaux* (Arles, Actes Sud, 1992), pp. 121–38.)

[61] Dominique Thouvénin, 'Autour du don et de la gratuité' (2002) *Revue générale de droit médical, Numéro spécial: droit santé* 99–108.

[62] Civil code, art. 894.

[63] See e.g., Bartha M. Knoppers, *et al.*, 'Ethical issues in international collaborative research on the human genome: the HGP and the HDGP' (1996) 34 *Genomics* 272–5 and B. M. Knoppers, 'Human genetic material: commodity or gift?' in R. F. Weir (ed.), *Stored Tissue Samples: Ethical, Legal and Public Policy Implications* (Iowa City, Iowa University Press, 1998), pp. 226–35 as well as the results of a Medical Research Council (UK) survey

In formal terms gift is so irrevocable as to require an agreement witnessed by a *notaire*. This level of finality and formality lends to the concept of gift of tissue or blood a weight for which there is no equivalent in common law, and against which there is no chance of appeal afterwards. As a protection for patients or research subjects, it is quite insufficient. As Thouvénin remarks, 'The law uses . . . the word gift, because expressing things in terms of gift . . . camouflages the incursion on the body's integrity, and privileges the generosity of the person who decides to give an ill person an organ vital for survival.'[64] Furthermore, the voluntariness of gift is largely fictitious, as is the opposition between gift and the market system.[65] Implicitly following Mauss, Thouvénin writes:

Gift implies counter-gift; we are concerned with a social system characterised by the double obligation of receiving and giving. Thus gift is not the opposite of the market model or of goods circulating without monetary counterpart . . . Just as there is no gift, there is no altruistic donation . . . [We must] distinguish between two situations both comprised under altruistic donation: the person from whom the tissues are taken may not receive any financial recompense, or the tissues once taken may be transferred for a market price, or may be used subject to the costs incurred in the taking.[66]

In Thouvénin's view, the French government has been concerned to preserve a tight distinction between 'altruistic donation', implying no further control by the donor, and the development of 'patrimonial collections' of tissue for the benefit of research and industry. This whited-sepulchre style of argument seems to be borne out by the recent ministerial decree allowing the importation of stem cell lines, not currently part of the 'patrimonial collections' because of the ongoing deadlock over the status of

---

indicating that doctors and nurses believe patients should retain some ongoing rights over donated material (Medical Research Council, *Public Perceptions of the Collection of Human Biological Samples* (2000)).

[64] Thouvénin, 'Autour du don et de la gratuité', 102 ('Le legislateur a utilisé . . . le mot *don*, parce que s'exprimer en termes de don . . . permet d'occulter l'atteinte à l'integrité corporelle pour privilégier la generosité de la personne qui déciderait que soient transmis à des malades ces organes si précieux pour leur survie.')

[65] This point is also made by another French commentator, P. Oliveiro, in 'La communication sociale des matériaux biologiques: sang, sperme, organs, cadavres' (1993) 18 *Cahiers internationauz de psychologie sociale* 21–51.

[66] Thouvénin, 'Autour du don et de la gratuité', 103–4: 'Le don appelle le contre-don; il s'agit donc d'un système social caracterisé par la double obligation de recevoir et de donner. Le don n'est donc pas l'envers du modèle marchand où des biens circuleraient sans contrepartie financière; ce qui le caracterise, c'est la création de liens de personne à personne . . . Pas plus qu'il n'y de don, il n'y de gratuité . . . Il faut . . . distinguer ces deux situations qui peuvent être resumées ainsi: la personne sur qui les éléments sont pris ne peut pas recevoir de contrepartie financière, tandis que les éléments une fois detachés peuvent soit être cédés moyennant un prix, soit être utilitsés moyennant une prise en charge des coûts générés par leur obtention.'

the embryo.[67] In order to preserve France's international research standing, both 'patrimonial collections' and imports of blood products from the USA,[68] or stem cell lines from less 'ethical' countries such as the United Kingdom, will allow France to preserve both her principles and her market position. Ironically, there is more than a passing resemblance between the policy of UK Biobank, say, and the French use of 'gift' as a mechanism to close down further ethical debate.

Is the body the person?

I began this chapter with a quotation from Jean-Pierre Baud, highlighting the official French doctrine that 'the body is the person'. Baud is an iconoclastic author, the first in a growing lineage, who insists that the body should actually be regarded in French jurisprudence as a thing and not as a person: 'but not just any thing: a thing which, by virtue of reality and its sacred nature, is the object of narrowly limited and controlled legal procedures'.[69] The physical person, he says, is regarded elsewhere in the law as separate from the legal person, which can be a corporation or other disembodied individual. It is only religious dogma, he charges, which keeps the supposedly anti-clerical French from acknowledging frankly that 'man' is master of his own body. Advocating abandonment of the doctrine that tissue separated from the body is mere waste, he asks, 'Which is more damaging for the human person: to consider his body and everything belonging to it as things rigorously protected by property law, or to admit that anything detached from the body has the same status as excrement, but excrement that can be turned to gold?'[70]

Many French scholars and critics of the French system appear to agree with Baud in regarding the equivalence of body and person as an insufficiently examined platitude. We have already seen that the rights of subjects over their own tissue are curtailed in the French system by the presumption that genetic endowments, and tissues to some extent, belong to the *patrimoine*. This assumption sets up a tension: if the body is the person, and yet the body in some sense belongs to the wider community, how are we to conceive of the embodied subject's rights? In the extreme, the claims of the community might be so pressing that the person becomes less a subject than the *patrimoine* itself. That would be an extreme reading, however: although it may be tempting to make the

---

[67] Ministère delegué à la Récherche, Communiqué de Presse, 'Cellules souches embryonnaires: présentation du decret autorisant l'importation', 19 October 2004, available at www.recherche.gouv.fr/discours/2004/decretembryon.htm.
[68] Steiner, 'Don du sang et don d'organes', 363.
[69] Baud, *L'affaire de la main volée*, p. 120.   [70] *Ibid.* p. 25.

patrimoine into a subject in its own right, as the French philosopher Martine Rémond-Gouilloud has written, that would be a category mistake. Yet if things belonging to the *patrimoine*, such as 'French DNA', are not subjects, they are not straightforward objects either.[71] Similarly, they are both property and not property. As Rabinow writes, 'one of the functions of the institution of patrimony is to provide a means of bridging the domains of property [*avoir*] and being [*l'être*]'.[72]

The 1994 French bioethics Law 94–654 may stipulate that the body cannot be the object of patrimonial rights, but we have already seen that there is presumed consent to the extraction of tissue in the case of cadaveric 'donors', in the name of the *patrimoine*. More broadly, there is a tension between the notion of *patrimoine* and that of the body as identified entirely with the subject. If the latter were infallibly true, even altruistic donation of blood or other tissue from one member of the *patrie* to another would be disallowed, and the *patrimoine* would dissolve into a loose Hobbesian collection of individual body-subjects. The response of French jurisprudence to this tension has been to allow certain usages, such as blood donation, while retaining an overall degree of control forbidding other usages, such as gamete sale, in the name of protecting the *patrimoine*. Although French judges continue to reiterate the principle that the body is the subject, in practice they have made a series of concessions to medical reality.[73]

In the view of many French commentators, including Baud and Marzano-Parisoli, the way ahead is not to insist doggedly on the equivalence between subject and body, but to admit that the body is an object, although a particular kind of object over which the full rights of *dominium* cannot be exercised. 'The body is not a simple worldly object, but rather the object which each of us both *has* and *is*; it is a thing, but *sui generis*; it is that over which we dispose, but not in an absolute manner.'[74] The effect of this 'rethinking the body' in the context of French civil law is actually rather similar to using the common-law concept of property as a bundle, as I have advocated. Certain property rights over the body then become permissible; others remain prohibited. The question, of course, is which uses of the body fall into which category. Marzano-Parisoli retains the official French insistence on a distinction between sale and gift, for example.

At the time of writing it appears highly likely that the result of the August 2004 bioethics laws will be to further weaken the once-sovereign

[71] Rémond-Gouilloud, 'L'affaire du patrimoine', cited in Rabinow, *French DNA*, p. 128.

[72] Rabinow, *French DNA*, p. 128.

[73] Maria M. Marzano-Parisoli, *Penser le corps* (Paris, Presses Universitaires de France, 2002), p. 124.

[74] *Ibid.* p. 138.

French insistence on non-commercialisation of the body. Indeed, my analysis in this chapter has already suggested that this supposedly sovereign principle was already something of a puppet monarch. Among the disturbing elements of the new legislation appear to be:

• the formal and explicit extension of the opt-out principle to commercially valuable tissue such as the placenta;[75]

• express permission for the utililisation of parts or 'products' of the human body for other scientific or medical purposes than those for which they were first intended, unless the patient explicitly objects;[76]

• the softening of the previously strong position against any incursion on the human body, so that the exemption in favour of the patient's own therapeutic needs is now augmented by 'the therapeutic needs of others, in exceptional instances';[77]

• the greatly expanded list of purposes for which tissue can be taken as a gift from a living person;[78]

• the removal of any distinction between different levels of transformation of human tissue through research techniques or industrial processes, and the inclusion of genetic material explicitly under the same heading as other biomaterial;[79]

• the lack of any distinction between public and private biotechnology 'operators'.[80]

The first effect of these concessions to commodification is greatly to undermine French exceptionalism. The French position on biobanks,

---

[75] Article L.1245-2: 'Les tissus, les cellules et les produits du corps humain, prélevés à l'occasion d'une intervention chirurgicale pratiquée dans l'intérêt de la personne operée, ainsi que le placenta, peuvent être utilisés a des fins thérapeutiques ou scientifiques, sauf opposition exprimée par elle après qu'elle à été informée des finalités de cette utilitsation.' The only restriction here is the catch-all phrase 'therapeutic or scientific ends' ('des fins thérapeutiques ou scientifiques'); almost any applied use of tissue will probably qualify as 'scientific', if ostensibly in the interests of further research.

[76] Title II, art. 7, revision of art. L.1211-2: 'L'utilisation d'éléments et de produits du corps humain à une fin médicale ou scientifique autre que celle pour laquelle ils ont été prélevés ou collectés est possible, sauf opposition exprimée par la personne sur laquelle a été opéré ce prélèvement ou cette collecte, dûment informée au préalable de cette autre fin.' The only exception is embryonic and fetal tissue.

[77] Article 9, A, revision of first paragraph of art. 16-3 of civil code: 'Il ne peut être porté atteinte à l'integrité du corps humain qu'en cas de nécessité médicale pour la personne ou à titre exceptionnel dans l'intérêt thérapeutique d'autrui.'

[78] Article 12, revising art. 1241-1 of the 1994 law to read: 'Le prélèvement de tissus ou de cellules ou la collecte de produits du corps humain sur une personne vivante en vue de don ne peut être opéré que dans un but thérapeutique ou scientifique ou de réalisation ou contrôle des dispositifs médicaux de diagnostic in vitro ou de contrôle de qualité des analyses de biologiemédicale ou dans le cadre des expertises et des contrôles techniques réalisés sur les tissus ou sur les cellules ou sur les produit du corps humain.'

[79] Article L.1243-1.   [80] Article 1243-3.

tissue collection and commercialisation of body 'product' increasingly resembles no system so much as the United Kingdom's, not least because the 2004 Law sets up a new Agence de la Biomédecine[81] with functions similar to (but wider than) those of the UK Human Tissue Authority and Human Fertilisation and Embryology Authority (to be merged in 2008 into a single agency). Much of the 2004 legislation seems at first glance to rely on this agency to ensure that no ill is done by the numerous relaxations of principle elsewhere in the statute. For example, no tissues or cells can be transferred to any other establishment without authorisation from the new agency, which may help to inhibit totally free global markets in biomaterial. However, the new French agency will encounter a much more commodified situation than the HFEA did when it began operations over fifteen years ago. Furthermore, generally speaking, France is accustomed to relying on the state to regulate, but where the actors to be regulated are not French citizens but multinational firms, the modes of governance required lie outside the state's previous experience.[82]

Even in the 1994 legislation, many French analysts had already noted the tension between the notion of the *corps-sujet* and *corps-outil*, body as subject and body as tool, particularly in the light of the doctrine of the *patrimoine*. The second effect of the 2004 laws is to move the position of the body even closer to the object end of the spectrum – despite the ostensibly immovable principle in French jurisprudence that the human subject is an embodied person and not a thing. This is a disappointing outcome. As Rabinow says in a backhanded compliment to the CCNE, 'the committee was instrumental in transforming France's official ethical mood from proud affirmation of acts of benevolent giving to a defensive one requiring vigilance against transgressive threats'.[83] Despite its vigilance, however, the threat of commodification has not been avoided in the French context.

[81] Article L.1418-1.   [82] Rabinow, *French DNA*, p. 73.   [83] *Ibid.*

8   Tonga, the Genetic Commons and *No Man's Land*

In the previous chapter I evaluated the extent to which the official French view of the body as *une chose hors commerce* has provided a bulwark against commodification. In contrast to that example from the developed world, here in this chapter I want to analyse an instance from the global South: the Tongans' resistance to commodification of their genome. Despite their different provenance, the two case studies offer striking parallels. Coincidentally, diabetes research, based on mapping population genomes, was the subject of both the research project analysed by Rabinow in his book *French DNA*[1] and the venture sought in Tonga by the Australian firm Autogen. In one case the government itself blocked the project – perhaps surprisingly, the French case. In the Tongan instance, it was left up to a popular resistance movement to scupper the proposal. Resistance to these particular ventures was successful in both cases, although as I suggested in the previous chapter, less than typical in the French instance. The two examples both demonstrate a view of the body as *tapu* or sacred, in contradistinction to the body as tool,[2] a distinction which can also be drawn in feminist terms, between sacred and 'open-access' bodies. Women's bodies are likewise nominally regarded as inviolable or sacred, but in practice are used in an instrumental fashion.

The Tongan example also suggests a tantalising and powerful analogy between the legal understanding of human tissue and the human genome as *res nullius* and the notion of *terra nullius*, recently developed by Carole Pateman as an extension of her thinking on the sexual contract.[3] Here again, feminist theory provides innovative and informative constructs with which to conceptualise human tissue in the context of the new biotechnologies. Pateman is interested in the ways in which the 'settler contract' with the indigenous inhabitants of colonised lands parallels

---

[1] This venture was a collaboration between the Centre d'Etude du Polymorphisme Humain and the US firm Millennium Pharmaceuticals.

[2] Dominique Memmi, *Les gardiens du corps: dix ans de magistère bioèthique* (Paris, Editions de l'Ecole des Hautes Etudes en Sciences Sociales, 1996), p. 20.

[3] Charles Mills and Carole Pateman, *Contract and Domination* (Cambridge, Polity, 2006).

the sexual contract; both impose civil subordination but justify it by means of the supposedly liberating notion of contract. Just as female bodies are rendered male property by the sexual contract, so are the lands and bodies of indigenous peoples feminised by the settler contract. Although Pateman does not extend her metaphor into bioethics, some scholars in that field have already likened the mapping of the genome to the exploration of a 'wilderness'.[4]

In this chapter I bring these two strands of thought together by positing the parallel between the genome or tissue as *terra nullius* and the way in which the *terra nullius* doctrine has been used to justify civil subordination. As the Kenyan scholar H. W. O. Okoth-Ogendo has written of a similar situation in Africa, 'the vast undocumented African Commons were, at the stroke of a pen, declared *terra nullius*, hence, under civil law principles, automatically vested in the imperial power'.[5] Similarly, one might argue, the courts have been too ready to invoke the doctrine of *res nullius* in regard to human tissue, automatically allowing extensive property rights in donated tissue and DNA to the 'imperial powers' of biotechnology – the firms and researchers who constitute the 'tissue-industrial complex'.

Peoples of the global South are doubly vulnerable to the genetic enclosures: first, because their lands have historically been regarded as open, as *terra nullius*, and secondly because the vestigial law of the colonial power prevents them from claiming a property in their own genomes, because of the doctrine of *res nullius*. (That phenomenon is particularly marked in countries formerly ruled by common law nations such as the United Kingdom, but civil law colonial powers like France likewise lacked any notion of individual property rights in the body.) The body's legal status as *res nullius* has left a vacuum, a sort of legal *terra nullius*, an unregulated domain which mimics the Hobbesian war of all against all. This vulnerability, which is particularly marked in the former colonial countries of the global South, chimes with the feminisation of all bodies in the new biotechnologies.

In examining the Tongan case and other relevant examples involving indigenous peoples, particularly the encounter between Maori and European *pakeha* culture, we see the after-effects of colonialism and its assumption that the lands colonised were *terra nullius*. The resistance to

---

[4] Paul Lauritzen, 'Stem cells, biotechnology and human rights: implications for a posthuman future' (2005) 35(2) *Hastings Center Report* 25–33. Lauritzen does not use the term 'wilderness' critically, however; we need to remember its colonialist overtones. A 'wilderness' is generally only a 'wilderness' to the colonial explorers and occupiers, not to its indigenous peoples.

[5] H. W. O. Okoth-Ogendo, 'The tragic African commons: a century of exploration, suppression and submersion' (2003) 1 *University of Nairobi Law Journal* 107–17, at 110.

colonialism continues to inform the resistance of such indigenous peoples to the 'new enclosures' by Western biotechnology firms. The notion of *terra nullius* is only tenable from an outsider's viewpoint, of course. Neither Maori nor Tongan society was in a state of nature at the time of colonisation; neither was in fact *terra nullius*. Rather, both possessed sophisticated codes and moral systems, but not codes and systems rooted in private ownership. However, our conventional property language does not apply fully to these cultures. This anomaly leads us naturally into a more searching analysis of the 'new enclosures' metaphor which has run like a thread throughout this book from the first paragraph. The genetic commons is actually unlike the agricultural commons of Western European pre-industrial societies in important respects. It will be the task of a section of this chapter to re-examine that metaphor.

Finally, in this chapter I will also explore some of the flexible and sophisticated Maori and Tongan concepts which are now beginning to be applied to human tissue and the human genome by members of those societies. These concepts accord neatly with embodied notions of subjectivity favoured by many feminist thinkers and contrast sharply with prevailing consequentialist and neo-liberal models in Western bioethics. The Tongan and Maori cultures examined in this chapter do not accept the liberal notion of self-ownership, even in the more limited format according to which the individual does not possess all the rights in the property bundle. Here again, there emerges an instructive parallel with much feminist theory, which is likewise alert to the complex effects inherent in embodied identity.

Catherine Waldby has argued that more and more areas of medicine involve tissue transfer and thus produce 'biotechnical fragmentation' of body image – a similar point to my claim in chapter 1 that the boundary between physical self and the outside world is increasingly undermined by modern biotechnology. '[B]iomedically engineered intercorporeality creates new circuits of relationship in ways that are often neither anticipated nor recognized by medical researchers or liberal bioethicists devoted to the defence of an autonomous self.'[6] Tissue, organs, limbs or even faeces taken from another body retain elements of the original person's identity for many recipients, however superstitious that view may appear to many doctors.[7] This way of understanding is actually closely akin to Tongan

---

[6] Catherine Waldby, 'Biomedicine, tissue transfer and intercorporeality' (2002) 3(3) *Feminist Theory* 239–54, at 252.

[7] F. Varela, 'Intimate distances: fragments for a phenomenology of organ transplantation' in E. Thompson (ed.), *Between Ourselves: Second-Person Issues in the Study of Consciousness* (Thorverton, Imprint Academic, 2001); M. Lock, *Twice Dead: Organ Transplants and the Reinvention of Death* (Berkeley, University of California Press, 2002).

and Maori concepts and, coincidentally, to some feminist work on body images.[8] Gail Weiss's concept of intercorporeality, cited by Waldby, draws our attention to the way in which our experience of embodiment emerges from a context of embodied relationships, rather than being developed in isolation.[9] Moira Gatens has likewise directed attention to 'imaginary anatomy', the model of body image developed by the subject in order to make her way in the world.[10] Many other feminist theorists have emphasised the formation of identity through relationship rather than in isolation,[11] although here the focus is specifically on the formation of embodied identity. Likewise, Luce Irigaray presents 'the entire speaking body of the subject' as 'archaeologically structured by an already spoken language'.[12] This view of embodied identity as formed in relationship, too, is consistent with Tongan and Maori concepts, as well as with a Hegelian understanding of the identity of the subject.

In this chapter, then, several different strands of thought, including feminist insights into mutual recognition and bodily identity formation, come together in the context of the beliefs and actions of indigenous peoples from the South Pacific who have resisted the 'new enclosures' on a global scale.

The Tongan and Maori cases

In November 2000, the Australian firm Autogen announced to the Australian media an agreement with the Tongan Ministry of Health, to collect tissue samples for the purpose of genomic research into the causes of diabetes (well-known for its high incidence, about 14 per cent, among the Tongan population).[13] As the press announcement declared, the firm was attracted to the 'unique population resources of the Kingdom of Tonga'. Such relatively homogeneous indigenous populations are

---

[8] Naomi Segal, 'Words, bodies and stone', inaugural lecture delivered at the Institute of Germanic and Romance Studies, University of London, 19 April 2005.

[9] Gail Weiss, *Body Images: Embodiment as Intercorporeality* (London and New York, Routledge, 1999).

[10] Moira Gatens, *Imaginary Bodies: Ethics, Power and Corporeality* (London, Routledge, 1996).

[11] *Property, Women and Politics*, ch. 6; Carol Gilligan, *In a Different Voice: Psychological Theory and Women's Development* (2nd edn, Cambridge, MA, Harvard University Press, 1993).

[12] Luce Irigaray,' L'invisible de la chair' ('The invisible of the flesh'), lecture on Maurice Merleau-Ponty, *Le visible et l'invisible*, in Luce Irigaray, *Ethique de la différence sexuelle* (Paris, Editions de Minuit, 1984), p. 143.

[13] I base my narrative on an account by the Director of the Tonga Human Rights and Democracy Movement, Lopeti Senituli ('They came for sandalwood'). Because the issue in this case was collection of tissue samples, I shall treat this case as dealing primarily with tangible property, although the purpose of the research was genomic analysis, which might also be thought to raise intellectual property issues.

likely to possess an increasing appeal not only in terms of research into the genetic basis of such conditions as diabetes, but also for pharmacogenomic and pharmacogenetic research, which is still in the very early days of learning how to tailor drug regimes on a individualised genetic basis. Randomised clinical trials testing the effects of pharmacogenomic drug regimes may well be cheaper to run on populations possessing a high degree of genetic similarity in both the experimental and control arms, since the required level of statistical significance will probably be available from smaller populations.

Although the Tongan public had not been informed of the initiative before the announcement in the Australian press, Autogen might have expected little resistance. It was offering several sorts of benefits: annual research funding for the Tongan Ministry of Health, royalties to the Tongan government from any commercially successful discoveries, and provision of drugs from such discoveries free of charge to the people of Tonga. However, although the Director of the Tonga Human Rights and Democracy Movement, Lopeti Senituli, had advocated similar benefits for indigenous peoples in a previous instance, when Smith Kline Beecham was pondering a bioprospecting agreement for *plant* samples in Fiji, he was wholly opposed to the Tongan government's agreement with Autogen concerning *human* tissue, despite its apparently lucrative benefits. As Senituli put it:

Existing intellectual property right laws favor those with the technology, the expertise and the capital. All we have is the raw material – our blood. We should not sell our children's blood so cheaply.[14]

It would be easy to dismiss this statement as a political war cry of dubious scientific accuracy. Of course the Tongans were not literally being asked to sell their children's blood. The DNA samples to be taken were renewable tissue in any case, and there was no theft of any individual's genome. But Senituli's position is mirrored in the views of many other peoples of the global South, to whom benefit-sharing smacks of trinket exchange.[15]

[14] Lopeti Senituli, 'They came for sandalwood, now the b . . . s are after our genes!', paper presented at the conference 'Research ethics, Tikanga Maori/indigenous and protocols for working with communities', Wellington, New Zealand, 10–12 June 2004, p. 3.

[15] Lori Andrews and Dorothy Nelkin, *Body Bazaar: The Market for Human Tissue in the Biotechnology Age* (New York, Crown, 2001), p. 79, in a chapter which discusses similar instances, including Tristan da Cunha, the Human Genome Diversity Project and the Hagahai of Papua/New Guinea. An anonymous article in *Nature*, 18 November 2004, describes a parallel attitude among the indigenous peoples of Vancouver Island, who donated blood for research into the genetic causes of rheumatoid arthritis, a disease that is rampant in their tribes. Twenty years later they were incensed to discover that the

The Tongans' primary stated objection to the Autogen proposal was that only individual informed consent was to be sought, in accordance with the dominant ethical model in genetic databanks. 'The Tongan family, the bedrock of Tongan society, would have no say, even though the genetic material donated by individual members would reflect the family's genetic make-up.'[16] They also had highly pragmatic objections: for example, they cannily surmised that Autogen would reap rewards, such as higher share values and provision of venture capital from the pharmaceutical industry, as soon as the agreement was announced, whether or not any therapies were eventually developed. By contrast, 'the promised royalties from any therapeutics and the provision of those therapeutics free of charge to the Tongan people were, we felt, prefaced by a huge "IF"'.[17] In the face of this opposition, Autogen quietly dropped its proposed Tongan DNA databank in 2002, announcing that it would conduct its research in Tasmania instead but then disappearing from view altogether.

If the issue of extended consent could have been solved, and if the benefits of the agreement had been made more secure, would the Tongan opposition have been placated? Senituli says no: ultimately the conflict with Tongan values was simply too great, and the threat from global commodification too vast:

The Tongan people in general still find it inconceivable that some person or Company or Government can own property rights over a human person's body or parts thereof. We speak of the human person as having 'ngeia', which means 'awe-inspiring, inspiring fear or wonder by its size or magnificence'. It also means 'dignity'. When we speak of 'ngeia o te tangata' we are referring to 'the dignity of the human person' derived from the Creator . . . Therefore the human person should not be treated as a commodity, as something that can be exchanged for another, but always as a gift from the Creator.[18]

Again, to dismiss these objections as biologically incorrect – because no individual human being is owned or exchanged as a commodity by a DNA databank – is to miss the point. Global ethics reminds us of the need to understand explanations such as this in their wider cultural context. Just as improved benefits or community consent would not have been sufficient counter-weight to the Tongans' core objections, so correction of 'misperceptions' about the science involved would be insufficient to balance the power of a host of core ethical beliefs in Polynesian cultures. In the closely related Maori culture of Aotearoa/New Zealand, the concept

---

specimens had been used for other research, including a project on the sensitive issue of the spread of lymphotropic viruses by intravenous drug abuse. Leaders of the Nuu-chah-nulth (Nootka) tribe described the research as another example of exploitation of indigenous peoples and demanded the return of the samples.

[16] Senituli, 'They came for sandalwood', p. 3.   [17] *Ibid.* p. 4.   [18] *Ibid.*

of human dignity to which Senituli refers is linked to the core values of *mana tipuna*, prestige and authority drawn from the ancestors; *tapu o te tangata*, the sanctity of the person; *whakapapa*, genealogy; and *mauri*, or life force. (The Maori language also uses the word *ira* for the life principle; it is the closest Maori translation to the word 'gene'.)[19]

As the eminent Maori cultural studies professor Hirini Moko Mead has written, Maori culture views one's personal *tapu* as the most important spiritual attribute of the individual. 'This attribute is inherited from the Maori parent and comes with the genes.'[20] The aim of a good life is to preserve and enhance *tapu*, keeping the self in a steady state of balance. Actions by self or others that take away *tapu* are to be avoided. In the Polynesian context, it might well be thought that allowing others to take away one's genetic material is a violation of *tapu*, resulting in a diminution of the *tapu* available to one's descendants and affronting one's ancestors, who have striven to preserve their own *tapu* as a legacy. The ultimate source of *tapu* is seen as the primeval parent gods Tangi and Papa and their divine children, and the greatest threat to the vitality of the entire Maori people, embodied in this legacy from the earliest parents, is perceived by Maori elders as the assaults of European *pakeha* culture on Maori customs. An earlier anthropological study recorded the powerful statement from one elder 'that the vitality of their race departed with the loss of *tapu*, leaving the people in a defenceless and helpless condition'.[21]

Although learning for its own sake is highly esteemed in Polynesian cultures, research for principally financial gain does not necessarily share the same high value. On the other hand, if it could be known definitely that the proposed research might have lowered the high Tongan rate of diabetes or provided more effective therapies, the value of *tapu* might be displaced from its usual pre-eminent position. The countervailing value of *mauri* or life force could arguably be enhanced, one might think. However, Maori and Polynesian values do not admit of the utilitarian calculus. Even if the benefit to be derived from the research were definite, there would still be qualms about sacrificing even a small part of some individuals' life force in order to benefit others.

Mead discusses a similar reluctance in the instance of xenotransplants. Although it might be thought that Maori values would allow the implantation of a pig's heart valve, for example, in order to save a human, Mead

---

[19] H. M. Mead, *Whakapapa and the Human Gene* (Wellington, Toi Te Taiao/The Bioethics Council of New Zealand, 2004).

[20] H. M. Mead, *Tikanga Maori: Living by Maori Values* (Wellington, Huia Publishers, 2003), p. 45.

[21] E. Best, *The Maori* (Wellington, The Polynesian Society, 1941), vol. 1, p. 39, cited in Mead, *Tikanga Maori*, p. 47.

is in fact unwilling to allow this sacrifice as unproblematic in terms of *mauri*, which pigs too possess. It is the offence against *mauri* as a life force which renders a consequentialist balancing of harms inapplicable – or, to translate into the utilitarian calculus, which requires us to set a value on *mauri* in the abstract, as an ultimate value to be maximised, regardless of where and how it is embodied. In the case of xenotransplantation, Mead argues:

> In the final analysis a *mauri* is sacrificed to save another and this is not an ideal situation. The rationalisation for sacrificing the pig is that we kill it and eat it anyway. But when we eat it we do not call it pig, but rather pork. Eating pork, however, is quite different from using living tissues of a pig to keep us alive . . . Many of us have qualms about employing living pig tissues to repair damaged human parts. Why is this? In the case of pork the pig is killed, prepared, cooked and eaten by us. The *mauri* of the pig is extinguished in the process . . . In contrast, living tissue used to repair human parts continues to live . . . Part of the *mauri* of pigs remain [sic] in human beings as living tissue . . . We doubt that the *mauri* and *tapu* of the pig are in fact completely extinguished, and this is a concern.[22]

In the case of DNA samples taken for the proposed Tongan research on diabetes, there is no cross-species violation of *mauri*; no research subjects are asked to sacrifice their *mauri* for the greater good of the community, or Autogen. I have already suggested, however, that they are being asked to infringe their personal *tapu*, and that a countervailing claim that *mauri* will instead be enhanced for the community as a whole would not be unproblematic. In other instances in bioethics where a Western analyst might employ a consequentialist, balancing mode of reasoning, such as xenotransplants, a Maori analyst is loath to let the benefit to some outweigh harm to the life force in other persons, or indeed any other creatures.

The subtle analysis suggested by Mead distinguishes between certain permissible uses of pigs, including eating pork, because *mauri* has already been extinguished in the pigs and can be enhanced in the humans who use pork as sustenance. In the case of genetic material, however, it is living tissue that is being taken, so that *mauri* is not extinguished. Not only is the taking of such tissue wrong in terms of both *tapu* and *mauri*; even the beneficial employment of Tongan DNA to produce more effective therapies for the Tongan population might be suspect, to the extent that living cell lines are involved. For example, an immortal cell line such as that produced through stem cell therapies would continue to contain the *mauri* of the individual who donated the genetic material, as well as the *mauri* of the woman who donated the enucleated ovum. The mixing

[22] Mead, *Tikanga Maori*, p. 339.

of these individuals' *mauri* with that of the recipient patients might be ethically problematic, even if the *mauri* of the recipient were enhanced.

Maori and other Polynesian values might appear to forbid any 'border crossings', to return to the terminology of property, liability and inalienability. However, there are also aspects of Maori culture concerned with repairing breaches of *tapu* and *mauri*, in effect compensating for border crossings once they have occurred, more in the manner of liability. In the *take* procedure, the starting point for repairing such breaches is to acknowledge that they have occurred and that a wrong has been committed. Had Autogen acknowledged that harm had been done to Tongan values, regardless of the benefits offered, the resultant breakdown of negotiations might not have occurred.

Possibly this seems an impossibly high price to exact of a Western company, particularly because the Polynesian sense of harm does not accept the Kantian excuse of good intentions. 'All offences appear to be offences of strict liability.'[23] It would not be sufficient for Autogen to claim that they intended no harm; once core values such as *ngeia* had been offended, harm had occurred. However, the subsequent process of *utu* or reparation does provide a blueprint for negotiation, in the hope of establishing *ea* or balance between the conflicting viewpoints. Complete value relativism is neither necessary nor desirable: accommodation between indigenous and Western values can in principle be reached, through recognition of the validity of indigenous frameworks. The Bioethics Council of Aotearoa/New Zealand has recently completed a consultative exercise on the use of human genes in other organisms, for example, in which both Maori and *pakeha* values were canvassed – although some Maori critics viewed this exercise as more top-down than bottom-up.[24]

As Mead notes, 'the debates are likely to be contested, and since we are now dealing with global rather than local issues, with believers and non-believers, and with Maori and non-Maori, it is much more difficult to reach agreement'.[25] This pessimism about the possibility of reaching accord between 'indigenous' and Western values is borne out by the

---

[23] J. Patterson, *Maori Values* (Palmerston North, Dunmore Press, 1992), p. 131.

[24] Toi Te Taiao/The Bioethics Council of New Zealand, *Reflections on the Use of Human Genes in Other Organisms: Ethical, Spiritual and Cultural Dimensions* (Wellington, Toi Te Taiao/The Bioethics Council of New Zealand, 2004). For example, one of the anonymous comments made to the Council in the run-up to the consultation was: 'They say they want Maori perspectives, but really they just want us to say yes or no to the questions they've already worked out. They don't realise that really getting Maori views would mean asking different questions.' It is to the credit of the Bioethics Council, however, that this comment is reproduced in the leaflet setting out the consultation exercise and inviting further similar or dissimilar opinions.

[25] Mead, *Tikanga Maori*, p. 341.

Tongan case, and in New Zealand by the rather formulaic hearing given to Maori beliefs during hearings by the Environmental Risk Management Authority (ERMA) over an application by the 'Dolly' firm, PPL Therapeutics, to field-test transgenic sheep in order to produce a cystic fibrosis treatment, human alpha-I-antitrypsin. Taking the position advanced by the Ngati Raukawa tribe's response to the consultation, the Maori advisors to the ERMA recommended that the application should be denied, representing as it did an unacceptable transgression against sacred values. However, the ERMA allowed the application after a 'balancing' test, holding that Maori cultural objections were outweighed by the possibility of relieving cystic fibrosis (which, it should be noted, disproportionately affects those of European descent). We have also seen that Maori values do not admit of this sort of utilitarian balancing; it is therefore rather mystifying that the ERMA denied that it had dismissed Maori objections and that the risks to Maori culture had been adequately considered.[26]

It is also a neo-colonialist error, however, to draw an overly black-and-white picture of the differences between indigenous and Western beliefs, or indeed to categorise those beliefs too rigidly into the very categories 'indigenous' and 'Western'. For patients and donors in the First World, human tissue has also been found in ethnographic surveys to retain elements of 'life force' or of personhood and identity.[27] A Quaker response to the New Zealand transgenic consultation exercise rejected the insertion of human genes in other organisms on grounds that independently echoed Maori beliefs, presenting the gene pool as a collective legacy for which we owe a collective responsibility.[28]

Communal ownership and the 'new enclosures': does the metaphor fit the human genome?

Although private ownership of tools, weapons and adornments was not unknown in the societies we have been examining, items such as fishing nets were joint property in Maori communities. Likewise, land was primarily conceived as a communal possession of the Maori tribe or *iwi*: more locally of the *hapu*, or village, and family group, or *whanua*.[29] Each

[26] M. Durie, '*Mana Tangata*: Culture, Custom and Transgenic Research' in Toi Te Taiao, *Reflections on the Use of Human Genes in Other Organisms*, pp. 20–5.

[27] Waldby, 'Biomedicine, tissue transfer and intercorporeality'.

[28] J. Moxon, 'Human Genes in Other Organisms: Ethical, Spiritual and Cultural Dimensions' in Toi Te Taiao, *Reflections on the Use of Human Genes in Other Organisms*, pp. 6–8.

[29] Makereti (Maggie Papakura), *The Old-Time Maori* (original edn T. K. Penniman (ed.), 1938, republished Auckland, New Women's Classics 1991), p. 34. I am endebted to Samaria Beaton of the Bluff *marae* for providing me with this hard-to-find text, the first example of an anthropological work by a member of the indigenous society under study.

whanua was allotted its own piece of ground, on which to build its dwelling and cooking shed. The largest house in the community, the *wharepuni*, was the property of the community, although the chief had the right to occupy it if he so desired.[30] Agricultural land was held in common by the members of the *hapu* and was worked communally.[31] Rules of *tapu* governed the planting and harvesting of crops, particularly the *kumara* or sweet potato, but these were not property-like rules of entitlement within the *whanua* and *hapu*. Rather, they concerned the gender associations of the crop (in the case of *kumara*, planted and harvested only by men, although weeded by women) and the ceremonies which had to be undergone in order to encourage its life force or *mauri*.

Property-like rules did exist, however, to protect the holdings of the village and family against trespass by outsiders. Each *hapu* had its own fishing ground, whose weirs were marked by carved figures. Trespass on another village's fishing ground was punishable by death.[32] Similarly, trespass by outsiders in the *kainga* or cluster of homes belonging to another *hapu* was forbidden; no outsider could settle in another *kainga*, although he might be welcomed as a guest.[33] Since trespassory prohibitions are a defining perquisite of property systems,[34] it seems correct to call these injunctions property rules. Indeed, the refusal to recognise customary laws concerning use of the commons as true property rules is often criticised by scholars in the developing world, who see it as a form of deliberate blindness which enabled the colonial powers to impose their own property systems, benefiting settlers at the expense of indigenous peoples.[35] Like the doctrine of *terra nullius*, the notion that indigenous peoples had no property rules is neo-colonial.

This combination of shared use within a geographically limited community and trespassory prohibitions against outsiders is typical of communitarian property systems,[36] but it is also radically different from what is generally meant by the genetic commons, where the community in question is often conceived as the entire human race. This disparity suggests that perhaps we have been too ready to accept the metaphor of the 'new enclosures', where, it is alleged, the genetic commons of the human species is at risk from trespass by outsiders. Since those 'outsiders' are

[30] Makareti, *The Old-Time Maori*, p. 289.
[31] *Ibid.* p. 184: 'A European would go to work [on the land] with his family, or even alone, but the Maori never did this. They always worked in companies. Their life was communal, and everything was for the community and not for the individual.'
[32] *Ibid.* p. 245.   [33] *Ibid.* p. 283.
[34] James W. Harris, *Property and Justice* (Oxford, Oxford University Press, 1996), p. 5.
[35] Okoth-Ogenda, 'The tragic African commons', 109.
[36] Harris, *Property and Justice*, p. 102.

also human, the genetic commons would then be nonsense. The concept might still have validity, however, if limited to the genome of a particular ethnic or local community, as in the Tongan instance. However, we have seen that the Tongans were asserting that no one, not even 'insiders', had the right to 'use' the resource of their genome, rejecting the entire notion of 'use' in this instance. Indeed, 'insiders' would have been the first to find the concept of 'use' of their genome or tissue wrongheaded. Presumably, they would not wish to assert a property in it, communitarian or otherwise; the concept of *ngeia* or dignity forbids doing so. So the 'new enclosures' metaphor begins to look doubly strained.

If the Tongan genome is not to be conceived as communal property of the Tongan people, however, then what protection can Tongans seek against illicit use of their genome? We, and they, risk tumbling into the void where human tissue is concerned in the common law; if the Tongan genome, like human tissue, is *res nullius*, no one's thing, because the Tongans are not asserting a claim to it, it seems hopelessly vulnerable to seizure by outsiders. Ironically, we would then be back in the *terra nullius* situation as well, with the Tongans and other indigenous peoples open to neo-colonial exploitation through the biotechnological equivalent of Pateman's 'settler contract'. Whereas indigenous peoples, particularly the Maori and Torres Strait Islanders, have sometimes been successful in using the colonisers' courts to enforce ancestral rights to communal lands against settlement,[37] no similar strategy has yet been applied to the genome. What makes this lack particularly frustrating is that in the Torres Strait case, the indigenous peoples were not required to prove that they viewed their relationship to the land as one of ownership.[38] Even if the Tongans likewise eschewed a property model of their genome, by analogy they might still profit from that model, because a court might well uphold such a claim.

In important respects the genome does differ from land, of course. We have seen over and over again that the common law does not regard bodily tissue, including DNA, as property; people cannot own their bodies in the same way that they can own land. Nevertheless the parallel still holds, because within the common law 'outsiders' can still be barred from trespassing on something which is a communal possession, even

---

[37] In *Mabo v. State of Queensland (No. 2)* [1982] 175 CLR 1, the High Court of Australia upheld the 'native title' of the Meriam people in the Torres Strait. The Treaty of Waitangi tribunal in New Zealand has dealt with similar claims, for example, under the recent Foreshore and Seabeds Legislation. The Bastion Point *marae* in Auckland was successful, after a long struggle, in upholding their land rights against seizure of their ancestral burial grounds.

[38] Harris, *Property and Justice*, p. 104.

if the community in question does not itself view that thing – land or genome – as a possession in a property framework. What is at issue here is the prohibitions and duties laid upon outsiders, not the indigenous people's own construction of either land or genome. In the Torres Strait case, it was held that the common law recognised a 'special defeasible interest' which the courts ought in justice to uphold. The proprietary interest of the Islanders in their land was defined explicitly but negatively by comparison with normal private property, but nevertheless was afforded trespassory protection.

The court also held that the Torres Strait people's native title could be surrendered to no other body than the Crown. If we consider the parallel with the Tongan genome, arguably their 'native title' in their own genome could only be surrendered to a public body, not to a private firm like Autogen. What the Tongans really disliked, as Senituli's statement reveals, was the commodification of that which should be beyond price, *ngeia*. Perhaps common state 'ownership' or management would alleviate some of that hostility: a non-market mechanism such as a state agency[39] or a charitable biotrust of the sort advocated in chapter 6.

Let us return now to the question of whether the 'new enclosures' is an appropriate metaphor for invasion of the 'genetic commons' and, by extension, for unauthorised takings of human tissue. Perhaps the appropriate comparison is not *communitarian* property, such as the Maori held in fishing rights and land, but rather *common* property.[40] Whereas in the Maori case there were trespassory protections against outsiders, but no other hallmarks of property and no conventional Western concept of ownership, in the case of common property there is a definite owner of the resource, such as a public authority or state agency. That agency is empowered to decide who has access to the property and under what conditions: for example, the general public will typically be allowed to use a public park at certain times of day and subject to rules preventing nuisance. This is closer to the meaning of 'commons', where uses by villagers were subject to rules concerning overgrazing and other abuses, regulated through a local court and upheld against other commoners, not only against outsiders in the manner of trespassory protections.[41]

---

[39] See e.g., Charlotte H. Harrison, 'Neither Moore nor the market' (2002) 28 *American Journal of Law and Medicine* 77–104; and G. Calabresi and A. D. Melamed, 'Property rules, liability rules and inalienability: one view of the cathedral' (1972) 85 *Harvard Law Review* 1089–1128.

[40] This distinction is made by Harris, in *Property and Justice*, p. 109.

[41] For example, in my own village, Beckley in Oxfordshire, rules governing use of the common lands of Otmoor were adjudicated by a local court serving 'the seven towns' of Otmoor. Owners who exceeded their quota for grazing rights could have surplus animals impounded, and other restraints also applied to regulate abuses. By a fascinating historical quirk, Makereti (n. 29 above) also once lived on Otmoor.

These protections are more akin to the privileges, duties and rights in a Hohfeldian model of property than is the Maori example, and it also becomes easier to see how they map against the notion of the 'genetic commons'. We are all 'genetic commoners'; we all hold rights, albeit probably not full-blown property rights, in the human genome. The protections against other 'commoners' which we require might include protections against commodification of the genome. We do not need to see other human beings as 'outsiders' to use the notion of the commons in this sense.[42]

That dispels one problem with the notion of the 'genetic commons' but raises another. We have no comparable authority to a state agency to police the genetic commons, which raises not only practical problems but also theoretical ones related to that old and by now familiar difficulty, the lack of a legal concept of property in the body. Where no one is registered as the owner of common land, any local authority in whose region the land is partially or wholly situated may take steps to protect the land against unlawful interference.[43] There is no comparable authority to protect the genetic commons at a global level, although arguably the state can fulfil that role at the national level. How successfully the state does in fact do so can be questioned in both the Tongan and the Icelandic genetic database cases. However, not even the state can, strictly speaking, be registered as the owner of the national genetic commons since, broadly speaking, no one can own human DNA or tissue in either civil or common law.

The metaphors of the commons and the enclosures have given rise to useful and sustained analysis, sometimes at a very high analytical level: for example, in Seana Valentine Shiffrin's sophisticated reversal of the neo-liberal arguments for patenting the genome.[44] Shiffrin has observed that the Lockean justification for the trespass on the commons entailed by any act of appropriation cannot be applied to intellectual property. Locke's initial presumption, she argues, is in favour of common property on the grounds of common equality:

Common ownership, for Locke, is not, I think, best seen as a mere starting point or an easily overturned default rule. It is also a concrete expression of the equal standing of, and the community relationship between, all people. Important resources may not be monopolized without good reason. They should, if possible, be available to all for use freely.[45]

---

[42] Carol Rose uses a similar notion of the commons as 'inherently public property' in her article 'The comedy of the commons: customs, commerce and inherently public property' (1986) 53 *University of Chicago Law Review* 742.

[43] Commons Registration Act 1965, s 9.

[44] Seana Valentine Shiffrin, 'Lockean arguments for private intellectual property' in Stephen R. Munzer (ed.), *New Essays in the Legal and Political Theory of Property* (Cambridge, Cambridge University Press, 2002), pp. 138–67.

[45] *Ibid.* p. 167.

That presumption can only be overturned when the nature of the good requires it. In the case of tangible property, such as an apple, an individual can only enjoy the benefits of the object by consuming it *as* an individual. Subject to the limitations of 'enough and as good' left for others and no wastage, Locke views that trespass on the commons not merely as permissible but as consistent with the will of God. 'For real property, private appropriation proceeds because it is necessary for proper and full use to be made of the commons.'[46]

In the case of intangible property, Shiffrin has perceptively noted, that justification does not hold. Even the Lockean possessive individual can enjoy the benefits of intellectual property better, in fact, if that property is held in common. The 'tragedy of the commons', whereby there is no incentive not to overuse a common resource, and therefore no bar to its degradation, simply does not apply in the case of the genome.[47] Otherwise, to apply Shiffrin's argument to biotechnology, holders of monopoly rights can and frequently do block access to researchers, as in the case of the patent taken out by Myriad Genetics on two genes implicated in some breast cancers, or to beneficial drugs such as anti-retrovirals, in the example of the South African litigation by pharmaceutical firms against the production and distribution of generic anti-retrovirals there.[48] Thus, the metaphors of enclosure and commons have given rise to productive further comparisons and analysis – one mark of a good theoretical construct.

I am not sure how much it matters that the enclosure metaphor does not fit the genome quite as well as it does land. Boyle's original use of the metaphor was directed at 'the relentless power of market logic to migrate to new areas, disrupting traditional social relationships, views of the self, and even the relationship of human beings to the environment.'[49] That seems to apply perfectly well to the Tongan and Maori cases, even if

---

[46] *Ibid.* p. 156.

[47] H. W. O. Okoth-Ogendo, in 'The tragic African commons: a century of exploration, suppression and submersion' (2003) 1 *University of Nairobi Law Journal* 107–17, questions whether it ever applied in the case of the African commons in land. Because the colonial authorities were eager to apply the doctrine of *terra nullius* in order to justify their seizure of communal lands, they effectively translated the 'tragedy of the commons' notion into public policy, claiming that private ownership was the only way to prevent degradation of the lands. This, according to Okoth-Ogendo, ignored the careful management of the commons in customary law.

[48] Alyna C. Smith, 'Intellectual property rights and the right to health: considering the case of access to medicines' in Christian Lenk, Nils Hoppe and Roberto Andorno (eds.), *Ethics and Law of Intellectual Property: Current Problems in Politics, Science and Technology* (Aldershot, Ashgate, 2006), ch. 3.

[49] James Boyle, 'Fencing off ideas: enclosure and the disappearance of the public domain', Interactivist Info Exchange, available at http://slash.autonomedia.org/analysis, p. 4. Boyle acknowledges that there are crucial differences between the 'commons of the

the metaphor is a little ragged at the edges. In other respects, too, the simile fits better. The defenders of land enclosures argued that enclosure avoided the 'tragedy of the commons' by eliminating incentives for overuse and transferring inefficiently managed common land into single ownership. Similarly, the advocates of new biotechnologies propound efficiency arguments about incentives for investment and long-term benefits for the entire population. These arguments have figured weightily in such decisions as *Moore* and continue to be used frequently in other contexts, including genomic research of the Tongan variety. As Boyle characterises these claims:

To the question 'should there be patents over human genes?' the answer will be 'private property saves lives'. Only by extending the reach of property right can the state guarantee the investment of time, ingenuity and capital necessary to produce new drugs and gene therapies. Private-property rights are a necessary incentive to research.[50]

The original enclosures, however, actually resulted in gross mismanagement in many cases, so that the efficiency argument is disproved. In the northwest Highlands, for example, enclosures for sheep-farming not only dispossessed crofters, but also nearly destroyed the Gaelic language and left large areas radically underpopulated to this day. Sheep-farming did not even prove economical, so that many large holdings were converted to deer parks for shooting purposes. When those in turn fell out of fashion, deer bred too rapidly, with the result that it is now being debated whether the grey wolf should be reintroduced to the Highlands. In the Scottish enclosures, overturning traditional rights of commons resulted in

mind' – intellectual property – and the original enclosure movement over tangible property in land, for example in non-rivalrousness, but he does not mention the differences I have drawn out between property in tissue or the genome and property in land. That omission gives the mistaken impression that the crucial difference is between tangible and intangible, but I have suggested that the metaphor even has its deficiencies in terms of tangible property in tissue, including DNA. Indeed, at one point Boyle suggests that genetic sequences, like MP3 files and photographic images, are inherently non-rivalrous (p. 12); that, however, was not the Tongans' view.

50 Boyle, 'Fencing off ideas', 7. For articles discussing the historical commons system, see A. Yelling (ed.), *Common Field and Enclosure in England, 1450–1850* (Hamden, CT, Archon Books, 1977). For other arguments concerning the applicability of the commons model to intellectual property, see, *inter alia*, A. C. Dawson, 'The intellectual commons: a rationale for regulation' (1998) 16(3) *Prometheus* 275–89; The Ecologist, *Whose Common Future? Reclaiming the Commons* (Philadelphia, New Society Publishers, 1998); Lawrence Lessing, *The Future of Ideas: the Fate of the Commons in a Connected World* (New York, Random House, 2001); Ossorio, 'Common heritage arguments against patenting human DNA' in A. Chapman (ed.), *Perspectives on Gene Patenting: Religion, Science and Industry in Dialogue* (Washington, DC, American Association for the Advancement of Science, 1999), pp. 89–108; and Vandana Shiva, *Biopiracy: The Plunder of Nature and Knowledge* (Boston, South End Press, 1997).

what has been called elsewhere 'the tragedy of the anti-commons'.[51] The premiss of the 'tragedy of the commons'[52] holds that common or communitarian property encourages overuse and inefficiency, to everyone's eventual loss. Conversely, underuse of a monopolised resource typifies the 'tragedy of the anti-commons', both in land use and potentially in genetic research, where one patent-holder may block valuable research by others. The argument from potential benefits cuts both ways, in part because the tragedy of the commons concerns the naturally scarce resource of land. Information, including genetic profiles, and some forms of biotechnological tangible property, such as easily reproduced cell lines, are not scarce; these goods are naturally non-rivalrous, capable of being used by many individuals without being used up. Where an artificially imposed scarcity is imposed through patents, the tragedy of the anti-commons ensues.

Likewise, we have yet to see the much-touted benefits of stem cell research, genetic therapy and many other new biotechnologies.[53] That is not to say that no benefits will materialise, rather that it is not yet certain either that benefits will definitely result or that no benefits will definitely result. Utilitarian arguments, extolling the welfare and efficiency benefits of the biotechnologies in which private market developers seek to extend property rights in tissue and genomes, are vulnerable to moral luck considerations because those benefits are uncertain. As I have argued elsewhere,[54] luck in outcomes radically undermines utilitarianism, whether we view the agent as responsible for the actual or the potential consequences of her actions. Where the probability of an outcome is less than 1.00, or total certainty, it is obviously ill-advised to rely on the certainty of that outcome as a justification for one's actions. Because utilitarianism does rely on the benefits of consequences, rather than the purity of the will in a Kantian framework, utilitarian arguments are open to the moral luck paradox. That, in brief, is the tension between holding people responsible for their actions according to how the actions turn out, and also maintaining that people are not responsible for outcomes beyond their control. How the new biotechnologies will turn out is not fully within anyone's control, precisely because they are new and full of imponderables.

---

[51] M. Heller and R. Eisenberg, 'Can patents deter biomedical research?' (280) *Science* 698–701.

[52] Garrett Hardin, 'The tragedy of the commons' (1968) 162 *Science* 124.

[53] Roger Highfield, 'Have we been oversold the stem cell dream?', *Daily Telegraph*, 29 June 2005.

[54] Donna Dickenson, *Moral Luck in Medical Ethics and Practical Politics* (Aldershot, Avebury, 1991) and *Risk and Luck in Medical Ethics* (Cambridge, Polity Press, 2003), ch. 3.

9   Afterword

> For if the body is a thing among things, it is so in a stronger and deeper sense than they.[1]

> The strangeness of the world itself . . . is in one way or another always presented to us through the strangeness of the flesh.[2]

I have argued throughout this book that much disquiet at the new biotechnological enclosures of the body derives from the fear that bodies are being objectified, commodified, and thus also feminised. In the last chapter I also suggested some deficiencies in the enclosure metaphor itself. Here is another one: the body is not a thing like land, even though land is not merely a thing either, particularly not to indigenous peoples such as the Maori. Land carries with it a set of connotations, rules and affections, none of which typify an object of ownership, if ownership is primarily conceived as the right to do whatever one wants with one's possessions.[3] Particularly because indigenous peoples were themselves treated as something less than full subjects by their colonisers, colonised peoples rarely view their land merely as a thing among things, or as the *terra nullius* of the occupying power.

True, I have drawn a parallel between *terra nullius* and *res nullius*. Yet the body is still not an object in the same way that land is an object, because we are embodied subjects, not 'enlanded' subjects. Consciousness itself is embodied, as Merleau-Ponty argues, and the body the primary locus of intentionality.[4] Baud's strategy of treating the body merely as an object among objects fails to capture the strangeness, strength and depth of the ways in which the body both does and does not constitute a thing.

---

[1] Maurice Merleau-Ponty, *The Visible and the Invisible* (Evanston, IL, Northwestern University Press, 1968), p. 137.

[2] Paul Ricœur, *Réflexion faite: autobiographie intellectuelle* (Paris, Editions Esprit, 1995), p. 106.

[3] James W. Harris, *Property and Justice* (Oxford, Oxford University Press, 1996).

[4] Iris Marion Young, *On Female Body Experience: 'Throwing like a Girl' and Other Essays* (Oxford, Oxford University Press, 2005), p. 7.

When genes are patented, ova are 'harvested' or cord blood is 'banked', that strangeness is ignored. Camouflaged only by the fig-leaf of the 'gift relationship', human tissue is increasingly treated merely as the source of free material for commercial use.[5] Even the bodies of the rich world's citizens may be appropriated in this fashion, as in the case of Alistair Cooke's bones. Insufficiently protected in both civil and common law systems, our bodies – 'our bodies, our selves', in the famous slogan from the woman's movement – are increasingly open to all comers.

On the other hand, modern biotechnology reconstructs the relationship between the body and the outside world so radically that the body can no longer be taken as a mere biological 'given'. That essentialist assumption has been a source of profound dissatisfaction to much feminist theory. Culturally dominant conceptions of the body, as remaining the same in whatever the historical period or culture it is situated, have even been accepted uncritically by some feminists themselves.[6] But the idea that the body has a fixed character, separate from its surroundings, is increasingly untenable when external objects such as pacemakers can be incorporated into the body and bodily tissues can become external objects such as biobank samples. If bioethics and feminist theory can engage in dialogue about these developments, as I have tried to make them do throughout this book, we can use the multiple occasions presented by new biotechnological developments to reconceptualise the question with which I opened the first chapter and to which I now return at the end of the book: whether the body is merely a thing, whether it is nearer to person or object.

Feminists or not, we all need to jettison the old metaphors about bodies as merely things to be appropriated or, particularly in the case of women's bodies, as empty receptacles to be filled. Unfortunately, treatment of the new biotechnologies in the popular media and academic literature alike has actually reinforced those tired old oversimplifications. When the crucial necessity of enucleated ova in the stem cell technologies is ignored, or when umbilical cord blood is seen as merely a waste product, components from female bodies are being treated as things among things, despite the strangeness, strength and depth of the body's nature. Denied credit for their agency and intentionality in what their bodies do and produce, as in the laborious processes involved in the donation of ova or the additional risk and effort to produce cord blood, women and their

---

[5] Catherine Waldby and Robert Mitchell, *Tissue Economies: Blood, Organs and Cell Lines in Late Capitalism* (Durham, NC, Clarendon Press, 1988), p. 24.

[6] Moira Gatens, *Imaginary Bodies: Ethics, Power and Corporeality* (London, Routledge, 1996), p. 49.

bodies are reduced in new ways to the old ascription, of being something less than full and genuine subjects.

Just as the passengers on the train in Hitchcock's film deny that anything amiss has occurred, even though Miss Froy has palpably disappeared,[7] so has too much bioethical analysis simply ignored the way in which 'the lady vanishes' in the stem cell technologies. Instead, most commentators have blindly and blithely accepted the myth of stem cells as bypassing women's central involvement in creating new life, even though stem cell technologies depend crucially on that most symbolically female tissue, eggs. The evangelical fervour surrounding the stem cell technologies derives from the old patriarchal myth of autogenesis, of the way in which a master cell reinscribes patriarchal power.[8]

Or perhaps that is an overstatement? Yet the myth of autogenesis and eternal resurrection through the stem cell technologies is promulgated by powerful interests, and it is to power that we must look to break through the impasse about whether the body is more akin to a subject or an object. As Moira Gatens has written, following Michel Foucault, 'Power differentially *constitutes* particular kinds of body and empowers them to perform particular kinds of task, thus constructing specific kinds of subject.'[9]

I have argued throughout this book that when the power of modern biotechnology reconstitutes bodies, it makes them all the more like women's bodies and thus less like subjects. But this process has become so extreme that it can no longer be ignored, particularly where it affects men's bodies as well, as in the cases of patenting and biobanking. That is in fact a good thing, because it compels us to take account of objectification and commodification, and to resist them.

---

[7] My thanks to Marli Huijer for helping me to explore the full meaning of this metaphor.

[8] Ruth Quiney, 'Autogenesis and the absent mother: cultural fantasies of maternal space and posthuman reproduction', paper delivered at the Open Forum on 'Posthuman bodies', Birkbeck, University of London, 18 March 2006.

[9] Gatens, *Imaginary Bodies*, p. 66, original emphasis.

Bibliography

Abouzahr, C., 'Antepartum and postpartum haemorrhage' in C. J. L. Murray and A. D. Lopez (eds.), *Health Dimensions of Sex and Reproduction* (Cambridge, MA, Harvard University Press, 1998), pp. 172–4

American College of Obstetricians and Gynecologists, *Opinion Number 183, Routine Storage of Umbilical Cord Blood for Potential Future Transplantation* (Washington, DC, ACOG, 1997)

Anderson, Elizabeth, 'Is women's labor a commodity?' (1990) 19 *Philosophy and Public Affairs* 71–92

Value in Ethics and Economics (Cambridge, MA, Harvard University Press, 1993)

Andorno, Roberto, 'Population genetic databases: a new challenge to human rights' in Christian Lenk, Nils Hoppe and Roberto Andorno (eds.), *Ethics and Law of Intellectual Property: Current Problems in Politics, Science and Technology* (Aldershot, Ashgate, 2006), ch. 2

Andrews, Lori B., 'Control and compensation: laws regulating extracorporeal generative materials' (1989) 14 *Journal of Medicine and Philosophy* 541–60

'Genes and patent policy: rethinking intellectual property rights' (2002) 3 *Nature Reviews Genetics* 803–8

'Harnessing the benefits of biobanks' (2005) 33 *Journal of Law, Medicine and Ethics* 1

'Shared patenting experiences: the role of patients', paper presented at the fifth workshop of the EC PropEur project, Bilbao, December 2005

Andrieu, Bernard, 'La santé biotechnologique du corps-sujet' (2004) 3 *Revue philosophique* 339–44

Annas, George J., 'Waste and longing: the legal status of placental blood banking' (1999) 340 *New England Journal of Medicine* 1521–4

Arendt, Hannah, *The Human Condition* (2nd edn, Chicago, University of Chicago Press, 1998)

Aristotle, *Politics* (Benjamin Jowett (tr.)) in *The Basic Works of Aristotle* (Richard McKeon (ed.), New York, Random House, 1941), pp. 1127–1324

The Generation of Animals (Arthur Platt (tr.)) in *The Basic Works of Aristotle* (Richard McKeon (ed.), New York, Random House, 1941), pp. 665–88

Armitage, S., Warwick, R., Fehily, D., Navarrete, C. and Contreras, M., 'Cord blood banking in London: the first 1000 collections' (1999) 24 *Bone Marrow Transplant* 139–45

Arneson, Richard, 'Lockean self-ownership: towards a demolition' (1991) 39
    Political Studies 54
'Commodification and commercial surrogacy' (1992) 21(2) *Philosophy and
    Public Affairs* 132–64
Attas, Daniel, 'Freedom and self-ownership' (2000) 26 *Social Theory and Practice*
    1–23
Aubry, C. M. and Rau, F. F., *Cours de droit civil français* (Brussels, Méline, Cans,
    1850)
Australian Law Reform Commission, *Genes and Ingenuity: Gene Patenting and
    Human Health*, report number 99, available at www.austlii.edu.au/other/alrc/
    publications/reports/99/01.html, accessed 8 September 2004
Ball, Nan T., 'The reemergence of Enlightenment ideas in the 1994 French
    bioethics debates' (2000) 50 *Duke Law Journal* 545–87
Barker, Juliet N. and Wagner, John E., 'Umbilical-cord blood transplantation for
    the treatment of cancer' (2003) 3 *Nature Reviews Cancer* 526–32
Barker, J. N., Weisdorf, D. J., DeFor, T. E., *et al.*, 'Rapid and complete donor
    chimerism in adult recipients of unrelated donor umbilical cord blood trans-
    plantation after reduced-intensity conditioning' (2003) 102 *Blood* 1915–19
Barnett, Antony and Smith, Helen, 'Cruel cost of the human egg trade', *Observer*,
    30 April 2006, pp. 6–7
Bartolini, Francesco, Battaglia, Manuela, De Iulio, Cinzia and Sirchia, Girolano,
    'Response' (1995) 86(12) *Blood* 4900
Bartolini, Francesco, Battaglia, M., De Julio, C., Sirchia, G. and Rosti, L., 'Pla-
    cental blood collection: effects on newborns' (1995) 85 *Blood* 3361–2
Bateman, Simone, 'La nature fait-elle (encore) bien les choses?' ('Does nature
    (still) know best?') in Patrick Pharo (ed.), *L'homme et le vivant: sciences de
    l'homme et sciences de la vie* (Paris, Presses Universitaires de France, 2004)
    pp. 391–404
    (as Simone Bateman Novaes) *Les passeurs de gamètes* (Nancy, Presses Univer-
    sitaires de Nancy, 1994)
Battersby, Christine, *The Phenomenal Woman: Feminist Metaphysics and the Patterns
    of Identity* (Cambridge, Polity Press, 1997)
Baud, Jean-Pierre, *L'affaire de la main volée: une histoire juridique du corps* (Paris,
    Editions du Seuil, 1993)
Beauchamp, Tom L. and Childress, James F., *Principles of Biomedical Ethics* (3rd
    edn, New York and Oxford, Oxford University Press, 1989)
Bellivier, Florence and Noiville, Christine, 'The commercialisation of human
    biomaterials: what are the rights of donors of biological materials?', paper
    presented at seminar at Faculté de Droit, Université de Paris-I, October 2004
'La circulation du vivant humain: modèle de la propriété ou du contrat?', paper
    presented at seminar at Faculté de Droit, Université de Paris-I, October 2004
Berg, Jessica W., 'Risky business: evaluating oocyte donation' (2001) 1(4)
    American Journal of Bioethics 18–19
Bertomeu, Maria Julia and Sommer, Susanna E., 'Patents on genetic material: a
    new originary accumulation' in Rosemarie Tong, Anne Donchin and Susan
    Dodds (eds.), *Linking Visions: Feminist Bioethics, Human Rights and ther Devel-
    oping World* (Lanham, MD, Rowman and Littlefield, 2004), pp. 183–202

Best, E., *The Maori* (Wellington, The Polynesian Society, 1941), vol. 1

Beyleveld, Derek and Brownsword, Roger, 'Patenting human genes: legality, morality and human rights' in J. W. Harris (ed.), *Property Problems: From Genes to Pension Funds* (London, Kluwer Law International, 1997), pp. 9–24

Birke, Lynda, *Feminism and the Biological Body* (Edinburgh, University of Edinburgh Press, 1999)

Bjorkmann, B. and Hansson, B. O., 'Bodily rights and property rights' (2006) 32 *Journal of Medical Ethics* 209–14

Boggio, Andrea, 'Charitable trusts and human research genetic databases: the way forward?' (2005) 1(2) *Genomics, Society and Policy* 41–9

Bok, H., Schill, K. E. and Faden, R., 'Justice, ethnicity and stem-cell banks' (2004) 364 *Lancet* 118–21

Bosely, Sarah, 'Doctors' concern over MS clinic', *Guardian*, 20 March 2006, p. 3

Bostyn, S. J. R., 'One patent a day keeps the doctor away? Patenting human genetic information and health care' (2000) 7 *European Journal of Health Law* 229–64

Bovenberg, Jasper A., 'Towards an international system of ethics and governance for biobanks: a "special status" for genetic data?' (2005) 15(4) *Critical Public Health* 369–83

Boyle, James, 'The second enclosure movement and the construction of the public domain' (2003) 66 *Law and Contemporary Problems* 33–74

'Fencing off ideas: enclosure and the disappearance of the public domain', Interactivist Info Exchange, available at http://slash.autonomedia. org/analysis, accessed 10 September 2004, p. 5

Boyle, Robert J. and Savulescu, Julian, 'Ethics of using preimplantation genetic diagnosis to select a stem cell donor for an existing person' (2001) 323 *British Medical Journal* 1240–3

Brace, Laura, *The Politics of Property: Labour, Freedom and Belonging* (Edinburgh, Edinburgh University Press, 2004)

Braidotti, Rosi, *Nomadic Subjects: Embodiment and Sexual Difference in Contemporary Feminist Theory* (New York, Columbia University Press, 1994)

Braverman, Andrea M., 'Exploring ovum donors' motivations and needs' (2001) 1(4) *American Journal of Bioethics* 16–17

Brenkert, George, 'Self-ownership, freedom and autonomy' (1998) 2 *Journal of Ethics* 27–55

Brownsword, Roger, 'Biobank governance – business as usual?', paper presented at the fourth workshop of the EC PropEur project, Tuebingen, 20 January 2005

'Biobank governance: property, privacy and consent' in Christian Lenk, Nils Hoppe and Roberto Andorno (eds.), *Ethics and Law of Intellectual Property: Current Problems in Politics, Science and Technology* (Aldershot, Ashgate, 2006), ch. 5

Burgio, G. R., Gluckman, Eliane and Locatelli, Franco, 'Ethical reappraisal of 15 years of cord-blood transplantation' (2003) 361 *Lancet* 250–2

Burgio, G. R. and Locatelli, F., 'Transplant of bone marrow and cord blood hematopoietic stem cells in pediatric practice, revisited according to the fundamental principles of bioethics' (1997) 19 *Bone Marrow Transplant* 1163–8

Butler, Judith, *Subjects of Desire: Hegelian Reflections on Twentieth-Century France* (New York, Columbia University Press, 1987)

Calabresi, G. and Melamed, A. D., 'Property rules, liability rules and inalienability: one view of the cathedral' (1972) 85 *Harvard Law Review* 1089–1128

Canadian Biotechnology Advisory Committee, *Patenting of Higher Life Forms and Related Issues: Report to the Government of Canada Biotechnology Ministerial Coordinating Committee* (Ottawa, Canadian Biotechnology Advisory Committee, 2002)

Canadian Royal Commission on New Reproductive Technologies, *Proceed with Care: Final Report of the Commission on New Reproductive Technologies* (Ottawa, Minister of Government Services Canada, 1993)

Carvel, John, 'With love at Christmas – a set of stem cells', *Guardian*, 6 December 2005, p. 7

Cassier, Maurice, 'Brevets et èthique: les controversies sur la brevetabilité des gênes humains' (2002) 56 *Revue française des affaires sociales* 235–59

Caulfield, Timothy, Gold, E. Richard and Cho, Mildred K., 'Patenting human genetic material: refocusing the debate' (2000) 1 *Nature Reviews Genetics* 227–31

Chadwick, Ruth, 'The Icelandic data base: do modern times need modern sagas?' (1999) 319 *British Medical Journal* 441–4

'Are genes us? Gene therapy and personal identity' in G. K. Becker, *The Moral Status of Persons* (Amsterdam, Rodopi, 2000), pp. 183–94

Christman, John, *The Myth of Property: Toward an Egalitarian Theory of Ownership* (Oxford, Oxford University Press, 1994)

Claeys, Alain, *Rapport sur les conséquences des modes d'appropriation du vivant sur les plans économique, juridique et éthique, Troisième partie*, report number 1487 (Paris, Office Parlementaire d'Evaluation des Choix Scientifiques et Technologiques, Assemblée Nationale, available at www.assemblee-nationale.fre/12/oecst/il1487.asp, accessed 23 September 2004

Cohen, G. A., *Self-Ownership, Freedom and Equality* (Cambridge, Cambridge University Press, 1995)

Coles, David, 'The European Union strategy on biotechnology, after the 2005 EC report', paper presented at the seventh workshop of the EC PropEur project, Paris, 6 May 2006

Comité Consultatif National d'Ethique (CCNE), *Opinion Number 1: On Sampling of Dead Human Embryonic and Foetal Tissue for Therapeutic, Diagnostic and Scientific Purposes* (22 May 1984), available at www.ccne-ethique.fr/english/avis/a_001.htm

Opinion Number 21: That the Human Body should not be Used for Commercial Purposes (13 December 1990)

Opinion Number 37: That the Human Genome should not be Used for Commercial Purposes (2 December 1991)

Opinion Number 64: L'avant-projet de loi portant transposition, dans le code de la propriété intellectuelle de la directive 98/44/CR du parlement Européen et du Conseil en date du 6 juillet 1998, relative à la protection juridique des inventions biotechnologiques (Paris, CCNE, 2000)

Opinion Number 70: Consentement en faveur d'un tiers (Paris, CCNE, 2001)

Opinion Number 74: Umbilical cord blood banks for autologous use or for research (Paris, CCNE, 2002)

Comité Consultatif National d'Ethique (CCNE) and Nationaler Ethikrat (German National Ethics Council), *Opinion No. 77: Ethical Problems Raised by the Collected Biological Material and Associated Information Data: 'Biobanks', 'Biolibraries'* (Paris, CCNE, 20 March 2003)

Commission on Intellectual Property Rights, *Integrating Intellectual Property Rights and Development Policy* (London, Department for International Development, 2002)

Connolly, William E., *Political Theory and Modernity* (Oxford, Blackwell, 1988)

Cornish, W. R., Llewelyn, M. and Adcock, M., *Intellectual Property Rights (IPRs) and Genetics: A Study into the Impact and Management of Intellectual Property Rights within the Healthcare Sector* (Cambridge, Cambridge Genetic Knowledge Park, July 2003)

Crignon-de Oliveira, Claire and Gaille-Nikodimov, Marie, *A qui appartient le corps humain? Médecine, politique et droit* (Paris, Les Belles Lettres, 2004)

Daar, Judith F., 'Regulating the fiction of informed consent in ART medicine' (2001) 1(4) *American Journal of Bioethics* 19–20

Danish Council on Ethics, *Patenting Human Genes* (Copenhagen, Danish Council on Ethics, 1994)

Davidoff, Leonore, 'The rationalisation of housework' in L. Davidoff, *Worlds Between: Historical Perspectives on Gender and Class* (Cambridge, Polity Press, 1995)

Dawson, A. C., 'The intellectual commons: a rationale for regulation' (1998) 16(3) *Prometheus* 275–89

De Beauvoir, Simone, *Le deuxième sexe* (Paris, Gallimard, 1986)

Delavigne, A. and Rozenberg, S., 'Epidemiology and prevention of ovarian hyperstimulation syndrome (OHSS): A review' (2002) 8 *Human Reproduction Update* 559–77

Delphy, Christine, *Close to Home: A Materialist Analysis of Women's Oppression* (D. Leonard (tr. and ed.), London, Hutchinson, in association with the Explorations in Feminism Collective, 1984)

Department of Health (UK), *Human Bodies, Human Choices: The Law on Human Organs and Tissue in England and Wales* (London, DOH, 2002)

Devalder, K., 'Preimplantation HLA typing: having children to save our loved ones' (2005) 31 *Journal of Medical Ethics* 582–6

Dickenson, Donna L., *Moral Luck in Medical Ethics and Practical Politics* (Aldershot, Avebury, 1991)

Property, Women and Politics (Cambridge, Polity Press, 1997)

'Procuring gametes for research and therapy: the case for unisex altruism' (1997) 23 *Journal of Medical Ethics* 93–5

'Property and women's alienation from their own reproductive labour' (2001) 15(3) *Bioethics* 203–17

'Commodification of human tissue: implications for feminist and development ethics' (2002) 2(1) *Developing World Bioethics* 55–63

Risk and Luck in Medical Ethics (Cambridge, Polity Press, 2003)

'Genetic research and the economic paradigm' ('Einwilligung, Kommodifizierung und Vortelsausgleich in der Genforschung') in L. Honnefelder, *et al.* (eds.), *Das Genetische Wissen und die Zukunft des Menschen* (Berlin, De Gruyter, 2003), pp. 139–51

'The threatened trade in human ova' (2004) 5(2) *Nature Reviews Genetics* 167

'Patently paradoxical? Public order and genetic patents' (2004) 5 *Nature Reviews Genetics* 86

'Human tissue and global ethics' (2005) 1(1) *Genomics, Society and Policy* 41–53

Dickenson, Donna L. and Vineis, Paolo, 'Evidence-based medicine and quality of care' (2002) 10(3) *Health Care Analysis* 243–59

Dienst, Paul van and Savulescu, Julian, 'For and against: no consent should be needed for using leftover body material for scientific purposes' (2002) 325 *British Medical Journal* 648–51

Dodds, Susan, 'Women, commodification and embryonic stem cell research' in James Humber and Robert F. Almeder (eds.), *Biomedical Ethics Reviews: Stem Cell Research* (Totowa, NJ, Humana Press, 2003), pp. 149–75

Dunn, John, 'Consent in the political theory of John Locke' in J. Dunn, *Political Obligation in its Historical Context* (Oxford, Oxford University Press, 1980)

Easton, Susan M., 'Hegel and feminism' in David Lamb (ed.), *Hegel and Modern Philosophy* (London, Croom Helm, 1987)

Ecker, Jeffrey L. and Greene, Michael F., 'The case against private umbilical cord blood banking' (2005) 105(6) *Obstetrics and Gynecology* 1282–4

Ecologist, The, *Whose Common Future? Reclaiming the Commons* (Philadelphia, New Society Publishers, 1998)

Eisenberg, Rebecca S., 'How can you patent genes?' (2002) 2 *American Journal of Bioethics* 3–11

Ende, Norman, 'Letter' (1995) 86(12) *Blood* 4699

English, Veronica, Mussell, Rebecca, Sheather, Julian and Sommerville, Ann, 'Ethics briefings: retention and use of human tissue' (2004) 30 *Journal of Medical Ethics* 235–6

European Commission Health and Consumer Protection Directorate-General, *Report on the Regulation of Reproductive Cell Donation in the European Union* (Brussels, European Commission, 2006)

European Group on Ethics and New Technologies (EGE), *Opinion on the Ethical Aspects of Umbilical Cord Blood Banking*, opinion number 19, IP/04/364 (Brussels, EGE, 2004)

Faden, Ruth R., *et al.*, 'Public stem cell banks: considerations of justice in stem cell research and therapy' (2003) 33(6) *Hastings Center Report* 13–27

Fagot-Largeault, Anne, 'Ownership of the human body: judicial and legislative responses in France' in Henk ten Have and Jos Welie (eds.), *Ownership of the Human Body: Philosophical Considerations on the Use of the Human Body and its Parts in Healthcare* (Dordrecht, Kluwer, 1998), pp. 115–40

Ferguson, Ann, *Sexual Democracy: Women, Oppression and Revolution* (Boulder, CO, Westview Press, 1991)

Ferguson, Kathy E., *The Man Question: Visions of Subjectivity in Feminist Theory* (Berkeley and Oxford, University of California Press, 1993)

Fernandez, M. N., Regidor, C. and Cabrera, R., 'Letter: Umbilical cord blood transplantation in adults' (2005) 352 *New England Journal of Medicine* 935

FIGO (International Federation of Gynaecology and Obstetrics), *Ethical Guidelines regarding the Procedure of Collection of Cord Blood* (1998), available at www.figo.org.

Foucault, Michel, *Power/Knowledge: Selected Interviews and Other Writings, 1972–1977* (Colin Gordon (ed.), New York, Pantheon, 1980)

Frow, John, 'Gift and commodity' in J. Frow, *Time and Commodity Culture: Essays in Cultural Theory and Postmodernity* (Oxford, Clarendon Press, 1997)

Gatens, Moira, *Feminism and Philosophy: Perspectives on Difference and Equality* (Cambridge, Polity Press, 1991)

Imaginary Bodies: Ethics, Power and Corporeality (London, Routledge, 1996)

Gerrand, Nicole, 'The misuse of Kant in the debate about a market in human body parts' (1999) 16(1) *Journal of Applied Philosophy* 59–67

Gilligan, Carol, *In a Different Voice: Psychological Theory and Women's Development* (2nd edn, Cambridge, MA, Harvard University Press, 1993)

Gluckman, E., Broxmeyer, H. A., Auerbach, A. D., *et al.*, 'Hematopoietic reconstitution in a patient with Fanconi's anemia by means of umbilical-cord blood from an HLA-identical sibling' (1989) 321 *New England Journal of Medicine* 1174–8

Gold, E. Richard, *Body Parts: Property Rights and the Ownership of Human Biological Materials* (Washington, DC, Georgetown University Press, 1996)

Gold, E. Richard and Gallochat, Alain, 'The European Biotech Directive: past as prologue' (2001) 7 *European Law Journal* 331–66

Gomez, Jean-Jacques, 'Intellectual property in human genetics: the French legal approach', paper presented at the first workshop of the EC PropEur project, Cardiff, July 2004

Gottlieb, Karen, 'Human biological samples and the law of property: the trust as a model for biological repositories' in R. F. Weir (ed.), *Stored Tissue Samples: Ethical, Legal and Public Policy Implications* (Iowa City, Iowa University Press, 1998), pp. 183–97

Grey, Thomas, "The disintegration of property" in J. P. Pennock and J. Chapman (eds.), *Nomos XXII: Property* (New York, New York University Press, 1980), pp. 69–85

Grubb, Andrew, '"I, me mine": bodies, parts and property' (1998) 3 *Medical Law International* 299–313

Gunning, Jennifer, 'Umbilical cord blood banking: a surprisingly controversial issue', unpublished report for Cardiff Centre for Ethics, Law and Science (CCELS, no date)

Gupta, Jayasna, 'Postmodern bodies, assisted reproduction and women's agency', paper presented at the Seventh World International Association of Bioethics conference, Sydney, November 2004

Gurmankin, Andrea D., 'Risk information provided to prospective oocyte donors in a preliminary phone call' (2001) 1(4) *American Journal of Bioethics* 3–13

Habermas, Juergen, *Between Facts and Norms: A Discourse Theory of Law and Democracy* (William Rehg (tr.), Cambridge, MA, MIT Press, 1996)

Haley, Rebecca, Horvath, Liana and Sugarman, Jeremy, 'Ethical issues in cord blood banking: summary of a workshop' (1997) 38 *Transfusion* 367–73

Hansen, Mogens Herman, *The Athenian Democracy in the Age of Demosthenes: Structures, Principles and Ideology* (Oxford, Blackwell, 1991)

Hanson, Mark M., 'Religious voices in biotechnology: the case of gene patenting' (1997) 27 *Hastings Center Report* 1–30

Haraway, Donna J., *Simians, Cyborgs and Women: The Reinvention of Nature* (New York, Routledge, 1991)

'Situated knowledges: the science question in feminism and the privilege of partial perspective' (1988) 14 *Feminist Studies* 3

Hardin, Garrett, 'The tragedy of the commons' (1968) 162 *Science* 1243

Harding, Sandra, 'Is gender a variable in conceptions of rationality? A survey of issues' in Carol C. Gould (ed.), *Beyond Domination: New Perspectives on Feminism and Philosophy* (Totowa, NJ, Rowman and Allanheld, 1984), pp. 43–63

Harris, James W., *Property and Justice* (Oxford, Oxford University Press, 1996)

Harris, John, *Wonderwoman and Superman: The Ethics of Human Biotechnology* (Oxford, Oxford University Press, 1992)

Harris, John and Sulston, John, 'Genetic Equity' (2004) 5 *Nature Reviews Genetics* 796–800

Harrison, Charlotte H., 'Neither Moore nor the market' (2002) 28 *American Journal of Law and Medicine* 77–104

Hegel, G. W. F., *Hegel's Philosophy of Right* (T. M. Knox (tr.), Oxford, Oxford University Press 1967)

Phenomenology of Spirit (A. V. Miller (tr.), Oxford, Oxford University Press, 1977)

Held, David, *Models of Democracy* (1st edn, Cambridge, Polity Press, 1987)

Heller, M. and Eisenberg, R., 'Can patents deter biomedical research?' (1998) 280 *Science* 698–701

Hermitte, Marie-Angèle, *Le sang et le droit: essai sur la transfusion sanguine* (Paris, Editions du Seuil, 1996)

Highfield, Roger, 'Have we been oversold the stem cell dream?', *Daily Telegraph*, 29 June 2005

Hofmeyr, G. K., Bex, P. J. M., Skapinker, R. and Delahunt, T., 'Hasty clamping of the umbilical cord may initiate neonatal intraventricular hemorrhage' (1989) 29 *Medical Hypotheses* 5

Hohfeld, Wesley Newcomb, *Fundamental Legal Conceptions as applied in Judicial Reasoning* (New Haven, CT, Yale University Press, 1919)

Holland, Suzanne, 'Contested commodities at both ends of life: buying and selling embryos, gametes and body tissues' (2001) 11 *Kennedy Institute of Ethics Journal* 263–84

Holm, Soren, 'Going to the roots of the stem cell controversy' (2002) 16(6) *Bioethics* 493–507

Honoré, A. M., 'Ownership' in *Making Law Bind: Essays Legal and Philosophical* (Oxford, Clarendon Press, 1987), pp. 161–92

Hottois, Gilbert, *Essais philosophie bioéthique et biopolitique* (Paris, Librairie Philosophique J. Vrin, 1999)

HUGO (Human Genome Organisation) Ethics Council, *Statement on Benefit-Sharing* (Vancouver, HUGO, 9 April 2000)

Irigaray, Luce, *Ethique de la différence sexuelle* (Paris, Editions de Minuit, 1984)
Le temps de la différence: pour une révolution pacifique (Paris, Livre de Poche, 1989)

Jacobs, Allen, Dwyer, James and Lee, Peter, 'Seventy ova' (2001) 31 *Hastings Center Report* 12–14

Jaggar, Alison, *Feminist Politics and Human Nature* (Totowa, NJ, Rowman and Allanheld, 1983)

Jensen, K. and Murray, F., 'International patenting: the landscape of the human genome' (2005) 310 *Science* 239–40

Kahn, Jeffrey, 'Can we broker eggs without making omelets?' (2001) 1(4) *American Journal of Bioethics* 14–15

Kaiser, Jocelyn, 'Court decides tissue samples belong to university, not patients' (2006) 312 *Science* 436

Kant, Immanuel, *Lectures on Ethics* (Indianapolis, Bobbs-Merrill, 1963)

Kattel, Rainer and Riivo, Anton, 'The Estonian genome project and economic development' (2004) 8(1–2) *Trames: Journal of the Humanities and Social Sciences* 106–28

Kaye, Jane, Helgason, Hordur Helgi, Nomper, Ants, *et al.*, 'Population genetic databases: a comparative analysis of the law in Iceland, Sweden, Estonia and the UK' (2004) 8(1–2) *Trames: Journal of the Humanities and Social Sciences* 15–33

Klein, Naomi, *No Logo* (London, Picador, 2000)

Knoppers, Bartha M., 'Status, sale and patenting of human genetic material: an international survey' (1999) 1 *Nature Reviews Genetics* 23
'DNA banking: a retrospective perspective' in J. Burley and J. Harris (eds.), *A Companion to Genethics* (Oxford, Blackwell, 2002), pp. 379–86

Knoppers, Bartha M., *et al.*, 'Ethical issues in international collaborative research on the human genome: the HGP and the HDGP' (1996) 34 *Genomics* 272–5

Knoppers, Bartha M., Hirtle, M. and Glass, K. C., 'Commercialization of genetic research and public policy' (1999) 286(5448) *Science* 2277–8

Koegler, Gesine, *et al.*, 'A new human somatic stem cell from placental cord blood with intrinsic pluripotent differentiation potential' (2004) 200(2) *Journal of Experimental Medicine* 123

Korts, Kuliki, Weldon, Sue and Gudmansdottir, Margaret Lilja, 'Genetic databases and public attitudes: a comparison of Iceland, Estonia and the UK' (2004) 8(1–2) *Trames: Journal of the Humanities and Social Sciences* 131–49

Lainez Villabona, B., *et al.*, 'Early or late umbilical cord clamping? A systematic review of the literature' (2005) 63(1) *Anales Pediatrica* 14–21

Lanzendorf, S. E., *et al.*, 'Use of human gametes obtained from anonymous donors for the production of human embryonic stem cell lines' (2001) 76 *Fertility and Society* 132–7

Laughlin, M. J., Eapen, M., Rubinstein, P., *et al.*, 'Outcomes after transplantation of cord blood or bone marrow from unrelated donors in adults with leukaemia' (2004) 351 *New England Journal of Medicine* 2265–75

Laurie, Graeme, *(Intellectual) Property: Let's Think about Staking a Claim to our own Genetic Samples* (Edinburgh, Arts and Humanities Board Research Centre, 2004)

Lauritzen, Paul, 'Stem cells, biotechnology and human rights: implications for a posthuman future' (2005) 35(2) *Hastings Center Report* 25–33

Le Dœuff, Michele, *Hipparchia's Choice: An Essay Concerning Women, Philosophy, etc.* (Trista Selous (tr.), Oxford, Blackwell, 1991)

Lessing, Lawrence, *The Future of Ideas: the Fate of the Commons in a Connected World* (New York, Random House, 2001)

Levitt, Mairi and Weldon, Sue, 'A well placed trust? Public perceptions of the governance of DNA databases' (2005) 15(4) *Critical Public Health* 311–21

Liddell, Kathleen and Wallace, Susan, 'Emerging regulatory issues for stem cell medicine' (2005) 1(1) *Genomics, Society and Policy* 54–73

Lock, Margaret, *Twice Dead: Organ Transplants and the Reinvention of Death* (Berkeley, University of California Press, 2002)

Locke, John, *The Second Treatise on Civil Government* (1689), in Howard R. Penniman (ed.), *John Locke: On Politics and Education* (New York, D. Van Nostrand, 1947)

Lorentzen, H. and Paterson, F., 'Le don des vivants: l'altruisme des Norvégiens et des Français?' in J. Elster and N. Herpin (eds.), *Ethique des choix médicaux* (Arles, Actes Sud, 1992), pp. 121–38

McDonald, S. J. and. Abbott, J. M., 'Effects of timing of umbilical cord clamping of term infants on maternal and neonatal outcomes (Protocol)', *Cochrane Database of Systematic Reviews*, issue 1, art. no. CD004074, first published online 20 January 2003

McGee, Glenn, 'Gene patents can be ethical' (1999) 7 *Cambridge Quarterly of Healthcare Ethics* 417–30

McGovern, Ann, 'Sharing our body and blood: organ donation and feminist critiques of sacrifice' (2003) 28(1) *Journal of Medicine and Philosophy* 89–114

McHale, Jean, 'Waste, ownership and bodily products' (2000) 8(2) *Health Care Analysis* 123–35

MacKenzie, Catriona, 'Conceptions of the body and conceptions of autonomy in bioethics', paper presented at the Seventh World International Association of Bioethics conference, Sydney, November 2004

MacKinnon, Catharine A., *Toward a Feminist Theory of the State* (Cambridge, MA, Harvard University Press, 1989)

McLeod, Carolyn 'Means and partial means: the full range of the objectification of women' (2003) 28 *Canadian Journal of Philosophy* 219–44

McLeod, Carolyn and Baylis, Francoise, 'Feminists on the inalienability of human embryos' (2006) 21(1) *Hypatia* 1–14

MacPherson, C. B., *The Political Theory of Possessive Individualism: Hobbes to Locke* (Oxford and New York, Oxford University Press, 1962)

Macklin, Ruth, 'What is wrong with commodification?' in C. R. Cohen (ed.), *New Ways of Making Babies: The Case of Egg Donation* (Bloomington, Indiana University Press, 1996), pp. 106–21

Mahoney, Joan, 'An Essay on Surrogacy and Feminist Thought' in Larry Gostin (ed.), *Surrogate Motherhood: Politics and Privacy* (Bloomington, Indiana University Press, 1990), pp. 183–97

Maio, Giovanni, 'The cultural specificity of research ethics – or why ethical debate in France is different' (2002) 28 *Journal of Medical Ethics* 147–50

Malone, T., Catalano, P. J., O'Dwyer, P. J. and Giantonio, B., 'High rate of consent to bank biologic samples for future research: the Eastern Cooperative Oncology Group experience' (2002) 94 *Journal of the National Cancer Institute* 769–71

Manson, Neil C., 'How not to think about genetic information' (2005) 35 *Hastings Center Report* 3

Marx, Karl, *Capital* (Samuel Moore and Edward Aveling (trs.), Frederick Engels (ed.), Moscow, Progress, 1954, original edn 1867)
  Early Writings (T. B. Bottomore (tr. and ed.), New York, McGraw-Hill, 1963)
  Grundrisse: Foundations of the Critique of Political Economy (Martin Nicolas (tr.), New York, Vintage Books, 1973)

Marzano-Parisoli, Maria M., *Penser le corps* (Paris, Presses Universitaires de France, 2002)

Mason, Ken and Laurie, Graeme, 'Consent or property? Dealing with the body and its parts in the shadow of Bristol and Alder Hey' (2001) 9 *Medical Law Review* 710–29

Matthijs, Gert, 'Editorial: Patenting genes' (2004) 329 *British Medical Journal* 1358–60

Mauss, Marcel, *The Gift: The Form and Reason for Exchange in Archaic Societies* (2nd edn, London, Routledge, 1990)

Mead, H. M., *Tikanga Maori: Living by Maori Values* (Wellington, Huia Publishers, 2003)
  Whakapapa and the Human Gene (Wellington, Toi Te Taiao/The Bioethics Council of New Zealand, 2004)

Medical Research Council, *Public Perceptions of the Collection of Human Biological Samples* (London, MRC, 2000)
  Human Tissue and Biological Samples for Use in Research: Operational and Ethical Guidelines (London, MRC, 2001)

Meek, James, 'Why you are first in the great gene race', *Guardian*, 15 November 2000, p. 4

Meilaender, Gilbert, 'The point of a ban, or, how to think about stem cell research' (2001) 31 *Hastings Center Report* 9–15

Memmi, Dominique, *Les gardiens du corps: dix ans de magistère bioéthique* (Paris, Editions de l'Ecole des Hautes Etudes en Sciences Sociales, 1996)

Mercer, Judith S. and Skovgaard, Rebecca L., 'Neonatal transitional physiology: a new paradigm' (2002) 15 *Journal of Perinatal and Neonatal Nursing* 56–75

Merchant, Jennifer, 'Confronting the consequences of medical technology: policy frontiers in the United States and France' in Marianne Givvens and Dorothy McBride Stetson (eds.), *Abortion Politics: Public Policy in Cross-Cultural Perspective* (New York and London, Routledge, 1996), pp. 189–210

Merle, Jean-Christophe, 'A Kantian argument for a duty to donate one's own organs: a reply to Nicole Gerrand' (2000) 17(1) *Journal of Applied Philosophy* 93–101

Merleau-Ponty, Maurice, *The Visible and the Invisible* (Evanston, IL Northwestern University Press, 1968)

Mills, Charles and Pateman, Carole, *Contract and Domination* (Cambridge, Polity Press, 2006)

Ministère délégué à la Recherche, Communiqué de Presse, 'Cellules souches embryonnaires: présentation du decret autorisant l'importation', 19 October 2004, available at www.recherche.gouv.fr/discours/2004/decretembryon.htm

Mitchell, Robert, 'Registered genes, patents and bio-circulation', paper presented at the BIOS 'Vital politics' conference, London School of Economics, September 2003

Moine, Isabelle, *Les choses hors commerce: une approche de la personne humaine juridique* (Paris, LGDJ-Monchrestien, Bibliothèque de droit privé, 1997)

Momberger, K., 'Breeder at law' (2002) 11 *Columbia Journal of Gender and Law* 127–74

Montgomery, Jonathan, *Health Care Law* (1st edn, Oxford, Oxford University Press, 1997)

Morley, G. M., 'Cord closure: can hasty clamping injure the newborn?' (1998) *Obstetrics and Gynaecology Management*, July

Munzer, Stephen R., *A Theory of Property* (Cambridge, Cambridge University Press, 1990)

'An uneasy case against property rights in human body parts' (1994) 11(2) *Social Philosophy and Policy* 259–86

'The special case of property rights in umbilical cord blood for transplantation' (1999) 51 *Rutgers Law Review* 493–568

(ed.), *New Essays in the Legal and Political Theory of Property* (Cambridge, Cambridge University Press, 2002)

'Property, patents and genetic material' in J. Burley and J. Harris (eds.), *A Companion to Genethics* (Oxford, Basil Blackwell, 2002), pp. 438–54

Murray, Thomas, 'Will new ways of creating stem cells dodge the objections?' (2005) 35(1) *Hastings Center Report* 8–9

National Academies, 'Report proposes structure for national network of cord blood stem cell banks', available at www.sciencedaily.com/releases/2005/04/050418095036.htm

Nelkin, Dorothy, *Dangerous Diagnostics: The Social Power of Biological Information* (Chicago, University of Chicago Press, 1994)

'Is bioethics for sale?' (2003) 24(2) *Tocqueville Review* 45–60

Nelkin, Dorothy and Lindee, Susan, *The DNA Mystique: The Gene as a Cultural Icon* (New York, W. H. Freeman and Co., 1995)

Nuffield Council on Bioethics, *Stem Cell Therapy: The Ethical Issues, A Discussion Paper* (London, Nuffield Council on Bioethics, 2000)

The Ethics of Patenting DNA (London, Nuffield Council on Bioethics, 2002)

Nussbaum, Martha, 'Objectification' (1995) 24(4) *Philosophy and Public Affairs* 249–91

Okin, Susan Moller, *Women in Western Political Thought* (London, Virago, 1980)

Okoth-Ogendo, H. W. O., 'The tragic African commons: a century of exploration, suppression and submersion' (2003) 1 *University of Nairobi Law Journal* 107–17

Oldham, Paul, 'The patenting of plant and animal genomes', paper presented at the seventh workshop of the EC PropEur project, Paris, May 2006

Oliveiro, P., 'La communication sociale des matériaux biologiques: sang, sperme, organs, cadavres' (1993) 18 *Cahiers internationaux de psychologie sociale* 21–51

Ossorio, Pilar, 'Common heritage arguments against patenting DNA' in A. Chapman (ed.), *Perspectives on Gene Patenting: Religion, Science and Industry in Dialogue* (Washington, DC, American Association for the Advancement of Science, 1999), pp. 89–108

'Legal and ethical issues in biotechnology patenting' in J. Burley and J. Harris, *A Companion to Genethics* (Oxford, Blackwell, 2002), pp. 408–19

Otten, J., Wyle, H. and Phelps, G., 'The charitable trust as a model for genomic banks' (2004) 350 *New England Journal of Medicine* 85–6

Palsson, Gisli and Rabinow, Paul, 'Iceland: the case of a national Human Genome Project' (1999) 15(3) *Anthropology Today* 14–18

Parfit, Tom, 'Beauty salons fuel trade in aborted babies', *Guardian Unlimited*, 17 April 2005, available at www.guardian.co.uk

Parry, Bronwyn, 'The new Human Tissue Bill: Categorization and Definitional Issues and their Implications' (2005) 1(1) *Genomics, Society and Policy* 74–85

Pateman, Carole, *The Sexual Contract* (Cambridge, Polity Press, 1988)

'The fraternal social contract' in *The Disorder of Women* (Stanford, CA, Stanford University Press, 1989), pp. 33–57

Patrick, M., Smith, A. L., Meyer, W. R. and Bashford, A., 'Anonymous oocyte donation: a follow-up questionnaire' (2001) 75 *Fertility and Sterility* 1034–6

Patterson, J., *Maori Values* (Palmerston North, Dunmore Press, 1992)

Peltonen, T., 'Placental transfusion: advantages and disadvantages' (1981) 137 *European Journal of Pediatrics* 141–6

Penner, James, *The Idea of Property in Law* (Oxford, Clarendon Press, 1997)

Plato, *Laws* (Paul Shorey (tr.)) in *The Collected Dialogues of Plato including the Letters* (Edith Hamilton and Huntington Cairns (eds.), New York, Pantheon Books, 1961)

Plato, *The Republic* (Paul Shorey (tr.)) in *The Collected Dialogues of Plato including the Letters* (Edith Hamilton and Huntington Cairns (eds.), New York, Pantheon Books, 1961)

Pottage, Alain, 'The inscription of life in law: genes, patents and biopolitics' (1998) 61 *Modern Law Review* 740–65

Prendiville, W. J. and Elbourne, D., 'Care during the third stage of labour' in I. Chalmers, M. Enkin and M. J. N. C. Keirse (eds.), *Effective Care in Pregnancy and Childbirth* (Oxford, Oxford University Press, 1989), pp. 1145–69

Prendiville, W. J., Elbourne, D. and McDonald, S., 'Active versus expectant management in the third stage of labour', *Cochrane Database of Systematic Reviews*, issue 3, art. no. CD000007, 24 July 2000

President's Council on Bioethics, *Alternative Sources of Human Pluripotent Stem Cells* (Washington, DC, President's Council on Bioethics, 2005)

Proctor, S. J., Dickinson, A. M., Parekh, T. and Chapman, C., 'Umbilical cord blood banks in the UK have proved their worth and now deserve a firmer foundation' (2001) 323 *British Medical Journal* 60–1

Quiney, Ruth, 'Autogenesis and the absent mother: cultural fantasies of maternal space and posthuman reproduction', paper delivered at the Open Forum on 'Posthuman bodies', Birkbeck, University of London, 18 March 2006

Rabe, H., Reynolds, G. and Diaz-Rossello, J., 'Early versus delayed umbilical cord clamping in preterm infants', *Cochrane Database of Systematic Reviews*, issue 4, art. no. CD003248pub2, 18 October 2004

Rabinow, Paul, *French Modern: Norms and Forms of the Social Environment* (Chicago and London, University of Chicago Press, 1989)

French DNA: Trouble in Purgatory (Chicago, University of Chicago Press, 1999)

Radin, Margaret J., *Contested Commodities: The Trouble with Trade in Sex, Children, Body Parts and Other Things* (Cambridge, MA, Harvard University Press, 1996)

Ragone, Helena, *Surrogate Motherhood: Conception in the Heart* (Boulder, CO, Westview Press, 1996)

Randerson, James, 'Rise and fall of clone king who doctored stem-cell research', *Guardian*, 24 December 2005

Rawls, John, *A Theory of Justice* (Ist edn, Cambridge, MA, Harvard University Press, 1971)

Remond-Gouilloud, Martin, 'L'avenir du patrimoine,' *Esprit*, November 1995, p. 216

Resnik, David, 'The morality of human gene patents' (1997) 7 *Kennedy Institute of Ethics Journal* 43–61

'The commodification of human reproductive materials' (1998) 24 *Journal of Medical Ethics* 288–93

'Regulating the market for human eggs' (2001) 15(1) *Bioethics* 1–26

'The commercialization of human stem cells: ethical and policy issues' (2002) 10 *Health Care Analysis* 127–54

Retained Organs Commission, *A Consultation Document on Unclaimed and Unidentifiable Organs and Tissue: A Possible Regulatory Framework* (NHS, February 2002)

Rheenen, Patrick van and Brabin, Bernard J., 'Late umbilical cord-clamping as an intervention for reducing iron deficiency anaemia in term infants in developing and industrialised countries: a systematic review' (2004) 24 *Annals of Tropical Paediatrics* 3–16

Richardson, Ruth, 'Fearful symmetry' in Stuart Younger, *et al.*, *Death, Dissection and the Destitute* (Chicago, University of Chicago Press, 2001)

Ricœur, Paul, *Oneself as Another* (Kathleen Blamey (tr.), University of Chicago Press, 1992)

Réflexion faite: autobiographie intellectuelle (Paris, Editions Esprit, 1995)

Rocha, V., *et al.*, 'Graft-versus-host disease in children who have received a cord-blood or bone marrow transplant from an HLA-identical sibling' (2000) 342(25) *New England Journal of Medicine* 1846–54

Rocha, V., Labopin, M., Sans, G., *et al.*, 'Transplants of umbilical cord blood or bone marrow from unrelated donors in adults with leukaemia' (2004) 351 *New England Journal of Medicine* 2276–85

Rogers, Ian and Casper, Robert F., 'Lifeline in an ethical quagmire: umbilical cord blood as an alternative to embryonic stem cells' (2004) 2(2) *Sexuality, Reproduction and Menopause* 64–70

Rose, Carol M., 'The comedy of the commons: customs, commerce and inherently public property' (1986) 53 *University of Chicago Law Review* 742

    Property and Persuasion: Essays on the History, Theory and Rhetoric of Ownership (Boulder, CO, Westview Press, 1994)

Rose, Hilary, 'Gendered genetics in Iceland' (2001) 20(2) *New Genetics and Society* 119–38

    'An ethical dilemma: the rise and fall of UmanGenomics – the model biotech company?' (2004) 425 *Nature* 123–4

Rothstein, Mark A., 'Expanding the ethical analysis of biobanks' (2005) 33(1) *Journal of Law, Medicine and Ethics* 89–101

Royal College of Obstetricians and Gynaecologists Scientific Advisory Committee, *Opinion Paper 2: Cord Blood Banking* (London, RCOG, 2001)

Rubinstein, P., Rosenfeld, R. E., Adamson, J. W. and Stevens, C. E., 'Stored placental blood for unrelated bone marrow reconstitution' (1993) 81 *Blood* 1679–90

Ryan, Alan, 'Locke, labour and the purposes of God' in A. Ryan, *Property and Political Theory* (Oxford, Blackwell, 1984)

    Property and Political Theory (Oxford, Blackwell, 1984)

    'Self-ownership, autonomy and property rights' (1994) 11 *Social Philosophy and Policy* 341

Sample, Ian, 'Stem cell pioneer accused of faking all his research, apart from the cloned dog', *Guardian*, 11 January 2006, p. 11

Sauer, M. V., 'Defining the incidence of serious complications experienced by oocyte donors: a review of 1,000 cases' (2001) 184 *American Journal of Obstetrics and Gynecology* 277–8

    'Egg donor solicitation: problems exist, but do abuses?' (2001) 1(4) *American Journal of Bioethics* 1–2

Sauer, M. V., Paulson, R. J. and Lobo, R. A., 'Rare occurrence of ovarian hyperstimulation syndrome in oocyte donors' (1996) 52 *International Journal of Gynecology and Obstetrics* 259–62

Scheper-Hughes, Nancy, 'Bodies for sale – whole or in parts' (2002) 7 *Body and Society* 1–8

Schneider, Ingrid and Schumann, Claudia, 'Stem cells, therapeutic cloning, embryo research: women as raw material suppliers for science and industry' in Svea Luise Herrmann and Margaretha Kurmann (eds.), *Reproductive Medicine and Genetic Engineering: Women between Self-Determination and Societal Standardisation*, proceedings of a conference held in Berlin, 15–17 November 2001 (Reprokult, 2002), pp. 70–9

Schneider, Susan Weidman, 'Jewish women's eggs: a hot commodity in the IVF marketplace' (2001) 26(3) *Lllith* 22

Schroeder, J. L., 'Chix nix bundle-o-stix: a feminist critique of the disaggregation of property' (1994) 83 *Michigan Law Review* 239

Scully, Jackie Leach, 'Normative ethics and non-normative embodiment', paper presented at the Feminist Approaches to Bioethics conference, Sydney, November 2004

Segal, Naomi, 'Words, bodies and stone', inaugural lecture delivered at the Institute of Germanic and Romance Studies, University of London, 19 April 2005

Senituli, Lopeti, 'They came for sandalwood, now the b . . . s are after our genes!', paper presented at the conference 'Research ethics, tikanga Maori/indigenous and protocols for working with communities', Wellington, New Zealand, 10–12 June 2004

Shiffrin, Seana Valentine, 'Lockean arguments for private intellectual property' in Stephen R. Munzer (ed.), *New Essays in the Legal and Political Theory of Property* (Cambridge, Cambridge University Press, 2002), pp. 138–67

Shiva, Vandana, *Biopiracy: The Plunder of Nature and Knowledge* (Boston, South End Press, 1997)

Sicard, Didier (ed.), *Travaux du Comité Consultatif National d'Ethique* (Paris, Quadrige/Presses Universitaires de France, 2003)

Sigurdsson, Skuli, 'Yin-yang genetics, or the HSD decode controversy' (2001) 20(2) *New Genetics and Society* 103–17

Simpson, Alan, Hildyard, Nicholas and Sexton, Sarah, 'No patents on life: a briefing on the proposed EU directive on the legal protection of biotechnological inventions', available at www.thecornerhouse.org.uk, first published September 1997, accessed 24 August 2004

Skloot, Rebecca, 'Taking the least of you: the tissue-industrial complex', *New York Times*, 16 April 2006, available at www.nytimes.com/2006/04/16/magazine/16tissuehtml, accessed 24 April 2006

Skolbekken, John-Arne, Ursin, Lars Oystein, Solberg, Berge, *et al.*, 'Not worth the paper it's written on? Informed consent and biobank research in a Norwegian context' (2005) 15(4) *Critical Public Health* 335–47

Smith, Alyna C., 'Intellectual property rights and the right to health: considering the case of access to medicines' in Christian Lenk, Nils Hoppe and Roberto Andorno (eds.), *Ethics and Law of Intellectual Property: Current Problems in Politics, Science and Technology* (Aldershot, Ashgate, 2006), ch. 3

Smith, Stephen A., *Contract Theory* (Oxford, Oxford University Press, 2004)

Steinbock, Bonnie, 'Alternative sources of stem cells' (2005) 35(4) *Hastings Center Report* 24–6

Steinbrook, Robert, 'Egg donation and human embryonic stem-cell research' (2006) 354 *New England Journal of Medicine* 324–6

Steiner, Philippe, 'Don du sang et don d'organes: le marché et les marchandises "fictives"' (2001) 42(2) *Revue française de sociologie* 357–73

Sterckx, Sigrid, *Biotechnology, Patents and Morality* (2nd edn, Aldershot, Ashgate, 2000)

    'Embryo stem cell patenting', paper presented at the fifth workshop of the EC PropEur project, Bilbao, December 2005

'Lack of access to essential drugs: a story of continuing global failure, with particular attention to the role of patents' in Christian Lenk, Nils Hoppe and Roberto Andorno (eds.), *Ethics and Law of Intellectual Property: Current Problems in Politics, Science and Technology* (Aldershot, Ashgate, 2006), ch. 9

Stock, Gregory, 'Eggs for sale: how much is too much?' (2001) 1(4) *American Journal of Bioethics* 26–7

Stranger, Mark, Chalmers, Donald and Nicol, Dianne, 'Capital, trust and consultation: databanks and regulation in Australia' (2005) 15(4) *Critical Public Health* 349–58

Sugarman, Jeremy, Reisner, Emily G. and Kurtzberg, Joanne, 'Ethical issues of banking placental blood for transplantation' (1995) 274 *Journal of the American Medical Association* 1763–85

Taylor, Robert S., 'A Kantian defense of self-ownership' (2004) 12(1) *Journal of Political Philosophy* 65–78

Thambisetty, Sivaramjani, *Human Genome Patents and Developing Countries* (London, Department for International Development, Commission on Intellectual Property Rights, 2002)

Théry, Jean-François, Salat-Baroux, Frédéric and Le Bihan-Graf, Christine, *Les lois de la bioéthique: cinq ans après* (Paris, La Documentation française, 1999)

Thouvénin, Dominique, 'Autour du don et de la gratuité' (2002) *Revue générale de droit médical, Numéro spécial: droit santé* 99–108

Titmuss, Richard M., *The Gift Relationship: From Human Blood to Social Policy* (Ann Oakley and J. Ashton (eds.), 2nd edn, London, LSE Books, 1997)

Tober, Diane, 'Semen as gift, semen as goods: reproductive workers and the market in altruism' (2001) 7 *Body and Society* 137–60

Toi Te Taiao/The Bioethics Council of New Zealand, *Reflections on the Use of Human Genes in Other Organisms: Ethical, Spiritual and Cultural Dimensions* (Wellington, Toi Te Taiao/The Bioethics Council of New Zealand, 2004)

Tromp, Saskia, 'Seize the Day, Seize the Cord', unpublished undergraduate medical dissertation (University of Maastricht, 2001)

United Kingdom Parliament, House of Commons, *Select Committee on Science and Technology Fifth Report*, available at www.publications.parliament.uk/pa/cm200405, accessed 20 April 2005

Varela, F., 'Intimate distances: fragments for a phenomenology of organ transplantation' in E. Thompson (ed.), *Between Ourselves: Second-Person Issues in the Study of Consciousness* (Thorverton, Imprint Academic, 2001)

Waldby, Catherine, 'Biomedicine, tissue transfer and intercorporeality' (2002) 3(3) *Feminist Theory* 239–54

Waldby, Catherine and Mitchell, Robert, *Tissue Economies: Blood, Organs and Cell Lines in Late Capitalism* (Durham, NC, Duke University Press, 2006)

Waldron, Jeremy, *The Right to Private Property* (Oxford, Clarendon Press, 1988)

Wallace, Susan and Stewart, Alison, 'Cord blood banking: guidelines and prospects', Cambridge Genetic Knowledge Park report, 22 November 2004, available at www.cambridgenetwork.co.uk/pooled/ articles, accessed 19 May 2005

Warren, Mary Anne, 'The moral significance of the gene' in J. Burley and J. Harris (eds.), *A Companion to Genethics* (Oxford, Blackwell, 2002), pp. 147–57

Watts, Jonathan and Semple, Ian, 'Cloning fraud hits search for stem cell cures', *Guardian*, 24 December 2005

Weiss, Gail, *Body Images: Embodiment as Intercorporeality* (London and New York, Routledge, 1999)

Wert, Guido de, Meulen, Ruud ter, Mordacci, Roberto and Tallachini, Mariachiara, *Ethics and Genetics: A Workbook for Practitioners and Students* (Oxford, Berghahn Books, 2003)

Widdows, Heather, 'The impact of new reproductive technologies on concepts of genetic relatedness and non-relatedness' in Heather Widdows, Itziar Alkorta Idiakez and Aitziber Emaldi Cirion (eds.), *Women's Reproductive Rights* (Basingstoke, Palgrave Macmillan, 2006), pp. 151–64

Wiemels, J. L., Cazzaniga, G., Daniotti, M., *et al.*, 'Prenatal origin of acute lymphoblastic leukaemia in children' (1999) 352 *Lancet* 1499–1503

Wilkinson, Stephen, 'Commodification arguments for the legal prohibition of organ sale' (2000) 8 *Health Care Analysis* 189–201

Williams, Garrath, 'Bioethics and large-scale biobanking: individualistic ethics and collective projects' (2005) 1(2) *Genomics, Society and Policy* 50–66

Williams, Patricia J., 'On being the object of property' in D. Kelly Weisberg (ed.), *Feminist Legal Theory: Foundations* (Philadelphia, Temple University Press, 1992), pp. 594–602

Williams-Jones, Bryn, 'History of a gene patent: tracing the development and application of commercial BRCA testing' (2002) 10 *Health Law Journal* 121–44

Winickoff, David E. and Neumann, Larissa B., 'Towards a social contract for genomics: property and the public in the "biotrust" model' (2005) 1(3) *Genomics, Society and Policy* 8–21

Winickoff, David E. and Winickoff, Richard N., 'The charitable trust as a model for genomic biobanks' (2003) 349(12) *New England Journal of Medicine* 1180–4

Xitaras, Mikhail, *La Propriété* (Paris, Fondements de la politique, Presses Universitaires de France, 2004)

Yelling, A. (ed.), *Common Field and Enclosure in England, 1450–1850* (Hamden, CT, Archon Books, 1977)

Young, Iris Marion, *On Female Body Experience: 'Throwing like a Girl' and Other Essays* (Oxford, Oxford University Press, 2005)

Younge, Gary, 'Embryo scientist quits team over ethics fear', *Guardian*, 14 November 2003, p. 19

Zilberstein, Moshe, Feingold, Michael and Selbel, Michelle M., 'Umbilical cord-blood banking: lessons learned from gamete donation' (1997) 349 *Lancet* 642–5

Index